D0683595

Our Daily Bread.

2020 ANNUAL EDITION

Contents   Page

© 2019 Our Daily Bread Ministries® • Grand Rapids, Michigan, USA
Internet address: ourdailybread.org • email: odb@odb.org
Printed in China

EDITORIAL TEAM

Monica Brands, Anne Cetas, Tom Felten, Tim Gustafson, Alyson Kieda,
Becky Knapp, and Peggy Willison

WRITERS

James Banks	Adam Holz	Amy Peterson
Monica Brands	Arthur Jackson	Amy Boucher Pye
Dave Branon	Cindy Hess Kasper	Patricia Raybon
Anne M. Cetas	Alyson Kieda	David H. Roper
Poh Fang Chia	Randy K. Kilgore	Lisa Samra
William E. Crowder	Leslie Koh	Julie Schwab
Lawrence Darmani	Julie Ackerman Link	Jennifer Benson Schuldt
Mart DeHaan	David C. McCasland	Joseph M. Stowell
Xochitl Dixon	Elisa Morgan	Linda Washington
H. Dennis Fisher	Keila Ochoa	Marvin L. Williams
Timothy Gustafson	Jeff Olson	Karen Wolfe
Kirsten Holmberg		Philip D. Yancey

ACKNOWLEDGMENTS

August 15 and *December 21* articles excerpted and adapted from
Meet the Bible: A Panorama of God's Word in 366 Daily Readings and Reflections,
by Philip D. Yancey and Brenda Quinn. © 2000 Zondervan.
Published by permission of Zondervan.

Dear friend of Our Daily Bread,

Thank you very much for your continuous support for Our Daily Bread Ministries.

We strongly apologize for the 2019 *Our Daily Bread* which was produced with 'Volume' edition. From the feedback we received from a lot of our readers so far; we found out that not only did this change come without prior notice from us, it was also not well received because our readers are so used to have the day of the week along with the day of the month.

We appreciate your feedback; it shows that you are committed to our resources which have helped us to know we can serve you better and we are not taking this for granted.

The feedback have made us to reconsider the decision to continue producing the Annual *Our Daily Bread* in 'Volume' and we are happy to inform you that from 2020 we will revert to the 'Year' edition.

Your purchase of the Annual Edition of *Our Daily Bread* devotional helps us to do more in distributing our resources to schools, prisons, hospital, military, etc.

We thank you for your loyalty over these 80 years we have made the life-changing wisdom of the Bible understandable and accessible to all. We hope you will continue this journey with us.

May God bless you and keep you.

Sincerely,

THE OUR DAILY BREAD STAFF

Journey into Healing

Feature Article

Impatience is a constant temptation for me. If something seems broken, in my life or the lives of those I love, my default is to want it fixed—*today*. Walking patiently with God *through* the ups and downs of life is usually not my first preference.

I don't think I'm alone in this. Dale S. Ryan, CEO of Christian Recovery International, writes about how one of the biggest roadblocks he's seen for Christians seeking healing is the belief that recovery—even from trauma or addiction—should happen quickly. Just as we often think of salvation primarily as a one-time event, believers also often expect God to bring instant healing.

> Scripture describes the life of faith, not as an instant fix, but as a slow journey in which God invites us to walk with Him into healing.

But Scripture describes the life of faith, not as an instant fix, but as a slow journey in which God invites us to walk *with* Him into healing (1 PETER 2:1–3). God invites us to bring our whole selves—the parts of ourselves we like *and* the parts of ourselves we're ashamed or afraid of—before Him. Because it's only when we come before Him in our weakness that we experience the healing power of His love.

This requires time, patience, and constant dependence on God in prayer, especially since many of us are uncomfortable with looking too deeply into the broken parts of ourselves.

But as the author of Hebrews reminds us, we have no reason to fear. God already knows us better than we know ourselves (4:12–13). Our Savior, who fully understands our struggles, invites us to courageously bring them before God's throne. As we do, we experience the wonder of His never-ending mercy and grace. ❧ *MONICA BRANDS, OUR DAILY BREAD MINISTRIES*

Our Daily Bread

Beginning Again

After Christmas festivities conclude at the end of December, my thoughts often turn to the coming year. While my children are out of school and our daily rhythms are slow, I reflect on where the last year has brought me and where I hope the next will take me. Those reflections sometimes come with pain and regret over the mistakes I've made. Yet the prospect of starting a new year fills me with hope and expectancy. I feel I have the opportunity to begin again with a fresh start, no matter what the last year held.

> **TODAY'S READING**
> **Ezra 1:1–11**
>
> **Everyone whose heart God had moved—prepared to go up and build the house of the LORD in Jerusalem.**
> Ezra 1:5

My anticipation of a fresh start pales in comparison to the sense of hope the Israelites must have felt when Cyrus, the king of Persia, released them to return to their homeland in Judah after seventy long years of captivity in Babylon. The previous king, Nebuchadnezzar, had deported the Israelites from their homeland. But the Lord prompted Cyrus to send the captives home to Jerusalem to rebuild God's temple (EZRA 1:2–3). Cyrus also returned to them treasures that had been taken from the temple. Their lives as God's chosen people, in the land God had appointed to them, began afresh after a long season of hardship in Babylon as a consequence for their sin.

No matter what lies in our past, when we confess our sin, God forgives us and gives us a fresh start. What great cause for hope! 🌱

KIRSTEN HOLMBERG

God's grace offers us fresh starts.

Pressing On

As I walked past an outside wall of the office building where I work, I was amazed to see a beautiful flower growing up through a crack between concrete slabs covering the ground. Despite its deprived circumstance, the plant had found a foothold, rooted itself in the dry crevice, and was flourishing. Later, I noticed that an air-conditioning unit located directly above the plant dropped water on it throughout the day. While its surroundings were hostile, the plant received the help it needed from the water above.

> **TODAY'S READING**
> **Philippians 3:7–14**
>
> **I press on toward the goal to win the prize.** Philippians 3:14

Growing in the Christian life can sometimes be difficult, but when we persevere with Christ, barriers are surmountable. Our circumstances may be unfavorable and discouragement may seem like an obstacle. Yet if we press on in our relationship with the Lord, we can flourish like that lone plant. This was the experience of the apostle Paul. Despite the severe hardships and challenges he faced (2 CORINTHIANS 11:23–27), he wouldn't give up. "I . . . take hold of that for which Christ Jesus took hold of me," he wrote. "I press on toward the goal to win the prize" (PHILIPPIANS 3:12, 14).

Paul realized he could do all things through the Lord who strengthened him (4:13), and so can we as we press on with the help of One who gives us strength. 🌱 *LAWRENCE DARMANI*

This is a day that You have made, Father.
Thank You that You'll be near me in whatever I face today.

God provides the strength we need to persevere and grow.

Breathtaking Glory

O ne of the pleasures of a trip to Europe is visiting the grand cathedrals that dot the landscape. They are breathtakingly beautiful as they soar toward the heavens. The architecture, art, and symbolism found in these amazing buildings present a spellbinding experience of wonder and magnificence.

As I thought about the fact that these structures were built to reflect God's magnificence and His all-surpassing splendor, I wondered how we could possibly recapture in our hearts and minds a similar feeling of God's grandeur and be reminded again of His greatness.

> TODAY'S READING
> **1 Chronicles 29:10–13**
>
> **Yours, LORD, is the greatness and the power and the glory and the majesty and the splendor.**
>
> 1 Chronicles 29:11

One way we can do that is to look beyond man's grand, regal structures and contemplate the greatness of what God Himself has created. Take one look at a starry night sky and think of God's power as He spoke the universe into existence. Hold a newborn baby in your arms and thank God for the miracle of life itself. Look at the snow-covered mountains of Alaska or the majestic Atlantic Ocean teeming with millions of God-designed creatures and imagine the power that makes that ecosystem work.

Mankind is not wrong to reach for the sky with structures that are intended to point us to God. But our truest admiration should be reserved for God Himself as we say to Him, "Yours, LORD, is the greatness and the power and the glory and the majesty and the splendor" (1 CHRONICLES 29:11). 🌑   *DAVE BRANON*

Lord, You do take our breath away with Your greatness. Thank You for reminding us of Your grandeur in Your world and in Your Word.

God alone is worthy of our worship.

What Do the Experts Say?

Boston Globe columnist Jeff Jacoby writes of the "uncanny ability of experts to get things hopelessly, cataclysmically wrong." A quick glance at recent history shows he's right. The great inventor Thomas Edison, for instance, once declared that talking movies would never replace silent films. And in 1928, Henry Ford declared, "People are becoming too intelligent ever to have another war." Countless other predictions by "experts" have missed the mark badly. Genius obviously has its limits.

> TODAY'S READING
> John 5:31–40
>
> **These are the very Scriptures that testify about me, yet you refuse to come to me to have life.** John 5:39–40

Only one Person is completely reliable, and He had strong words for some so-called experts. The religious leaders of Jesus's day claimed to have the truth. These scholars and theologians thought they knew what the promised Messiah would be like when He arrived.

Jesus cautioned them, "You study the Scriptures diligently because you think that in them you have eternal life." Then He pointed out how they were missing the heart of the matter. "These are the very Scriptures that testify about me, yet you refuse to come to me to have life" (JOHN 5:39–40).

As another new year gets underway, we'll hear predictions ranging from the terrifying to the wildly optimistic. Many of them will be stated with a great deal of confidence and authority. Don't be alarmed. Our confidence remains in the One at the very heart of the Scriptures. He has a firm grip on us and on our future. ❦ *TIM GUSTAFSON*

Father, whenever we are troubled or alarmed, help us to seek You. We commit this coming year and all it holds to You.

*Knowing the future is uncertain;
knowing the One who holds the future is a sure thing.*

Just Like My Father

My father's dusty, heeled-over, cowboy boots rest on the floor of my study, daily reminders of the kind of man he was.

Among other things, he raised and trained cutting horses—equine athletes that move like quicksilver. I loved to watch him at work, marveling that he could stay astride.

TODAY'S READING
1 Peter 5:8–12

It is written: "Be holy, because I am holy." 1 Peter 1:16

As a boy, growing up, I wanted to be just like him. I'm in my eighties, and his boots are still too large for me to fill.

My father's in heaven now, but I have another Father to emulate. I want to be just like Him—filled with His goodness, fragrant with His love. I'm not there and never will be in this life; His boots are much too large for me to fill.

But the apostle Peter said this: "The God of all grace, who called you to his eternal glory in Christ . . . will himself restore you and make you strong, firm and steadfast" (1 PETER 5:10). He has the wisdom and power to do that, you know (V. 11).

Our lack of likeness to our heavenly Father will not last forever. God has called us to share the beauty of character that is His. In this life we reflect Him poorly, but in heaven our sin and sorrow will be no more and we'll reflect Him more fully! This is the "true grace of God" (V. 12). 🌱

DAVID H. ROPER

Father God, we want to be just like You.
Help us to grow more and more like You each day!

Through the cross, believers are made perfect in His sight.

The Gift of the Magi

A **young married couple** had more love than money. As Christmas neared, both struggled to find a gift that would show how much they cared for the other. Finally, on Christmas Eve, Della sold her long, knee-length hair to buy Jim a platinum chain for the watch he'd inherited from his father and grandfather. Jim, however, had just sold the watch to buy a set of expensive combs for Della's hair.

Author O. Henry called the couple's story *The Gift of the Magi*. His creation suggests that even though their gifts became useless and may have caused them to look foolish on Christmas morning, their love made them among the wisest of those who give gifts.

> **TODAY'S READING**
> **Matthew 2:1–12**
>
> **We saw his star when it rose and have come to worship him.**
> Matthew 2:2

The wise men of the first Christmas story also could have looked foolish to some as they arrived in Bethlehem with gifts of gold, frankincense, and myrrh (MATTHEW 2:11). They weren't Jewish. They were outsiders, Gentiles, who didn't realize how much they would disturb the peace of Jerusalem by asking about a newly born king of the Jews (V. 2).

As with Jim and Della's experience, the magi's plans didn't turn out the way they expected. But they gave what money cannot buy. They came with gifts, but then bowed to worship One who would ultimately make the greatest of all loving sacrifices for them—and for us. 🍃

MART DEHAAN

Father in heaven, please help us in this season to learn what it means to give what money cannot buy.

God's gift of grace is priceless.

One Name

Cleopatra, Galileo, Shakespeare, Elvis, Pelé. They are all so well known that they need only one name to be recognized. They have remained prominent in history because of who they were and what they did. But there is another name that stands far above these or any other name!

Before the Son of God was born into this world, the angel told Mary and Joseph to name Him *Jesus* because "he will save his people from their sins" (MATTHEW 1:21), and "he . . . will be called the Son of the Most High" (LUKE 1:32). Jesus didn't come as a celebrity but as a servant who humbled Himself and died on the cross so that anyone who receives Him can be forgiven and freed from the power of sin.

> **TODAY'S READING**
> **Philippians 2:5–11**
>
> **At the name of Jesus every knee should bow, in heaven and on earth and under the earth.**
> Philippians 2:10

The apostle Paul wrote, "God exalted him to the highest place and gave him the name that is above every name, that at the name of Jesus every knee should bow, in heaven and on earth and under the earth, and every tongue acknowledge that Jesus Christ is Lord, to the glory of God the Father" (PHILIPPIANS 2:9–11).

In our times of greatest joy and our deepest need, the name we cling to is *Jesus*. He will never leave us, and His love will not fail. 🔖

DAVID C. MCCASLAND

Jesus, You are the name above all names, our Savior and Lord.
We lift our praise to You as we celebrate Your presence and
power in our lives today.

Jesus Christ is not valued at all until He is valued above all. AUGUSTINE

The Debt Eraser

blinked back tears as I reviewed my medical bill. Considering my husband's severe cut in salary after a lengthy unemployment, even paying half of the balance would require years of small monthly installments. I prayed before calling the doctor's office to explain our situation and request a payment plan.

After leaving me on hold for a short time, the receptionist informed me the doctor had zeroed out our account.

I sobbed a thank you. The generous gift overwhelmed me with gratitude. Hanging up the phone, I praised God. I considered saving the bill, not as a reminder of what I used to owe but as a reminder of what God had done.

> **TODAY'S READING**
> **Psalm 103:1–12**
>
> **As far as the east is from the west, so far has he removed our transgressions from us.** Psalm 103:12

My physician's choice to pardon my debt brought to mind God's choice to forgive the insurmountable debt of my sins. Scripture assures us God is "compassionate and gracious" and "abounding in love" (PSALM 103:8). He "does not treat us as our sins deserve" (V. 10). He removes our sins "as far as the east is from the west" (V. 12), when we repent and accept Christ as our Savior. His sacrifice erases the debt we once owed. Completely.

Once forgiven, we aren't defined by or limited by our past debt. In response to the Lord's extravagant gift, we can acknowledge all He's done. Offering our devoted worship and grateful affection, we can live for Him and share Him with others. 🖋

XOCHITL DIXON

Thank You for erasing our debt completely
when we place our confidence in You, Lord.

Our greatest debt, caused by sin, is erased by our greater God.

Stones of Remembrance

Some mornings when I go online, Facebook shows me "memories"—things I've posted on that day in previous years. These memories, such as photos from my brother's wedding or a video of my daughter playing with my grandmother, usually make me smile. But sometimes they have a more profound emotional effect. When I see a note about a visit to my brother-in-law during his chemotherapy or a picture of the staples across my mother's scalp after her brain surgery three years ago, I am reminded of God's faithful presence during difficult circumstances. These Facebook memories nudge me towards prayer and gratitude.

> TODAY'S READING
> Joshua 3:14–4:7
>
> **Remember the wonders he has done, his miracles, and the judgments he pronounced.**
>
> Psalm 105:5

All of us are prone to forget the things God has done for us. We need reminders. When Joshua led God's people towards their new home, they had to cross the Jordan River (JOSHUA 3:15–16). God parted the waters, and His people walked through on dry land (V. 17). To create a memorial of this miracle, they took twelve stones from the middle of the riverbed and stacked them on the other side (4:3, 6–7). When others asked what the stones meant, God's people would tell the story of what God had done that day.

Physical reminders of God's faithfulness in the past can remind us to trust Him in the present—and with the future. 🌿

AMY PETERSON

God, thank You for Your faithfulness to me over many years! Help me to trust You with the present and the future as well.

Growing a Servant's Heart

t was a long day at work. But when I got home, it was time to start my "other" job: being a good dad. Greetings from my wife and kids soon became, "Dad, what's for dinner?" "Dad, can you get me some water?" "Dad, can we play soccer?"

I just wanted to sit down. And even though *part* of me really wanted to be a good dad, I didn't *feel* like serving my family's needs. That's when I saw it: a thank-you card my wife had received from someone at church. It pictured a bowl of water, a towel, and dirty sandals. Across the bottom were these words from Luke 22:27: "I am among you as one who serves."

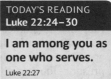

TODAY'S READING
Luke 22:24–30

I am among you as one who serves.

Luke 22:27

That statement of Jesus's mission, to serve those He came to seek and save (LUKE 19:10), was *exactly* what I needed. If Jesus was willing to do the dirtiest of jobs for His followers—like scrubbing His followers' no doubt filthy feet (JOHN 13:1–17)—I could get my son a cup of water without grumbling about it. In that moment, I was reminded that my family's requests to serve them weren't merely an *obligation*, but an *opportunity* to reflect Jesus's servant heart and His love to them. When requests are made of us, they are chances to become more like the One who served His followers by laying down His life for us. ❧   *ADAM HOLZ*

Lord, sometimes it's hard to serve others' needs. Help us to become more like You, willing to express Your love in the many opportunities we have to serve those around us each day.

God's love for us empowers us to serve others.

What's Inside?

"**D**o you want to see what's inside?" my friend asked. I had just complimented her on the old-fashioned rag doll her daughter held in her small arms. Instantly curious, I replied that yes, I very much wanted to see what was inside. She turned the doll face down and pulled open a discreet zipper sewn into its back. From within the cloth body, Emily gently removed a treasure: the rag doll she'd held and loved throughout the years of her own childhood more than two decades prior. The "outer" doll was merely a shell without this inner core to give it strength and form.

> **TODAY'S READING**
> 2 Corinthians 4:7–18
>
> **But we have this treasure in jars of clay to show that this all-surpassing power is from God and not from us.**
>
> 2 Corinthians 4:7

Paul describes the truth of Jesus's life, death, and resurrection as a treasure, carried about in the frail humanity of God's people. That treasure enables those who trust in Him to bear up under unthinkable adversity and continue in their service. When they do, His light—His life—shines brightly through the "cracks" of their humanness. Paul encourages us all not to "lose heart" (2 CORINTHIANS 4:16) because God strengthens us to do His work.

Like the "inner" doll, the gospel-treasure within us lends both purpose and fortitude to our lives. When God's strength shines through us, it invites others to ask, "What's inside?" We can then unzip our hearts and reveal the life-giving promise of salvation in Christ. ❧

KIRSTEN HOLMBERG

Thank You, Lord, for saving me. Please shine Your light brightly through my broken life so others will be invited to know You too.

The gospel of truth shines through the brokenness of God's people.

Fitting In

Lee is a diligent and reliable bank employee. Yet he often finds himself sticking out like a sore thumb for living out his faith. This reveals itself in practical ways, such as when he leaves the break room during an inappropriate conversation. At a Bible study, he shared with his friends, "I fear that I'm losing promotion opportunities for not fitting in."

Believers during the prophet Malachi's time faced a similar challenge. They had returned from exile and the temple had been rebuilt, but there was skepticism about God's plan for their future. Some of the Israelites were saying, "It is futile to serve God. What do we gain by carrying out his requirements . . . ? But now we call the arrogant blessed. Certainly evildoers prosper, and even when they put God to the test, they get away with it" (MALACHI 3:14–15).

> TODAY'S READING
> **Malachi 3:13–18**
>
> **Then those who feared the LORD talked with each other, and the LORD listened and heard.**
>
> Malachi 3:16

How can we stand firm for God in a culture that tells us we will lose out if we don't blend in? The faithful in Malachi's time responded to that challenge by meeting with like-minded believers to encourage each other. Malachi shares this important detail with us: "The LORD listened and heard" (V. 16).

God notices and cares for all who fear and honor Him. He doesn't call us to "fit in" but to draw closer to Him each day as we encourage each other. Let's stay faithful! 🕮   *POH FANG CHIA*

Lord, help us to keep on encouraging one another to
stay faithful to You in this faithless world.

Our faith may be tested so that we may trust God's faithfulness.

     Our Daily Bread

An Angry God?

When I studied Greek and Roman mythology in college, I was struck by how moody and easily angered the mythological gods were in the stories. The people on the receiving end of their anger found their lives destroyed, sometimes on a whim.

I was quick to scoff, wondering how anyone could believe in gods like that. But then I asked myself, *Is my view of the God who actually exists much different? Don't I view Him as easily angered whenever I doubt Him?* Sadly, yes.

That's why I appreciate Moses's request of God to "show me your glory" (EXODUS 33:18). Having been chosen to lead a large group of people who often grumbled

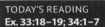

TODAY'S READING
Ex. 33:18–19; 34:1–7

The LORD, the LORD, the compassionate and gracious God, slow to anger, abounding in love and faithfulness.
Exodus 34:6

against him, Moses wanted to know that God would indeed help him with this great task. Moses's request was rewarded by a demonstration of God's glory. God announced to Moses His name and characteristics. He is "the compassionate and gracious God, slow to anger, abounding in love and faithfulness" (34:6).

This verse reminded me that God is not impulsive, suddenly striking out in anger. That's reassuring, especially when I consider the times I've lashed out at Him in anger or impatience. Also, He continually works to make me more like Himself.

We can see God and His glory in His patience with us, the encouraging word of a friend, a beautiful sunset, or—best of all—the whisper of the Holy Spirit inside of us. 🌿 *LINDA WASHINGTON*

Father God, I'm grateful that You are always compassionate, forgiving, and faithful.

Though we often change, God never does.

Knowing and Loving

"**J**esus loves me,** this I know, for the Bible tells me so" is the message of one of Christian music's most enduring songs, particularly for children. Written by Anna B. Warner in the 1800s, this lyric tenderly affirms our relationship with Him—we are loved.

Someone gave my wife a plaque for our home that gives these words a fresh twist by flipping that simple idea. It reads, "Jesus *knows* me, this I *love*." This provides a different perspective on our relationship with Him—we are known.

In ancient Israel, loving and knowing

TODAY'S READING
John 10:7-16

My sheep listen to my voice; I know them, and they follow me. John 10:27

the sheep distinguished a true shepherd from a hired hand. The shepherd spent so much time with his sheep that he developed an abiding care for and a deep knowledge of his lambs. Little wonder then that Jesus tells His own, "I am the good shepherd; I know my sheep and my sheep know me.... My sheep listen to my voice; I know them, and they follow me" (JOHN 10:14, 27).

He knows us and He loves us! We can trust Jesus's purposes for us and rest in the promise of His care because His Father "knows what [we] need before [we] ask him" (MATTHEW 6:8). As you deal with the ups and downs of life today, be at rest. You are known and loved by the Shepherd of your heart. 🌿

BILL CROWDER

Dear Lord, thank You for how You tenderly love and care for me.
Help me to trust You in all areas of my life.

The wonder of it all—just to think that Jesus loves me!

Pursuing Unity

G rowing up during the 1950s, I never questioned racism and the segregation practices that permeated daily life in the city where we lived. In schools, restaurants, public transportation, and neighborhoods, people with different shades of skin color were separated.

My attitude changed in 1968 when I entered US Army Basic Training. Our company included young men from many different cultural groups. We soon learned that we needed to understand and accept each other, work together, and accomplish our mission.

When Paul wrote to the first-century church at Colossae, he was well aware of the diversity of its members. He reminded them, "Here there is no Gentile or Jew,

> TODAY'S READING
> **Colossians 3:9–17**
>
> **Here there is no Gentile or Jew, circumcised or uncircumcised, barbarian, Scythian, slave or free, but Christ is all, and in all.** Colossians 3:11

circumcised or uncircumcised, barbarian, Scythian, slave or free, but Christ is all, and in all" (COLOSSIANS 3:11). In a group where surface as well as deeper differences could easily divide people, Paul urged them to "clothe [themselves] with compassion, kindness, humility, gentleness and patience" (V. 12). And over all these virtues, he told them to put on love "which binds them all together in perfect unity" (V. 14).

Putting these principles into practice may often be a work in progress, but that is what Jesus calls us to. What we as believers hold in common is our love for Him. On that basis, we pursue understanding, peace, and unity as members of the body of Christ.

Amid all our wonderful diversity, we pursue an even greater unity in Christ. 🌿

DAVID C. MCCASLAND

Christ's love creates unity in the midst of diversity.

The Power of Prayer

One day, when I was deeply concerned about the welfare of one close to me, I found encouragement in part of the Old Testament story of Samuel, a wise leader of the Israelites. As I read how Samuel interceded for God's people as they faced trouble, I strengthened my resolve to pray for the one I loved.

The Israelites faced the threat of the Philistines, who had previously defeated them when God's people didn't trust in Him (see 1 Samuel 4). After repenting of their sins, they heard that the Philistines were about to attack. This time, however, they asked Samuel to continue praying for them (7:8), and the Lord answered clearly by throwing their enemy into confusion (V. 10). Though the Philistines may have been mightier than the Israelites, the Lord was the strongest of them all.

> **TODAY'S READING**
> **1 Samuel 7:7–14**
>
> **Do not stop crying out to the LORD our God for us, that he may rescue us.** 1 Samuel 7:8

When we ache over the challenges facing those we love, and fear the situation won't change, we may be tempted to believe that the Lord will not act. But we should never underestimate the power of prayer, for our loving God hears our pleas. We don't know how He will move in response to our petitions, but we know that as our Father He longs for us to embrace His love and to trust in His faithfulness.

Do you have someone you can pray for today?

AMY BOUCHER PYE

Father God, the way You hear and answer my prayers amazes me. Strengthen my faith, that I will always believe in Your goodness and love.

God hears us when we pray.

Growing Gratitude

Would you like to cultivate a greater sense of gratitude? George Herbert, a seventeenth-century British poet, encourages readers toward that goal in his poem "Gratefulness": "Thou that hast given so much to me, give one thing more: a grateful heart."

Herbert recognized the only thing he needed in order to be thankful was simply an awareness of the blessings God had already given him.

TODAY'S READING
Romans 11:33–36

For from him and through him and for him are all things. Romans 11:36

The Bible declares Christ Jesus as the source of all blessing in Romans 11:36, "For from him and through him and for him are all things." "All things" encompasses both the extravagant and the mundane, everyday gifts in our lives. Everything we receive in life comes directly from our heavenly Father (JAMES 1:17), and He willingly gives us those gifts out of His love for us.

To expand my awareness of God's blessings in my life, I am learning to cultivate a heart that acknowledges the source of all the joys I experience each day, but especially the ones I often take for granted. Today those included a crisp morning to run, the anticipation of an evening with friends, a stocked pantry so I could make French toast with my daughters, the beauty of the world outside my window, and the aroma of freshly brewed coffee.

What is the "so much" that God has already given to you? Opening our eyes to those blessings will help us to develop grateful hearts. 🌿

LISA SAMRA

Take a few minutes to thank God for what comes to your mind right now.
Try to do that throughout the day as well.

When you think of all that's good, thank God.

Dealing with Delay

A global computer system outage causes widespread flight cancellations, stranding hundreds of thousands of passengers at airports. During a winter storm, multiple auto accidents close major highways. The person who promised to send a reply "right away" has failed to do so. Delays can often produce anger and frustration, but as followers of Jesus, we have the privilege of looking to Him for help.

TODAY'S READING
Genesis 45:1–8

So then, it was not you who sent me here, but God.

Genesis 45:8

One of the Bible's great examples of patience is Joseph, who was sold to slave traders by his jealous brothers, falsely accused by his employer's wife, and imprisoned in Egypt. "But while Joseph was there in the prison, the LORD was with him" (GENESIS 39:20–21). Years later, when Joseph interpreted Pharaoh's dreams, he was made second in command in Egypt (CH. 41).

The most remarkable fruit of his patience occurred when his brothers came to buy grain during a famine. "I am your brother Joseph," he told them, "the one you sold into Egypt! And now, do not be distressed and do not be angry with yourselves for selling me here, because it was to save lives that God sent me ahead of you. . . . So then, it was not you who sent me here, but God" (45:4–5, 8).

In all our delays, brief or long, may we, like Joseph, gain patience, perspective, and peace as we trust in the Lord. 🌿

DAVID C. MCCASLAND

Father in heaven, in all of our delays may we trust Your faithful hand of guidance and experience Your presence with us in every situation.

Confidence in God enables us to live out our faith patiently.

Our Daily Bread

By the Spirit's Power

What do you do when there is a mountain in your way? The story of Dashrath Manjhi can inspire us. When his wife died because he was unable to get her to the hospital to receive urgent medical care, Manjhi did what seemed impossible. He spent twenty-two years chiseling a massive gap in a mountain so other villagers could get to the local hospital to receive the medical care they needed. Before he died, the government of India celebrated him for his achievement.

> **TODAY'S READING**
> **Zechariah 4:1–7**
>
> **What are you, mighty mountain? Before Zerubbabel you will become level ground.**
> Zechariah 4:7

Rebuilding the temple must have looked impossible to Zerubbabel, one of the leaders of Israel who returned from exile. The people were discouraged, faced opposition from their enemies, and lacked resources or a big army. But God sent Zechariah to remind Zerubbabel that the task would take something more powerful than military strength, individual power, or man-made resources. It would take the Spirit's power (ZECHARIAH 4:6). With the assurance of divine aid, Zerubbabel trusted that God would level any mountain of difficulty that stood in the way of rebuilding the temple and restoring the community (V. 7).

What do we do when there is a "mountain" before us? We have two options: rely on our own strength or trust the Spirit's power. When we trust His power, He will either level the mountain or give us the strength and endurance to climb over it. 🌱

MARVIN WILLIAMS

Human power is inadequate to accomplish God's purposes.

My Help!

For decades the renowned Brooklyn Tabernacle Choir has blessed multitudes through their soul-refreshing gospel songs. One example is their recording from Psalm 121 titled "My Help."

Psalm 121 begins with a personal confession of faith in the Lord who brought all things into existence, and He was the source of the psalmist's help (VV. 1–2). Just what did this mean? Stability (V. 3), around-the-clock care (VV. 3–4), constant presence and protection (VV. 5–6), and

> **TODAY'S READING**
> **Psalm 121**
>
> **My help comes from the LORD, the Maker of heaven and earth.** Psalm 121:2

preservation from all kinds of evil for time and eternity (VV. 7–8).

Taking their cues from Scripture, God's people through the ages have identified the Lord as their source of "help" through their songs. My own worship experience includes lifting my voice with others who sang a soulful rendition of Charles Wesley's, "Father, I stretch my hands to Thee, no other help I know; if Thou withdraw Thyself from me, ah! whither shall I go." The great reformer Martin Luther got it right when he penned the words, "A mighty fortress is our God, a bulwark never failing; our helper He amid the flood of mortal ills prevailing."

Do you feel alone, forsaken, abandoned, confused? Ponder the lyrics of Psalm 121. Allow these words to fill your soul with faith and courage. You're not alone, so don't try to do life on your own. Rather, rejoice in the earthly and eternal care of God as demonstrated in the life, death, resurrection, and ascension of the Lord Jesus Christ. And whatever the next steps, take them with His help. 🌱

ARTHUR JACKSON

Father, how grateful we are that Scripture and song remind us that You are our source of help. Help me to not forget that this day.

The Maker of the universe is the helper of God's people!

Promises, Promises

My youngest daughter and I have a game we call "Pinchers." When she goes up the stairs, I'll chase her and try to give her a little pinch. The rules are that I can only pinch her (gently, of course!) when she's on the stairs. Once she's at the top, she's safe. Sometimes, though, she's not in the mood to play. And if I follow her up the stairs, she'll sternly say, "No pinchers!" I'll respond, "No pinchers. I *promise*."

Now, that promise may seem a little thing. But when I *do* what I say, my daughter begins to understand something of my character. She experiences my consistency. She knows my word is good, that she can trust me. It's a little thing, keeping such a promise. But promises—or, keeping them, I should say—are the glue of relationships. They lay a foundation of love and trust.

> **TODAY'S READING**
> **2 Peter 1:1–9**
>
> **He has given us his very great and precious promises, so that through them you may participate in the divine nature.**
>
> 2 Peter 1:4

I think that's what Peter meant when he wrote that God's promises enable us to "participate in the divine nature" (2 PETER 1:4). When we take God at His Word, trusting what He says about Himself and about us, we encounter His heart toward us. It gives Him an opportunity to reveal His faithfulness as we rest in what He says is true. I'm thankful Scripture brims with His promises, these concrete reminders that "his compassions never fail. They are new every morning" (LAMENTATIONS 3:22–23). 🌿 *ADAM HOLZ*

Lord, thank You so much for Your "great and precious promises."
Help us to recognize and to rest in what You say is true,
that we might fully experience Your tender goodness.

God's Word to us reveals His heart toward us.

It's in the Attitude

Regina drove home from work discouraged and tired. The day had started with tragic news in a text message from a friend, then spiraled downward in meetings with co-workers who refused to work with any of her ideas. As Regina was talking to the Lord, she thought it best to put the stress of the day aside and made a surprise visit with flowers to an elderly friend at a care center. Her spirits lifted as Maria shared how good the Lord was to her. She said, "I have my own bed and a chair, three meals a day, and help from the nurses here. And occasionally God sends a cardinal to my window just because He knows I love them and He loves me."

TODAY'S READING
James 1:1–12

Consider it pure joy... whenever you face trials of many kinds. James 1:2

Attitude. Perspective. As the saying goes, "Life is 10 percent what happens to us and 90 percent how we react to it." The people James wrote to were scattered because of persecution, and he asked them to consider their perspective about difficulties. He challenged them with these words: "Consider it pure joy... whenever you face trials of many kinds" (JAMES 1:2).

We are each on our own journey of learning to trust God with hard circumstances. The kind of joy-filled perspective James talked about comes as we learn to see that God can use struggles to produce maturity in our faith. ❦   *ANNE CETAS*

> Lord, please change my attitude about hard times.
> Bring about joy, perseverance, and maturity in me.

God can bring times of growth out of our times of heartache.

A "Yes" of Love

On August 21, 2016, Carissa posted photos on social media of a devastating flood in Louisiana. The next morning she included a note from someone in the flooded area pleading for help. Five hours after that, she and her husband, Bobby, sent out a call for others to join them on their 1,000-mile trip to provide help. Less than twenty-four hours later, thirteen people were on their way to serve those whose homes had been severely damaged.

What motivates people to drop everything and drive seventeen hours to move appliances, do demolition work, and provide hope in a place they've never been before? It's love.

> **TODAY'S READING**
> **1 John 3:16–24**
>
> **Let us not love with words or speech but with actions and in truth.** 1 John 3:18

Think about this verse, which she posted along with her call for help: "Commit your way to the LORD; trust in him and he will do this" (PSALM 37:5). This is especially true when we follow God's call to help. The apostle John said, "If anyone... sees a brother or sister in need but has no pity on them, how can the love of God be in that person?" (1 JOHN 3:17). It may be a daunting task—but we have God's promise of help when we "do what pleases him" (V. 22).

When a need arises, we can honor God by being willing to offer a "yes" of love to what we sense He is asking us to do for others. 🌸

DAVE BRANON

Lord, please open our eyes to the needs of others,
open our hearts to those people, and open our hands
so we can provide help in the time of need.

*We show God's love when we are willing to help others; we show His
strength when we take on the task He gives us to do.*

God of Life

A **few winters ago,** my hometown experienced an unusually long blast of bone-chilling temperatures that finally gave way to the warmer weather of spring. For two weeks straight, the outside thermometer dipped well below the sub-zero degree mark (-20 C; -5 F).

On one particularly bitter cold morning, the sound of chirping birds broke the silence of night. Dozens, if not hundreds, sang their hearts out. If I didn't know any better, I could have sworn the little creatures were crying out to their Creator to please warm things up!

Bird experts tell us that the multitude of birdsongs we hear during late winter mornings are mostly male birds, attempting to attract mates and claim their territories. Their chirping reminded me that God fine-tuned His creation to sustain and flourish life—because He is a God of life.

> TODAY'S READING
> Ps. 104:1–12, 24–30
>
> **LORD my God, you are very great; you are clothed with splendor and majesty.** Psalm 104:1

In a psalm that marvels at God's flourishing earth, the author begins, "Let all that I am praise the LORD" (PSALM 104:1 NLT). He went on to write, "The birds of the sky nest by the waters; they sing among the branches" (V. 12).

From singing and nesting birds to a vast ocean "teeming with creatures beyond number" (V. 25), we see reasons to praise the Creator for the lengths He's gone to ensure that all of life thrives. 🌱   *JEFF OLSON*

Thank God for the world He has made. List the parts of His creation that
You especially enjoy. Thank Him for them one by one.

He is before all things, and in him all things hold together. COLOSSIANS 1:17

True Hope

Not long ago I visited the Empire State Building with a friend. The line looked short—just down the block and around the corner. Yet as we entered the building, we discovered the line of people stretching through the lobby, up the stairs, and into another room. Every new turn revealed more distance to go.

TODAY'S READING
Romans 5:1–11

The Spirit himself testifies with our spirit that we are God's children.

Romans 8:16

Attractions and theme parks carefully route their crowds to make the lines seem shorter. Yet disappointment can lurk "just around the bend."

Sometimes life's disappointments are much more severe. The job we hoped for doesn't materialize; friends we counted on let us down; the romantic relationship we longed for fails to work out. But into these heartbreaks, God's Word speaks a refreshing truth about our hope in Him. The apostle Paul wrote, "Suffering produces perseverance; perseverance, character; and character, hope. And hope does not put us to shame [or disappoint us], because God's love has been poured out into our hearts through the Holy Spirit, who has been given to us" (ROMANS 5:3–5).

As we place our trust in Him, through His Spirit, God whispers the truth that we are unconditionally loved and will one day be with Him—regardless of the obstacles we face. In a world that may often disappoint us, how good it is to know that God gives genuine hope. ✿

JAMES BANKS

Abba, Father, thank You that I can always trust in Your perfect, never-ending love.

In Christ, the hopeless find hope.

Holy, Holy, Holy

"**ime flies when** you're having fun." This cliché has no basis in fact, but experience makes it seem true.

When life is pleasant, time passes all too quickly. Give me a task that I enjoy, or a person whose company I love, and time seems irrelevant.

My experience of this "reality" has given me a new understanding of the scene described in Revelation 4. In the past, when I considered the four living creatures seated around God's throne who keep repeating the same few words, I thought, What a boring existence!

I don't think that anymore. I think about the scenes they have witnessed with their many eyes (V. 8). I consider the view they have from their position around God's throne (V. 6). I think of how amazed they are at God's wise and loving involvement with wayward earthlings. Then I think, What better response could there be? What else is there to say but, "Holy, holy, holy"?

Is it boring to say the same words over and over? Not when you're in the presence of the one you love. Not when you're doing exactly what you were designed to do.

Like the four creatures, we were designed to glorify God. Our lives will never be boring if we're focusing our attention on Him and fulfilling that purpose.

> TODAY'S READING
> **Revelation 4**
>
> **Day and night they never stop saying: " 'Holy, holy, holy is the Lord God Almighty,' who was, and is, and is to come."** Revelation 4:8

JULIE ACKERMAN LINK

Holy, holy, holy, Lord God Almighty! Early in the morning
our song shall rise to Thee; holy, holy, holy! Merciful and mighty!
God in three Persons, blessed Trinity! *REGINALD HEBER*

The author of this article, Julie,
is now worshiping her Lord in heaven.

A heart in tune with God can't help but sing His praise.

The Last Word

One day during a university philosophy class, a student made some inflammatory remarks about the professor's views. To the surprise of the other students, the teacher thanked him and moved on to another comment. When he was asked later why he didn't respond to the student, he said, "I'm practicing the discipline of not having to have the last word."

This teacher loved and honored God, and he wanted to embody a humble spirit as he reflected this love. His words remind me of another Teacher—this one from long ago, who wrote the book of Ecclesiastes. Although not addressing how to handle an angry person, he said

TODAY'S READING
Ecclesiastes 5:1–7

Do not be quick with your mouth, do not be hasty in your heart.

Ecclesiastes 5:2

that when we approach the Lord we should guard our steps and "go near to listen" rather than being quick with our mouths and hasty in our hearts. By doing so we acknowledge that God is the Lord and we are those whom He has created (ECCLESIASTES 5:1–2).

How do you approach God? If you sense that your attitude could use some adjustment, why not spend some time considering the majesty and greatness of the Lord? When we ponder His unending wisdom, power, and presence, we can feel awed by His overflowing love for us. With this posture of humility, we too need not have the last word.    *AMY BOUCHER PYE*

Lord God, I want to honor You and I bow before You now in silence.
Teach me how to pray and how to listen.

Carefully chosen words honor God.

Joy

I 'm fast approaching a new season—the "winter" of old age—but I'm not there yet. Even though the years are galloping by and sometimes I'd like to slow them down, I have joy that sustains me. Each day is a new day given me by the Lord. With the psalmist, I can say, "It is good to praise the LORD . . . proclaiming your love in the morning and your faithfulness at night"! (PSALM 92:1–2).

TODAY'S READING
Psalm 92

I sing for joy at what your hands have done. Psalm 92:4

Even though my life has its struggles and the pain and difficulties of others sometimes overwhelms me, God enables me to join the psalmist in "[singing] for joy at what [His] hands have done" (V. 4). Joy for blessings given: family, friends, and satisfying work. Joy because of God's wondrous creation and His inspired Word. Joy because Jesus loved us so much He died for our sins. And joy because He gave us the Spirit, the *source* of true joy (ROMANS 15:13). Because of the Lord, believers in Him can "flourish like a palm tree . . . [and] still bear fruit in old age" (PSALM 92:12–14).

What fruit is that? No matter our circumstances or season of life, we can be examples of His love through the life we lead and the words we say. There is joy in knowing and living for the Lord and telling others about Him. 🌿   *ALYSON KIEDA*

> Dear Lord, thank You for the joy
> that is ours through the Spirit.

God is the giver of joy.

Like a Little Child

One evening many years ago, after saying a goodnight prayer with our two-year-old daughter, my wife was surprised by a question. "Mommy, where is Jesus?"

Luann replied, "Jesus is in heaven and He's everywhere, right here with us. And He can be in your heart if you ask Him to come in."

"I want Jesus to be in my heart."

"One of these days you can ask Him."

"I want to ask Him to be in my heart *now*."

So our little girl said, "Jesus, please come into my heart and be with me." And that started her faith journey with Him.

When Jesus's disciples asked Him who was the greatest in the kingdom of heaven, He called a little child to come and join them (MATTHEW 18:1–2). "Unless you change and become like little children," Jesus said, "you will never enter the kingdom of heaven. . . . And whoever welcomes one such child in my name welcomes me" (VV. 3–5).

> TODAY'S READING
> Matt. 18:1–5; 19:13–14
>
> **Unless you change and become like little children, you will never enter the kingdom of heaven.** Matthew 18:3

Through the eyes of Jesus we can see a trusting child as our example of faith. And we are told to welcome all who open their hearts to Him. "Let the little children come to me," Jesus said, "and do not hinder them, for the kingdom of heaven belongs to such as these" (19:14).

DAVID C. MCCASLAND

Lord Jesus, thank You for calling us to follow You
with the confident faith of a child.

Our faith in Jesus is to be like that of a trusting child.

Able and Available

My husband was at work when I received news about my mom's cancer diagnosis. I left him a message and reached out to friends and family. None were available. Covering my face with trembling hands, I sobbed. "Help me, Lord." A resulting assurance that God was with me comforted me through those moments when I felt utterly alone.

I thanked the Lord when my husband came home and support from friends and family trickled in. Still, the calming awareness of God's presence I sensed in those first few hours of lonely grieving affirmed that God is readily and faithfully available wherever and whenever I need help.

> **TODAY'S READING**
> **Psalm 46**
>
> **God is our refuge and strength, an ever-present help in trouble.** Psalm 46:1

In Psalm 46, the psalmist proclaims God is our sanctuary, strength, and steadfast supporter (V. 1). When it feels as if we're surrounded by chaos or everything we thought was stable crashes down around us, we don't have to fear (VV. 2–3). God doesn't falter (VV. 4–7). His power is evident and effective (VV. 8–9). Our eternal Sustainer gives us confidence in His unchanging character (V. 10). The Lord, our secure stronghold, remains with us forever (V. 11).

God created His followers to prayerfully support and encourage one another. But He also affirms He is always able and available. When we call on God, we can trust Him to keep His promises to provide for us. He will comfort us through His people as well as through His personal presence. 🌿 *XOCHITL DIXON*

Lord, thank You for assuring us You're always accessible
because You're always with us.

God is always able and available to help us.

White as Snow

Last December, my family and I went to the mountains. We had lived in a tropical climate all our lives, so it was the first time we could see snow in all its magnificence. As we contemplated the white mantle covering the fields, my husband quoted Isaiah, "Though your sins are like scarlet, they shall be as white as snow" (ISAIAH 1:18).

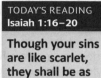

TODAY'S READING
Isaiah 1:16–20

Though your sins are like scarlet, they shall be as white as snow.
Isaiah 1:18

After asking about the meaning of scarlet, our three-year-old daughter asked, "Is the color red bad?" She knows sins are things God dislikes, but this verse is not talking about colors. The prophet was describing the bright red dye obtained from the eggs of a small insect. Clothes would be double-dyed in this bright red so the color became fixed. Neither rain nor washing would remove it. Sin is like that. No human effort can take it away. It's rooted in the heart.

Only God can cleanse a heart from sin. And as we looked at the mountains, we admired the pure whiteness that scrubbing and bleaching a piece of cloth dyed in scarlet red can't achieve. When we follow Peter's teaching, "Repent, then, and turn to God, so that your sins may be wiped out" (ACTS 3:19), God forgives us and gives us a new life. Only through Jesus's sacrifice can we receive what no one else can give—a pure heart. What a wonderful gift! 🌱   *KEILA OCHOA*

Father, thank You for forgiving our sins and wiping them clean.

When God forgives, He purifies us too.

National Treasure

When an advertiser altered a photo of Michelangelo's famous marble sculpture of the biblical hero David, Italy's government and gallery officials objected. Picturing David with a military rifle slung over his shoulder (instead of his slingshot) would be a violation—"like taking a hammer to it or worse," a cultural official said.

In first-century Jerusalem, David was remembered as the shepherd-songwriter and soldier-king of Israel's fondest memories and greatest hopes. Prophets foretold that David's descendant would finally defeat the enemies of Israel. So, centuries later, when crowds welcomed Jesus as *the Son of David* (MATTHEW 21:6–9), they were expecting Him to lead the revolt that

> TODAY'S READING
> **Matthew 21:12–16**
>
> **Hosanna to the Son of David! Blessed is he who comes in the name of the Lord!** Matthew 21:9

would overthrow their Roman occupiers. Instead Jesus knocked over the tables of temple money-changers to restore His Father's house as a house of prayer for all nations. Israel's leaders were furious. This wasn't the kind of Messiah and *son of David* they were looking for. So without realizing what they were doing, they called for Roman executioners to take a hammer to the hands and feet of the true glory of Israel.

Instead of stopping them, Jesus let Himself be lifted up on a cross of shame—defaced and disgraced. Only by resurrection would it be known that the true Son of David had defeated His enemies with love and enlisted the children of all nations to spread the word. ❧

MART DEHAAN

Father in heaven, it's hard to admit. But it's true. We get so confused.
We try to protect the images we love more than the love
You consider priceless.

Jesus shows that God is always better than our expectations.

Stepping into Opportunity

Like lots of people, I struggle to get enough exercise. So I recently got something to motivate myself to move: a pedometer that counts steps. It's a simple thing. But it's amazing how much difference this gadget makes in my motivation. Instead of grumbling when I have to get off the couch, I see it as an opportunity to get a few more steps.

Mundane tasks, like getting one of my kids a cup of water, become opportunities that help me work toward a larger goal. In that sense, my pedometer has changed my perspective *and* my motivation. Now I look to get extra steps in whenever possible.

> TODAY'S READING
> **Colossians 4:2–6**
>
> **Be wise in the way you act toward outsiders; make the most of every opportunity.**
> Colossians 4:5

I wonder if our Christian life isn't a bit like that. There are opportunities to love and serve and interact with people every day, as Paul exhorts in Colossians 4:5. But am I always aware of those moments? Am I paying attention to opportunities to be an encourager in seemingly mundane interactions? God is at work in the lives of every person I relate to, from my family and coworkers to a clerk at the grocery store. Each interaction offers a chance for me to pay attention to what God might be doing—even if it's something as seemingly "small" as kindly asking a server at a restaurant how she's doing.

Who knows how God might work in those moments when we're alert to the opportunities He sends our way. 🌐 *ADAM HOLZ*

Lord, there are so many opportunities to love, listen, and serve those around us each day. Please help us to become people who notice the needs of others.

Take every opportunity to serve someone.

How to Change a Life

Sometimes our lives can change in a moment through the powerful impact of others. For rock 'n' roll legend Bruce Springsteen, it was the work of musical artists that helped him through a difficult childhood and a persistent struggle with depression. He found meaning in his own work through the truth he'd experienced firsthand, that "You can change someone's life in three minutes with the right song."

Like a compelling song, others' well-chosen words can also give us hope, even change the course of our lives. I'm sure most of us could share stories of a conversation that forever impacted our lives—words from a teacher that changed the way we saw the world, words of encouragement that restored our confidence, gentle words from a friend that carried us through a difficult time.

> **TODAY'S READING**
> Prov. 15:4; 16:24; 18:21
>
> **Gracious words are a honeycomb, sweet to the soul and healing to the bones.** Proverbs 16:24

Perhaps this is why the book of Proverbs spends so much time emphasizing our responsibility to treasure words and use them wisely. Scripture never treats speech as if it's "just talk." Instead, we are taught that our words can have life-or-death consequences (18:21). In just a few words we could crush someone's spirit, or, through words of wisdom and hope, nourish and strengthen others (15:4).

Not all of us have the ability to create powerful music. But we each can seek God's wisdom to serve others through our speech (PSALM 141:3). With just a few well-chosen words, God can use us to change a life.    MONICA BRANDS

Lord, help us never to take for granted the powerful gift of language.
May we use our words wisely to heal and strengthen others
and point to the hope we have in You.

God has given us the power to have an impact on lives through our words.

Our Daily Bread

It Is Amazing!

In our natural state, we all fall short of *it* (ROMANS 3:23).

Jesus was the radiance of *it* (HEBREWS 1:3), and those who knew Him saw *it* (JOHN 1:14).

In the Old Testament, *it* filled the tabernacle (EXODUS 40:34–35), and the Israelites were led by *it*.

And we are promised that at the end of time, heaven will shine with *it* in splendor so great there will be no need for the sun (REVELATION 21:23).

What is the "it" in all those statements above?

"It" is *the glory of God*. And He is amazing!

TODAY'S READING
Rev. 21:1–3, 10–11, 23

Let the whole earth be filled with His glory. Amen and Amen.

Psalm 72:19 NKJV

Throughout the Bible we are told that we can enjoy glimpses of God's magnificent glory as we dwell on this earth He has created. God's glory is described as the external display of His being. Because we cannot see God, He gives us clear pictures of His presence and His work in things like the majesty of the universe, the greatness of our salvation, and the presence of the Holy Spirit in our lives.

Today, look for God's glory—for the evidence of His greatness. You'll see it in nature's beauty, a child's laughter, and the love of others. God still fills the earth with His glory. 🌿

DAVE BRANON

Thank You, heavenly Father, for the glimpse of Your glory that we see now, for the glory that we know exists in our Savior, and for the sure hope of the full knowledge of glory that we will experience in heaven.

We can see and enjoy the glory of God both now and forever.

Listening to His Voice

'm hard of hearing—"deaf in one ear and can't hear out of the other," as my father used to say. So I wear a set of hearing aids.

Most of the time the devices work well, except in environments where there's a lot of surrounding noise. In those settings, my hearing aids pick up every voice in the room and I cannot hear the person in front of me.

So it is with our culture: a cacophony of sounds can drown out God's quiet voice. "Where shall the Word be found, where will the Word resound?" poet T.S. Eliot asks. "Not here, there is not enough silence."

> **TODAY'S READING**
> **John 10:25–30**
>
> **My sheep hear My voice, and I know them, and they follow Me.**
>
> John 10:27 NKJV

Fortunately, my hearing aids have a setting that cuts out the surrounding sounds and enables me to hear only the voices I want to hear. In the same way, despite the voices around us, if we quiet our souls and listen, we will hear God's "still small voice" (1 KINGS 19:11–12 NKJV).

He speaks to us every day, summoning us in our restlessness and our longing. He calls to us in our deepest sorrow and in the incompleteness and dissatisfaction of our greatest joys.

But primarily God speaks to us in His Word (1 THESSALONIANS 2:13). As you pick up His book and read it, you too will hear His voice. He loves you more than you can ever know, and He wants you to hear what He has to say. 🌾

DAVID H. ROPER

Dear Lord, thank You for giving us Your Word. Help me to listen to Your voice as I spend time alone with You.

God speaks through His Word when we take time to listen.

Our Daily Bread

Praising Through Problems

"**I**t's cancer." I wanted to be strong when Mom said those words to me. But I burst into tears. You never want to hear those words even one time. But this was Mom's third bout with cancer. After a routine mammogram and biopsy, Mom learned that she had a malignant tumor under her arm.

Though Mom was the one with bad news, she had to comfort me. Her response was eye-opening for me: "I know God is always good to me. He's always faithful." Even as she faced a difficult surgery, followed up by radiation treatments, Mom was assured of God's presence and faithfulness.

TODAY'S READING
Job 1:13–22

Shall we accept good from God, and not trouble?

Job 2:10

How like Job. Job lost his children, his wealth, and his health. But after hearing the news, Job 1:20 tells us "he fell to the ground in worship." When advised to curse God, he said, "Shall we accept good from God, and not trouble?" (2:10). What a radical initial response. Though Job later complained, ultimately he accepted that God had never changed. Job knew that God was still with him and that He still cared.

For most of us, praise is not our first response to difficulties. Sometimes the pain of our circumstances is so overwhelming, we lash out in fear or anger. But watching Mom's response reminded me that God is still present, still good. He will help us through hard times. 🍃

LINDA WASHINGTON

Lord, prepare me for the times when praise is most difficult to utter.

Even at our lowest point, we can lift our eyes to the Lord.

A Blanket for Everyone

Linus Van Pelt, better known as simply "Linus," was a mainstay in the *Peanuts* comic strip. Witty and wise, yet insecure, Linus constantly carried a security blanket. We can identify. We have our fears and insecurities too.

The disciple Peter knew something about fear. When Jesus was arrested, Peter displayed courage by following the Lord into the courtyard of the high priest. But then he began to show his fear by lying to protect his identity (JOHN 18:15–26). He spoke disgraceful words that denied his Lord. But Jesus never stopped loving Peter and ultimately restored him (SEE JOHN 21:15–19).

Peter's emphasis on love in 1 Peter 4:8 came from one who had experienced the deep love of Jesus. And he, in turn, stressed the importance of love in our relationships with the words, "above all." The intensity of the verse continues with the encouragement to "love each other deeply, because love covers over a multitude of sins."

> **TODAY'S READING**
> **John 18:15–18, 25–27**
>
> **Above all, love each other deeply, because love covers over a multitude of sins.**
>
> 1 Peter 4:8

Have you ever needed that kind of "blanket"? I have! After saying or doing something I later regretted, I have felt the chilly draft of guilt and shame. I have needed to be "covered" in the manner that Jesus covered disgraced, shame-filled people in the Gospels.

To followers of Jesus, love is a blanket to be graciously and courageously given away for the comfort and reclamation of others. As recipients of such great love, let us be givers of the same. 🌿   *ARTHUR JACKSON*

Father, Your love, in and through Jesus, has rescued us time and time again. Help me to be an instrument of Your saving love for others.

God loves you and me—let's love each other.

The Problem with Pride

People who achieve an extraordinary level of fame or reputation while they are still alive are often called "a legend in their own time." A friend who played professional baseball says he met many people in the world of sports who were only "a legend in their own mind." Pride has a way of distorting how we see ourselves while humility offers a realistic perspective.

The writer of Proverbs said, "Pride goes before destruction, a haughty spirit before a fall" (16:18). Viewing ourselves in the mirror of self-importance reflects a distorted image. Self-elevation positions us for a fall.

TODAY'S READING
Proverbs 16:16–22

Pride goes before destruction, a haughty spirit before a fall.
Proverbs 16:18

The antidote to the poison of arrogance is true humility that comes from God. "Better to be lowly in spirit along with the oppressed than to share plunder with the proud" (V. 19).

Jesus told His disciples, "Whoever wants to become great among you must be your servant, and whoever wants to be first must be your slave—just as the Son of Man did not come to be served, but to serve, and to give his life as a ransom for many" (MATTHEW 20:26–28).

There is nothing wrong with receiving accolades for achievement and success. The challenge is to stay focused on the One who calls us to follow Him saying, "for I am gentle and humble in heart, and you will find rest for your souls" (11:29). 🌱

DAVID C. MCCASLAND

Lord Jesus, give us Your humility as we interact with others today.
May we honor You in all we do and say.

True humility comes from God.

Unlikely Friends

My Facebook friends often post endearing videos of unlikely animal friendships, such as a recent video I watched of an inseparable pup and pig, another of a deer and cat, and yet another of an orangutan mothering several tiger cubs.

When I view such heartwarmingly unusual friendships, it reminds me of the description of the garden of Eden. In this setting, Adam and Eve lived in harmony with God and each other. And because God gave them plants for food, I imagine even the animals lived peacefully together (GENESIS 1:30). But this idyllic scene was disrupted when Adam and Eve sinned (3:21–23). Now in both human relationships and the creation, we see constant struggle and conflict.

> TODAY'S READING
> **Isaiah 11:1–10**
>
> **The wolf will live with the lamb, the leopard will lie down with the goat, the calf and the lion and the yearling together.**
>
> Isaiah 11:6

Yet the prophet Isaiah reassures us that one day, "The wolf will live with the lamb, the leopard will lie down with the goat, the calf and the lion and the yearling together" (11:6). Many interpret that future day as when Jesus comes again to reign. When He returns, there will be no more divisions and "no more death . . . or pain, for the old order of things has passed away" (REVELATION 21:4). On that renewed earth, creation will be restored to its former harmony and people of every tribe, nation, and language will join together to worship God (7:9–10; 22:1–5).

Until then, God can help us to restore broken relationships and to develop new, unlikely friendships. 🌾   *ALYSON KIEDA*

Dear Father, help us to break down barriers and to seek to befriend others; and as we do, enable us to be bearers of the gospel of peace.

One day God will restore the world to perfect peace.

Everywhere and Nowhere

A **family friend who,** like us, lost a teenager in a car accident wrote a tribute to her daughter, Lindsay, in the local paper. One of the most powerful images in her essay was this: After mentioning the many pictures and remembrances of Lindsay she had put around their house, she wrote, "She is everywhere, but nowhere."

Although our daughters still smile back at us from their photos, the spirited personalities that lit up those smiles are nowhere to be found. They are everywhere—in our hearts, in our thoughts, in all those photos—but nowhere.

TODAY'S READING
Psalm 139:7–12

Where can I go from your Spirit? Where can I flee from your presence? Psalm 139:7

But Scripture tells us that, in Christ, Lindsay and Melissa are not really nowhere. They are in Jesus's presence, "with the Lord" (2 CORINTHIANS 5:8). They are with the One who, in a sense, is "nowhere but everywhere." After all, we don't see God in a physical form. We certainly don't have smiling pictures of Him on our mantel. In fact, if you look around your house, you may think He is nowhere. But just the opposite is true. He is everywhere!

Wherever we go on this earth, God is there. He's there to guide, strengthen, and comfort us. We cannot go where He is not. We don't see Him, but He's everywhere. In each trial we face, that's incredibly good news. 🌱 *DAVE BRANON*

Thank You, Lord, that You are present with me here,
right now. Teach me to lean on You.

Our greatest comfort in sorrow is knowing God is with us.

Fault Lines

An influx of refugees to our community has led to new growth in area churches. That growth brings challenges. Church members must learn how to welcome these newcomers as they adjust to a strange culture, new language, and different worship styles. All this change can create some awkward situations.

Misunderstandings and disagreements occur everywhere we find people. Church is no exception. If we don't handle our differences in a healthy way, they can harden into divisions.

The early church in Jerusalem was growing when a dispute arose that broke along a cultural fault line. The Greek-speaking Jews (the Hellenists) had a complaint against those Jews who spoke Aramaic. The Hellenist widows "were being overlooked in the daily distribution of food" (ACTS 6:1). So the apostles said, "Choose seven men from among you who are known to be full of the Spirit and wisdom" (V. 3). The seven chosen all had Greek names (V. 5). In other words, they were *Hellenists*, members of the group being neglected. They best understood the problem. The apostles prayed over them and the church thrived (VV. 6–7).

> TODAY'S READING
> **Acts 6:1–7**
>
> **They presented these men to the apostles, who prayed and laid their hands on them. So the word of God spread.**
> Acts 6:6–7

Growth brings challenges, in part because it increases interactions across traditional barriers. But as we seek the Holy Spirit's guidance, we'll find creative solutions as potential problems turn into opportunities for more growth. 🌱   *TIM GUSTAFSON*

*Coming together is a beginning; keeping together is progress;
working together is success.*

Trust Me

After graduation from college, I had a low-paying job. Money was tight, and sometimes I didn't even have enough for my next meal. I learned to trust God for my *daily* provision.

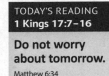

TODAY'S READING
1 Kings 17:7–16

Do not worry about tomorrow.
Matthew 6:34

It reminded me of the prophet Elijah's experience. During his prophetic ministry, he learned to trust God to meet his daily needs. Shortly after Elijah pronounced God's judgment of a drought in Israel, God sent him to a deserted place, Kerith Ravine, where He used the ravens to bring Elijah his daily meals and refresh him with water from the brook (1 KINGS 17:1–4).

But a drought occurred. The brook shrank to a tiny stream, and slowly became a mere trickle. It was only when the brook had dried up that God said: "Go at once to Zarephath . . . . I have directed a widow there to supply you with food" (V. 9). Zarephath was in Phoenicia, whose inhabitants were enemies of the Israelites. Would anyone offer Elijah shelter? And would a poor widow have food to share?

Most of us would rather God provided in abundance long before our resources were depleted rather than just enough for each day. But our loving Father whispers, *Trust Me.* Just as He used ravens and a widow to provide for Elijah, nothing is impossible for Him. We can count on His love and power to meet our daily needs. ❧

POH FANG CHIA

Faithful Father, thank You for knowing exactly what we need before we even ask. Help us to trust You for our daily needs.

God supplies all our needs—one day at a time.

A Blessing Bowl

The familiar bing of an arriving email caught my attention while I wrote at my computer. Usually I try to resist the temptation to check every email but the subject line was too enticing: "You are a blessing."

Eagerly, I opened it to discover a faraway friend telling me she was praying for my family. Each week, she displays one Christmas card photo in her kitchen table "Blessing Bowl" and prays for that family. She wrote, "I thank my God every time I remember you" (PHILIPPIANS 1:3) and then highlighted our efforts to share God's love with others—our "partnership" in the gospel.

TODAY'S READING
Romans 1:1–10

I thank my God every time I remember you.

Philippians 1:3

Through my friend's intentional gesture, the apostle Paul's words to the Philippians came trickling into my inbox, creating the same joy in my heart I suspect readers received from his first-century thank-you note. It seems Paul made it a habit to speak his gratitude to those who worked alongside him. A similar phrase opens many of his letters: "I thank my God through Jesus Christ for all of you, because your faith is being reported all over the world" (ROMANS 1:8).

In the first century, Paul blessed his co-laborers with a thank-you note of prayerfulness. In the twenty-first century, my friend used a Blessing Bowl to bring joy into my day. How might we thank those who serve in the mission of God with us today? ❧

ELISA MORGAN

Father, help us to intentionally bless those who serve alongside us.

Who can you thank today?

The Advance Team

A friend recently prepared to relocate to a city more than 1,000 miles from her current hometown. She and her husband divided the labor of moving to accommodate a short timeline. He secured new living arrangements, while she packed their belongings. I was astounded by her ability to move without previewing the area or participating in the house hunt, and asked how she could do so. She acknowledged the challenge but said she knew she could trust her husband because of his attention to her preferences and needs over their years together.

> **TODAY'S READING**
> **John 14:1–14**
>
> **My Father's house has many rooms; …I am going there to prepare a place for you.** John 14:2

In the upper room, Jesus spoke with His disciples of His coming betrayal and death. The darkest hours of Jesus's earthly life, and that of the disciples as well, lay ahead. He comforted them with the assurance that He would prepare a place for them in heaven, just as my friend's husband prepared a new home for their family. When the disciples questioned Jesus, He pointed them to their mutual history and the miracles they'd witnessed Him perform. Though they would grieve Jesus's death and absence, He reminded them He could be counted on to do as He'd said.

Even in the midst of our own dark hours, we can trust Him to lead us forward to a place of goodness. As we walk with Him, we too will learn to trust increasingly in His faithfulness. 🌱

KIRSTEN HOLMBERG

Help me, Lord, to lean on You when my life feels uncertain and hard.
You are trustworthy and good.

We can trust God to lead us through difficult times.

Following Where He Leads

As a child, I looked forward to our church's Sunday evening services. They were exciting. Sunday night often meant we got to hear from missionaries and other guest speakers. Their messages inspired me because of their willingness to leave family and friends—and at times, homes, possessions, and careers—to go off to strange, unfamiliar, and sometimes dangerous places to serve God.

TODAY'S READING
1 Kings 19:19–21

Then [Elisha] set out to follow Elijah and became his servant. 1 Kings 19:21

Like those missionaries, Elisha left many things behind to follow God (1 KINGS 19:19–21). Before God called him into service through Elijah, we don't know much about Elisha—except that he was a farmer. When the prophet Elijah met him in the field where he was plowing, he threw his cloak over Elisha's shoulders (the symbol of his role as prophet) and called him to follow. With only a request to kiss his mother and father goodbye, Elisha immediately sacrificed his oxen, burned his plowing equipment, said goodbye to his parents—and followed Elijah.

Though not many of us are called to leave family and friends behind to serve God as fulltime missionaries, God wants all of us to follow Him and to "live as a believer in whatever situation the Lord has assigned to [us], just as God has called [us]" (1 CORINTHIANS 7:17). As I've often experienced, serving God can be thrilling and challenging no matter where we are—even if we never leave home. 🌱

ALYSON KIEDA

Dear Lord, equip us to be Your missionaries wherever You have placed us—near or far, at home or abroad.

God will show us how to serve Him wherever we are.

Loving All

worship in a church located in a large, open field—a rare commodity on the island of Singapore (we're just twenty-five miles long and fifteen miles wide). Some time back, people from abroad who work in my country started gathering on the church property for a picnic every Sunday.

This evoked a range of responses from fellow churchgoers. Some fretted about the mess the visitors would leave behind. But others saw this as a divine opportunity to extend hospitality to a wonderful group of strangers—without even leaving the church grounds!

> TODAY'S READING
> **Leviticus 19:33–34**
>
> **The foreigner residing among you must be treated as your native-born. Love them as yourself.**
> Leviticus 19:34

The Israelites must have faced similar issues in their time. After they settled in their new land, they had to grapple with how to relate to other peoples. But God expressly commanded them to treat foreigners like their own kind, and to love them as themselves (LEVITICUS 19:34). Many of His laws made special mention of foreigners: they were not to be mistreated or oppressed, and they were to be loved and helped (EXODUS 23:9; DEUTERONOMY 10:19). Centuries later, Jesus would command us to do the same: to love our neighbor as ourselves (MARK 12:31).

May we have God's heart to love others as ourselves, remembering that we too are sojourners on this earth. Yet we have been loved as God's people, treated as His own. ● *LESLIE KOH*

Father, You have made each and every one of us in Your likeness.
May we love those from elsewhere and seek to reach out to them
with Your love.

Embracing God's love for us is the key to loving others.

Fleeing to Strength

"**P**arry four!"

When I began fencing in high school, my coach would shout the correct defensive position ("parry") against the move he was making. When he extended his weapon and lunged, to repel the attack I had to listen and respond immediately.

That active listening brings to mind the prompt obedience Scripture calls for in the area of sexual temptation. In 1 Corinthians 6:18 Paul writes to believers tempted to solicit pagan temple prostitutes, telling them to "flee from sexual immorality." Sometimes we are to "stand firm" in challenging circumstances (GALATIANS 5:1; EPHESIANS 6:11), but here the Bible practically shouts our best defense: *"Run away!"*

> TODAY'S READING
> **1 Corinthians 6:12–20**
>
> **You were bought at a price. Therefore honor God with your bodies.**
>
> 1 Corinthians 6:20

Immediate action guards against compromise. Small compromises can lead to devastating defeats. An unrestrained thought, a glance in the wrong place on the Internet, a flirting friendship when you're already married—each are steps that take us where we shouldn't go and put distance between us and God.

When we flee temptation, God also provides a place to run. Through Jesus's death on the cross for our sins, He offers us hope, forgiveness, and a new beginning—no matter where we've been or what we've done. When we run to Jesus in our weakness, He sets us free to live in His strength.  *JAMES BANKS*

Lord Jesus, out of love You gave Yourself on the cross for us.
I give myself to You in obedience to Your will.

God alone can meet our deepest needs and give us soul-deep satisfaction.

Courage to Be Faithful

Fear is Hadassah's constant companion. Hadassah, a young Jewish girl living in the first century, is a fictional character in Francine Rivers' book *A Voice in the Wind*. After Hadassah becomes a slave in a Roman household, she fears persecution for her faith in Christ. She knows that Christians are despised, and many are sent to their execution or thrown to the lions in the arena. Will she have the courage to stand for the truth when she is tested?

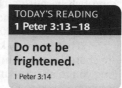

TODAY'S READING
1 Peter 3:13–18

Do not be frightened.
1 Peter 3:14

When her worst fear becomes reality, her mistress and other Roman officials who hate Christianity confront her. She has two choices: recant her faith in Christ or be taken to the arena. Then, as she proclaims Jesus as the Christ, her fear falls away and she becomes bold even in the face of death.

The Bible reminds us that sometimes we will suffer for doing what is right—whether for sharing the gospel or for living godly lives that are against today's values. We are told not to be frightened (1 PETER 3:14), but to "revere Christ as Lord" in our hearts (V. 15). Hadassah's main battle took place in her heart. When she finally made up her mind to choose Jesus, she found the courage to be faithful.

When we make the decision to honor Christ, He will help us to be bold and to overcome our fears in the midst of opposition. 🌸

KEILA OCHOA

Father, give me boldness to stand firm in difficult times.

Let us be bold as we witness for God.

Not Enough?

On the way home from church, my daughter sat in the backseat enjoying Goldfish crackers as my other children implored her to share. Trying to redirect the conversation, I asked the hoarder of snacks, "What did you do in class today?" She said they made a basket of bread and fish because a child gave Jesus five loaves and two fish that Jesus used to feed more than 5,000 people (JOHN 6:1–13).

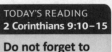

TODAY'S READING
2 Corinthians 9:10–15

Do not forget to do good and to share with others.

Hebrews 13:16

"That was very kind of the little boy to share. Do you think maybe God is asking you to share your fish?" I asked. "No, Momma," she replied.

I tried to encourage her not to keep all the crackers to herself. She was unconvinced. "There is not enough for everyone!"

Sharing is hard. It is easier to hold onto what we see in front of us. Perhaps we do the calculation and reason there is simply not enough for everyone. And the assumption is that if I give, I will be left wanting.

Paul reminds us that all we have comes from God, who wants to enrich us "in every way so that [we] can be generous" (2 CORINTHIANS 9:10–11). The math of heaven isn't a calculation of scarcity but of abundance. We can share joyfully because God promises to care for us even as we are generous to others. ❧

LISA SAMRA

Father, You take good care of me. Help me to think of others today
and to share Your goodness with them.

***When we believe that God is good, we can learn to
open our hands to others.***

The Great Physician

When Dr. Rishi Manchanda asks his patients, "Where do you live?" he's looking for more than an address. He has seen a pattern. Those who come to him for help often live in conditions of environmental stress. Molds, pests, and toxins are making them sick. So Dr. Manchanda has become an advocate of what he calls Upstream Doctors. These are health care workers who, while providing urgent medical care, are working with patients and communities to get to the source of better health.

> TODAY'S READING
> **Matthew 4:23–5:12**
>
> **Remain in me, as I also remain in you.**
> John 15:4

As Jesus healed those who came to Him (MATTHEW 4:23-24), He lifted their eyes beyond the need for urgent physical and material care. With His Sermon on the Mount He offered more than a medical miracle (5:1-12). Seven times Jesus described attitudes of mind and heart that reflect a well-being that begins with a new vision and promise of spiritual well-being (VV. 3-9). Two more times he called blessed those who experience relentless persecution and find their hope and home in Him (VV. 10-12).

Jesus's words leave me wondering. Where am I living? How aware am I of my need for a well-being that is greater than my urgent need for physical and material relief? As I long for a miracle, do I embrace as enviable the poor, broken, hungry, merciful, peacemaking heart that Jesus calls blessed? ❀

MART DEHAAN

Father in heaven, it's so hard to see beyond our pain. Please let us sense Your mercy in this moment. Lift our eyes beyond ourselves. Let us find a new vision and source of health in the care of Christ, who heals.

When God is our home, our hope is in Him.

Of Spiders and God's Presence

Spiders. **I don't** know any kid who likes them. At least not in their rooms … at bedtime. But as she was getting ready for bed, my daughter spied one dangerously close to her bed. "Daaaad!!!!! Spiiiderrr!!!!!" she hollered. Despite my determination, I couldn't find the eight-legged interloper. "He's not going to hurt you," I reassured her. She wasn't convinced. It wasn't until I told her I'd stay next to her top bunk and stand guard that she agreed to get in bed.

As my daughter settled in, I held her hand. I told her, "I love you so much. I'm right here. But you know what? God loves you even more than Daddy and Mommy. And He's very close. You can always pray to Him when you're scared." That seemed to comfort her, and peaceful sleep came quickly.

> **TODAY'S READING**
> **Ephesians 3:14–19**
>
> I pray that out of his glorious riches he may strengthen you with power through his Spirit in your inner being. Ephesians 3:16

Scripture repeatedly reassures us God is always near (PSALM 145:18; ROMANS 8:38–39; JAMES 4:7–8), but sometimes we struggle to believe it. Perhaps that's why Paul prayed for the believers in Ephesus to have *strength* and *power* to grasp that truth (EPHESIANS 3:16). He knew that when we're frightened, we can lose track of God's proximity. But just as I lovingly held my daughter as she went to sleep that night, so our loving heavenly Father is always as close to us as a prayer. 🌱 *ADAM HOLZ*

Lord, thank You for always being close by.
Please give us strength and power in our hearts to remember
You are near, You love us deeply, and we can always call out to You.

God is always near in spite of our fears.

Our Daily Bread

Buckling Up!

"**T**he captain has** turned on the seat belts sign, indicating that we are entering an area of turbulence. Please return to your seats immediately and securely fasten your seat belts." Flight attendants give that warning when necessary because in rough air, unbuckled passengers can be injured. Secured in their seats, they can safely ride out the turbulence.

TODAY'S READING
Hebrews 4:11–16

Let us then approach God's throne of grace with confidence.

Hebrews 4:16

Most of the time, life doesn't warn us of the unsettling experiences coming our way. But our loving Father knows and cares about our struggles, and He invites us to bring our cares, hurts, and fears to Him. The Scriptures tell us, "This High Priest of ours understands our weaknesses, for he faced all of the same testings we do, yet he did not sin. So let us come boldly to the throne of our gracious God. There we will receive his mercy, and we will find grace to help us when we need it most" (HEBREWS 4:15–16 NLT).

In seasons of turbulence, going to our Father in prayer is the best thing we can do. The phrase "grace to help us when we need it"—means that in His presence we can be "buckled" in peace during threatening times, because we bring our concerns to the One who is greater than all! When life feels overwhelming, we can pray. He can help us through the turbulence. *BILL CROWDER*

Father, sometimes life is overwhelming. Help me to trust You with all the turbulent moments, knowing how deeply You care for my life.

Although we cannot anticipate the trials of life, we can pray to our Father who fully understands what we face.

Mercy over Judgment

When my children were squabbling and came to me to tattle on one another, I took each child aside separately to hear their account of the problem. Since both were guilty, at the end of our chat I asked them each what they felt would be an appropriate, fair consequence for their sibling's actions. Both suggested swift punishment for the other. To their surprise, I instead gave them each the consequence they had intended for their sibling. Suddenly, each child lamented how "unfair" the sentence seemed now that it was visited upon them—despite having deemed it appropriate when it was intended for the other.

TODAY'S READING
James 2:1–13

Speak and act as those who are going to be judged by the law that gives freedom.

James 2:12

My kids had shown the kind of "judgment without mercy" that God warns against (JAMES 2:13). James reminds us that instead of showing favoritism to the wealthy, or even to one's self, God desires that we love others as we love ourselves (V. 8). Instead of using others for selfish gain, or disregarding anyone whose position doesn't benefit us, James instructs us to act as people who know how much we've been given and forgiven—and to extend that mercy to others.

God has given generously of His mercy. In all our dealings with others, let's remember the mercy He's shown us and extend it to others. 🌱
KIRSTEN HOLMBERG

Lord, I'm grateful for the great mercy You've shown me.
Help me to offer similar mercy to others as a measure of
my gratitude to You.

God's mercy prompts us to be merciful.

Our Daily Bread

Blooming in the Right Spot

A "**weed is any plant** that grows where you don't want it," my father said, handing me the hoe. I wanted to leave the corn plant that had "volunteered" among the peas. But Dad, who had grown up on a farm, instructed me to pull it out. That lone cornstalk would do nothing but choke the peas and rob them of nutrients.

Human beings aren't plants—we have minds of our own and God-given free will. But sometimes we try to bloom where God doesn't intend us to be.

King Saul's son, the warrior-prince Jonathan, could have done that. He had every reason to expect to be king. But he saw God's blessing on David, and he recognized the envy and pride of his own father (1 SAMUEL 18:12–15). So rather than grasping for a throne that would never be his, Jonathan became David's closest friend, even saving his life (19:1–6; 20:1–4).

> TODAY'S READING
> **1 Samuel 20:30–34**
>
> **So Jonathan made a covenant with the house of David.** 1 Samuel 20:16

Some would say that Jonathan gave up too much. But how would we prefer to be remembered? Like the ambitious Saul, who clung to his kingdom and lost it? Or like Jonathan, who protected the life of a man who would become an honored ancestor of Jesus?

God's plan is always better than our own. We can fight against it and resemble a misplaced weed. Or we can accept His direction and become flourishing, fruitful plants in His garden. He leaves the choice with us. ❧

TIM GUSTAFSON

Lord, please forgive us for those times when we act as if
You have planted us in the wrong place. Help us see what You
have for us to do today.

God invites us to participate with Him in taking the gospel to our world.

Our Sure Foundation

For many years, people in our city built and bought homes in areas subject to landslides. Some knew about the risk of the unstable land, while others were not told. "Forty years of warnings from geologists and city regulations created to ensure safe homebuilding" were unexplained or ignored (*The Gazette,* Colorado Springs, April 27, 2016). The view from many of those homes was magnificent, but the ground beneath them was a disaster in the making.

TODAY'S READING
Isaiah 33:2–6

[The LORD] will be the sure foundation for your times, a rich store of salvation and wisdom and knowledge; the fear of the LORD is the key to this treasure. Isaiah 33:6

Many people in ancient Israel ignored the Lord's warnings to turn from idols and seek Him, the true and living God. The Old Testament records the tragic results of their disobedience. Yet, with the world crumbling around them, the Lord continued reaching out to His people with a message of forgiveness and hope if they would turn to Him and follow His way.

The prophet Isaiah said, "[The LORD] will be the sure foundation for your times, a rich store of salvation and wisdom and knowledge; the fear of the LORD is the key to this treasure" (ISAIAH 33:6).

Today, as in the Old Testament era, God has given us a choice about the foundation on which we will build our lives. We can follow our own desires, or we can embrace His eternal principles revealed in the Bible and in the person of Jesus Christ. "On Christ, the solid rock, I stand—all other ground is sinking sand" (EDWARD MOTE). ❖

DAVID C. MCCASLAND

Father in heaven, we acknowledge You as our sure foundation. Our security and hope are in You.

The Lord Himself is our strong foundation in life.

Fearless Giving

When my son Xavier was six years old, a friend brought her toddler to visit and Xavier wanted to give him a few toys. I delighted in our little giver's generosity, until he offered a stuffed animal my husband had searched several stores in different cities to find. Recognizing the high-demand toy, my friend tried to politely decline. Still, Xavier placed his gift into her son's hands and said, "My daddy gives me lots of toys to share."

> **TODAY'S READING**
> **Malachi 3:8–12**
>
> **Bring the whole tithe into the storehouse, that there may be food in my house.**
> Malachi 3:10

Though I'd like to say Xavier learned his confident giving from me, I've often withheld my resources from God and others. But when I remember that my heavenly Father gives me everything I have and need, it's easier to share.

In the Old Testament, God commanded the Israelites to trust Him by giving a portion of all He had supplied to the Levite priests, who would in turn help others in need. When the people refused, the prophet Malachi said they were robbing the Lord (MALACHI 3:8–9). But if they gave willingly, showing they trusted the Lord's promised provision and protection (VV. 10–11), others would recognize them as God's blessed people (V. 12).

Whether we're managing our finances, our schedules, or the gifts God entrusted to us, giving can be an act of worship. Giving freely and fearlessly can show our confidence in the care of our loving Father—the ultimate generous Giver. XOCHITL DIXON

Lord, please help us live with full confidence in Your faithful provision, so we can give freely and fearlessly to You and others.

Fearless giving to God and others reveals our trust in the Lord's promises and provision.

The Release of Fear

Our bodies react to our feelings of dread and fear. A weight in the pit of our stomachs, along with our hearts pounding as we gulp for breath, signal our sense of anxiety. Our physical nature keeps us from ignoring these feelings of unease.

TODAY'S READING
Mark 6:45–53

Take courage! It is I. Don't be afraid.

Mark 6:50

The disciples felt shockwaves of fear one night after Jesus had performed the miracle of feeding more than five thousand people. The Lord had sent them ahead to Bethsaida so He could be alone to pray. During the night, they were rowing against the wind when suddenly they saw Him walking on the water. Thinking He was a ghost, they were terrified (MARK 6:49–50).

But Jesus reassured them, telling them not to be afraid and to take courage. As He entered their vessel, the wind died down and they made it to the shore. I imagine that their feelings of dread calmed as they embraced the peace He bestowed.

When we're feeling breathless with anxiety, we can rest assured in Jesus's power. Whether He calms our waves or strengthens us to face them, He will give us the gift of His peace that "transcends all understanding" (PHILIPPIANS 4:7). And as He releases us from our fears, our spirits and our bodies can return to a state of rest. 🌸 *AMY BOUCHER PYE*

Lord Jesus Christ, help me when the dread seems to cling to me.
Release me from my fears and give me Your peace.

The Lord releases us from fear.

Lost but Found

When we discovered that my mother-in-law had gone missing while shopping with a relative, my wife and I were frantic. Mom suffered from memory loss and confusion, and there was no telling what she might do. Would she wander the area, or hop onto any bus thinking it would take her home? Worst-case scenarios spun through our minds as we began to search for her, crying out to God, "Please find her."

TODAY'S READING
Luke 15:1–9

Rejoice with me; I have found my lost sheep. Luke 15:6

Hours later, my mother-in-law was spotted stumbling along a road, miles away. How God blessed us in being able to find her. Several months later, He blessed her: at eighty years of age, my mother-in-law turned to Jesus Christ for salvation.

Jesus, comparing humans to lost sheep, gives us this illustration: "Suppose [a shepherd] has a hundred sheep and loses one of them. Doesn't he leave the ninety-nine in the open country and go after the lost sheep until he finds it? And when he finds it, . . . he calls his friends and neighbors together and says, 'Rejoice with me; I have found my lost sheep'" (LUKE 15:4–6).

Shepherds counted their sheep to make sure every one was accounted for. In the same way, Jesus, who likens himself to that shepherd, values each of us, young and old. When we're wandering in life, searching, wondering about our purpose, it's never too late to turn to Christ. God wants us to experience His love and blessings. 🌿

LESLIE KOH

Lord, You search for us and find us.
Thank You for making us Your own.

Amazing grace! . . . I once was lost, but now am found. JOHN NEWTON

On Eagles' Wings

saiah's words about patiently waiting for the Lord anticipate the future with confident hope. From our place of trial, we wait for salvation that is certain to come. Jesus assured His followers, "Blessed are those who mourn, for they will be comforted" (MATTHEW 5:4).

TODAY'S READING
Isaiah 40:27–31

Those who hope in the LORD will renew their strength. They will soar on wings like eagles. Isaiah 40:31

Knowing that our destiny is glorious, which is the sure hope of heaven, we're able to pick up our pace here on earth. Though weary, we can stretch the wings of our faith and fly! We can walk the path of obedience and not get tired. We can move through routine days and not grow weary. A better world is coming, when our spirits will call us to action and our bodies will run and leap and fly! This is our hope.

In the meantime, what will be true one day can begin to be true now. We can be steadfast, patient, and joyful in spite of deep weariness; kind and calm, less focused on our frailty and fatigue; more concerned about others than we are about ourselves; ready to speak a loving word to those who are struggling. We can get ready now for the day our souls will take flight. *DAVID ROPER*

Dear Lord, thank You for the strength You offer me.
Help me to trust in You.

When you're weary in life's struggles, find your rest in the Lord.

We Won't Break

As a native Californian and lover of all things sunny, I shy away from all things cold. I do, however, enjoy beautiful photos of snow. So I couldn't help but smile when my friend from Illinois shared a winter picture of a sapling outside her window. Admiration turned to sadness when I noticed its bare, knotted branches bowing under the heavy fringe of sparkling icicles.

How long could those bending boughs endure before breaking under their icy burdens? The heaviness threatening to crack the tree's limbs reminded me of my shoulders, hunched beneath the weight of worries.

TODAY'S READING
Matthew 6:25–34

Can any one of you by worrying add a single hour to your life? Matthew 6:27

After Jesus affirms that the greatest treasures are not earthly or temporary, He encourages us to release our anxious thoughts. The Creator and Sustainer of the universe loves and provides for His children, so we don't have to waste our precious time worrying. God knows our needs and will care for us (MATTHEW 6:19–32).

He also knows we'll be tempted to succumb to worry. He tells us to come to Him first, trust His presence and provision in the present, and live by faith one day at a time (VV. 33–34).

In this life, we'll face overwhelming troubles and uncertainties that can make our shoulders droop. We may temporarily bend under the weight of worrying. But when we trust God, we won't break. 🌱

XOCHITL DIXON

Thanks for assuring us that we never have to worry, Lord,
because You never fail to meet our deepest needs.

Worry won't break us when we trust the Giver of all good things.

Phone Zone

One of the benefits of cell phones is that we now have virtually unlimited access to others. As a result, many people talk on the phone or text even while driving—sometimes resulting in terrible car crashes. To avoid such disasters, many areas of the world have made distracted driving illegal. In the United States, highway signs are popping up to remind drivers of special cell phone zones where they can pull off the road to safely talk and text to their heart's delight.

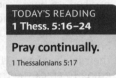

TODAY'S READING
1 Thess. 5:16–24

Pray continually.
1 Thessalonians 5:17

While it is a good idea to restrict mobile phone communication for drivers, there is another kind of communication that has no restrictions: prayer. God invites us to call on Him whether we are coming, going, or sitting still. In the New Testament, Paul's words advise each person who wants to communicate with God to "pray continually" (1 THESSALONIANS 5:17). Paul brackets this divine open-door policy by encouraging us to "rejoice always" (V. 16) and to "give thanks in all circumstances" (V. 18). God calls us to joy and thanksgiving—expressions of faith in God through Christ anchored in continual prayer.

God is available for our quick cry or for a lengthy conversation. He welcomes us into a relationship with Him, a constant and endless sharing of our joys and gratitude, needs, questions, and concerns (HEBREWS 4:15–16). We are always in the prayer zone. 🌿   *BILL CROWDER*

I'm grateful, Lord, that You want to hear from me.
I need You today.

Access to God's throne is always open.

Precious to God

His name was David, but most just called him "the street fiddler." David was a disheveled, older man who was a regular fixture in popular places in our city, serenading passers-by with unusual skill at his violin. In exchange for his music, listeners would sometimes place a dollar in the open instrument case before them on the sidewalk. David would smile and nod his head in thanks as he continued to play.

TODAY'S READING
Genesis 1:26–31

Dear friends, since God so loved us, we also ought to love one another.
1 John 4:11

When David died recently and his obituary appeared in a local paper, it was revealed that he spoke several languages, was the graduate of a prestigious university, and had even run for the state senate years ago. Some expressed surprise at the extent of his accomplishments, having assessed him on the basis of appearance alone.

Scripture tells us that "God created mankind in his own image" (GENESIS 1:27). This reveals an inherent worth within each of us, regardless of how we look, what we have achieved, or what others may think of us. Even when we chose to turn from God in our sinfulness, God valued us so much that He sent His only Son to show us the way to salvation and eternity with Him.

We are loved by God, and all around us are those who are precious to Him. May we express our love for Him in return by sharing His love with others. 🌱 *JAMES BANKS*

Heavenly Father, thank You for Your wonderful love for me.
I pray that others may see Your love in my words and actions today.

God's love is meant to be shared.

When God Fills Us

"**W**hat had I done?**"** It should have been one of the most exciting times of my life. Instead, it was one of the loneliest. I'd just gotten my first "real" job after college, in a city hundreds of miles from where I grew up. But the thrill of that big step quickly faded. I had a tiny apartment. No furniture. I didn't know the city. I didn't know *anyone*. The job was interesting, but the loneliness felt *crushing*.

One night, I sat at home with my back against the wall. I opened my Bible and stumbled onto Psalm 16, where verse 11 promises God will fill us. "Lord," I prayed, "I thought this job was the right thing, but I feel so alone. Please fill me with a sense of Your nearness." I offered variants of that plaintive plea for weeks. Some nights, my sense of loneliness eased, and I had a deep experience of God's presence. Other nights, I still felt achingly isolated.

> **TODAY'S READING**
> **Psalm 16:5–11**
>
> **You make known to me the path of life; you will fill me with joy in your presence, with eternal pleasures at your right hand.**
>
> Psalm 16:11

But as I returned to that verse, anchoring my heart in it night by night, God gradually deepened my faith. I experienced His faithfulness in a way I never had before. And I learned that my job was simply to pour out my heart to Him . . . and humbly await His faithful response, trusting His promise to fill us with His Spirit. 🌱

ADAM HOLZ

Lord, we can feel so empty at times. But You've made known the path of life. You long for us to trust You. Help us to cling to Your promise to fill us in our desperate moments.

Anchor your heart in God.

Grass or Grace

My friend Archie came home from vacation to find his neighbor had erected a wooden fence five feet inside his property line. Several weeks went by during which Archie tried to work with his neighbor to remove the fence. He offered to help and to split the cost of the work, but to no avail. Archie could have appealed to civil authorities, but he chose to forgo that right in this instance and allow the fence to stand—to show his neighbor something of the grace of God.

> TODAY'S READING
> **Genesis 13:1–18**
>
> **Lot chose for himself the whole plain of Jordan.**
> Genesis 13:11

"Archie is a wimp!" you say. No, he was man of towering strength, but he chose grace over a patch of grass.

I think of Abraham and Lot, who fell into conflict because their flocks and herds overwhelmed the land. "Quarreling arose between Abram's herders and Lot's. The Canaanites and the Perizzites [the unbelieving community] were also living in the land at that time" (GENESIS 13:7). Lot chose the best of the land and lost everything in the end. Abraham took what was left over and gained the promised land (VV. 12–17).

We *do* have rights and we *can* claim them, especially when other's rights are involved. And sometimes we *should* insist on them. Paul did when the Sanhedrin acted unlawfully (SEE ACTS 23:1–3). But we can choose to set them aside to show the world a better way. This is what the Bible calls "meekness"—not weakness. Strength under God's control. 🍂   DAVID H. ROPER

Dear Lord, I am prone to look out for myself.
Give me wisdom to know when giving up my rights would best
demonstrate Your love and grace to others.

My life helps paint my neighbor's picture of God.

Like a Little Child

The little girl moved joyfully and gracefully to the music of praise. She was the only one in the aisle but that didn't keep her from spinning and waving her arms and lifting her feet to the music. Her mother, a smile on her lips, didn't try to stop her.

My heart lifted as I watched, and I longed to join her—but didn't. I'd long ago lost the unselfconscious expression of joy and wonder of my childhood. Even though we are meant to grow and mature and put *childish* ways behind us, we were never meant to lose the joy and wonder, especially in our relationship with God.

> TODAY'S READING
> **Mark 10:13–16**
>
> **Let the little children come to me, and do not hinder them.**
> Mark 10:14

When Jesus lived on Earth, He welcomed little children to Him and often referred to them in His teaching (MATTHEW 11:25; 18:3; 21:16). On one occasion, He rebuked His disciples for attempting to keep parents from bringing their children to Him for a blessing, saying, "Let the little children come to me, and do not hinder them, for the kingdom of God belongs to such as these" (MARK 10:14). Jesus was referring to the *childlike* characteristics that ready us to receive Christ—joy and wonder, but also simplicity, dependence, trust, and humility.

Childlike wonder and joy (and more) open our hearts to be more receptive to Him. He is waiting for us to run into His arms. *ALYSON KIEDA*

Abba (Daddy), Father, help us to be more childlike in our relationship with You. We long to be filled with wonder at all You have done.

Faith shines brightest in a childlike heart.

Goodbye for Now

My granddaughter Allyssa and I have a regular routine we go through when we say goodbye. We wrap our arms around each other and begin to loudly wail with dramatic sobs for about twenty seconds. Then we step back and casually say, "See ya," and turn away. Despite our silly practice, we always expect that we will see each other again—*soon*.

But sometimes the pain of separation from those we care about can be difficult. When the apostle Paul said farewell to the elders from Ephesus, "They all wept as they embraced him . . . . What grieved them most was [Paul's] statement that they would never see his face again" (ACTS 20:37–38).

TODAY'S READING
1 Thess. 4:13–18

You do not grieve like the rest of mankind, who have no hope.

1 Thessalonians 4:13

The deepest sorrow, however, comes when we are parted by death and say goodbye for the last time in this life. That separation seems unthinkable. We mourn. We weep. How can we face the heartbreak of never again embracing the ones we have loved?

Still . . . we do not grieve like those who have no hope. Paul writes of a future reunion for those who "believe that Jesus died and rose again" (1 THESSALONIANS 4:13–18). He declares: "The Lord himself will come down from heaven, with a loud command, with the voice of the archangel," and those who have died, along with those who are still alive, will be united with our Lord. What a reunion!

And—best of all—we will be *forever* with Jesus. That's an eternal hope.

CINDY HESS KASPER

Thank You, Lord, for the assurance that this world is not all we have but that a blessed eternity awaits all who trust in You.

At death, God's people don't say "goodbye," but "we'll see you later."

Age-Old Wisdom

In 2010, a newspaper in Singapore published a special report that contained life lessons gleaned from eight senior citizens. It opened with these words: "While aging brings challenges to mind and body, it can also lead to an expansion in other realms. There is an abundance of emotional and social knowledge; qualities which scientists are beginning to define as wisdom . . . the wisdom of elders."

Indeed, wise older people have much to teach us about life. But in the Bible, we meet a newly crowned king who failed to recognize this.

King Solomon had just died, and in 1 Kings 12:3, we read that "the whole assembly of Israel went to Rehoboam" with a petition. They asked the new king to lighten the harsh labor and heavy taxes his father Solomon had demanded of them. In return, they would loyally serve Rehoboam.

> **TODAY'S READING**
> **1 Kings 12:1–7, 12–17**
>
> **Is not wisdom found among the aged? Does not long life bring understanding?**
> Job 12:12

At first the young king consulted the elders (V. 6). But he rejected their advice and accepted the foolish counsel of the young men who had grown up with him (V. 8). He made the burden on the people even greater! His rashness cost him most of his kingdom.

All of us need the counsel that comes with years of experience, especially from those who have walked with God and listened well to His counsel. Think of the accumulated wisdom God has given them! They have much to share with us about the Lord. Let's seek them out and give a listening ear to their wisdom. 🌱

POH FANG CHIA

To avoid the mistakes of youth, draw from the wisdom of age.

Direct Instructions

My second child was eager to sleep in a "big-girl bed" in her sister's room. Each night I tucked Britta under the covers, issuing strict instructions to stay in bed, warning her I'd return her to the crib if she didn't. Night after night, I found her in the hallway and had to escort my discouraged darling back to her crib. Years later I learned her customarily-sweet older sister wasn't excited about having a roommate and repeatedly told Britta that she'd heard me calling for her. Britta heeded her sister's words, went to look for me, and thus landed herself back in the crib.

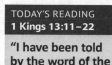

TODAY'S READING
1 Kings 13:11–22

"I have been told by the word of the LORD." 1 Kings 13:17

Listening to the wrong voice can have consequences for us all. When God sent a man to Bethel to speak on His behalf, He gave explicit instructions for him to not eat or drink while there, nor return home by the same route (1 KINGS 13:9). When King Jeroboam invited him to share a meal, the prophet declined, following God's command. When an older prophet extended an invitation to dine, the man initially declined, but relented and ate when his elder deceived him, saying an angel told him it was okay. Just as I wanted Britta to enjoy her "big-girl bed," I imagine God was saddened the man didn't heed His instructions.

We can trust God completely. His words are our path to life; we are wise to listen and obey. 🌿

KIRSTEN HOLMBERG

Thank You, Lord, for speaking to me through Your Word.
Help me to tune my ears to Your voice and obey.

God's words are the ones that matter most.

Lead Me to the Rock

While shopping for a humidifier, I noticed an older woman walking back and forth down the aisle. Wondering if she was shopping for humidifiers also, I moved aside to allow her to draw near. Soon we chatted about a flu virus in our area, one that left her with a lingering cough and headache.

A few minutes later, she launched into a bitter tirade, expressing her theory about the origin of the virus. I listened, unsure what to do. She soon left the store, still angry and frustrated. Though she had expressed her frustration, I couldn't do anything to take away that pain.

> TODAY'S READING
> **Psalm 61**
>
> **I call as my heart grows faint; lead me to the rock that is higher than I.**
> Psalm 61:2

David, Israel's second king, wrote psalms to express his anger and frustration to God. But David knew that God not only listened, He could also do something about his pain. In Psalm 61, he writes, "I call as my heart grows faint; lead me to the rock that is higher than I" (V. 2). God was his "refuge" (V. 3)—the "rock" to which David ran.

When we're in pain, or come in contact with someone in pain, David's example is a good one to follow. We can head to "the rock that is higher" or lead someone there. I wish I had mentioned God to the woman at the store. While God may not take away all our pain, we can rest in the peace He provides and the assurance that He hears our cry. 🌱 *LINDA WASHINGTON*

Father God, make me mindful of those in need of a listening ear
and the hope of Your presence.

Rest on the Rock.

Unashamed Loyalty

Sports fans love to sing their teams' praises. By wearing logos, posting notes on Facebook about their beloved teams, or talking about them with friends, fans leave no doubt where their loyalty stands. My own Detroit Tigers caps, shirts, and conversations indicate that I am right there with those who do this.

Our sports loyalties can remind us that our truest and greatest loyalty must be to our Lord. I think of such unashamed loyalty when I read Psalm 34, where David draws our attention to Someone vastly more vital than anything else on earth.

> **TODAY'S READING**
> **Psalm 34:1–4**
>
> **Glorify the LORD with me; let us exalt his name together.** Psalm 34:3

David says, "I will extol the LORD at all times" (V. 1), and we are left to wonder about the gaps in our lives when we live as if God is not our source of truth, light, and salvation. He says, "His praise will always be on my lips" (V. 1), and we think about how many times we praise things of this world more than we praise Him. David says, "My soul shall make its boast in the LORD" (V. 2 NKJV), and we realize that we boast about our own small successes more than what Jesus has done for us.

It's not wrong to enjoy our teams, our interests, and our accomplishments. But our highest praise goes to our Lord. "Glorify the LORD with me; let us exalt his name together" (V. 3).

DAVE BRANON

Lord, help me to have Your praise be on my lips and to boast in You.
Help me to keep my focus on You.

Loyalty is the test of true love.

Three-Lettered Faith

With a tendency toward pessimism, I quickly jump to negative conclusions about how situations in my life will play out. If I'm thwarted in my efforts on a work project, I'm easily convinced none of my other projects will be successful either and—even though utterly unrelated—I will probably never be able to touch my toes comfortably. And, woe is me, I'm an awful mother who can't do anything right. Defeat in one area unnecessarily affects my feelings in many.

> **TODAY'S READING**
> **Habakkuk 3:17–19**
>
> Yet I will rejoice in the LORD; I will be joyful in God my Savior. Habakkuk 3:18

It's easy for me to imagine how the prophet Habakkuk might have reacted to what God showed him. He had great cause for despair after having seen the coming troubles for God's people; long and arduous years lay ahead. Things really *did* look dismal: no fruit, no meat, and no creature comforts. His words lure me into a pessimistic bed of hopelessness until he jars me awake again with a small three-letter word: *yet*. "Yet I will rejoice in the LORD" (HABAKKUK 3:18). Despite all the hardships he anticipated, Habakkuk found cause for rejoicing simply because of who God is.

While we might be prone to exaggerate our problems, Habakkuk truly faced some extreme hardships. If he could summon praise for God in those moments, perhaps we can too. When we're bogged down in the depths of despair, we can look to God who lifts us up. 🌱

KIRSTEN HOLMBERG

Lord, You are the reason for all my joy. Help me to fix my eyes on You when my circumstances are painful and hard.

God is our cause for joy in the midst of despair.

Pulling Together

Why do more than five million people a year pay money to run several miles over an obstacle course where they must ascend vertical walls, slog through mud, and climb up inside a vertical pipe with water pouring down on them? Some see it as a personal challenge to push their limit of endurance or conquer their fears. For others, the attraction is teamwork where competitors help and support each other. One person called it "a no-judgment zone" where people who are strangers will reach out to help each other finish the race (Stephanie Kanowitz, *The Washington Post*).

> TODAY'S READING
> **Hebrews 10:19–25**
>
> **Let us consider how we may spur one another on toward love and good deeds.**
>
> Hebrews 10:24

The Bible urges us to pursue teamwork as a model of living out our faith in Jesus. "Let us consider how we may spur one another on toward love and good deeds, not giving up meeting together, as some are in the habit of doing, but encouraging one another—and all the more as you see the Day approaching" (HEBREWS 10:24–25).

Our goal is not to "finish first" in the race of faith, but to reach out in tangible ways of encouragement by setting an example and lending a helping hand along the way.

The day will come when we complete our life on earth. Until then, let's spur each other on, be ready to help, and keep pulling together every day. 🌿

DAVID C. MCCASLAND

Father in heaven, give us eyes to see and strength to
help each other in the race of faith today.

We run together in the race of faith.

Giving the Gift of Prayer

" **didn't realize** what a gift prayer was until my brother was sick and you all prayed for him. I cannot tell you what a comfort your prayers were!"

Laura had tears in her eyes as she thanked me for the prayers of the people in our church for her brother, who was facing a cancer diagnosis. She continued, "Your prayers have strengthened him in this difficult time and have been an encouragement to our entire family."

TODAY'S READING
Romans 8:28–34

You help us by your prayers.
2 Corinthians 1:11

One of the best ways to love others is to pray for them. Jesus is our ultimate example in this. The New Testament tells us about Jesus praying for others on many occasions, and even shows us that He continues to come to the Father on our behalf. Romans 8:34 says that He "is at the right hand of God and is also interceding for us." Even after showing such selfless love at the cross, the risen and ascended Lord Jesus Christ continues to express His care for us by praying for us at this very moment.

All around us are people who need us to follow Jesus's example and love them with our prayers, inviting God's help and intervention in their lives. We can ask God to help us pray for them, and He will! May our loving Lord strengthen us to generously give the gift of our prayers for others today. 🕊

JAMES BANKS

Thank You, Lord Jesus, for praying for me. Help me to serve You and others through faithfully praying today.

Prayer is a gift to be shared.

Revealed to Be Healed

As a boy, I watched my father plow fields that had never been cultivated. On the first pass the plowshare would turn up large rocks that he hauled away. Then, he would plow the field again, and then again, to further break up the soil. With each pass the plow turned up other, smaller rocks that he cast aside. The process continued, requiring many passes through the field.

Growth in grace can look like a similar process. When we first become believers, some "big" sins may be exposed. We confess them to God and accept His forgiveness. But as the years pass by, and as God's Word passes through us and sinks into our innermost being, the Holy Spirit

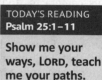

TODAY'S READING
Psalm 25:1–11

Show me your ways, LORD, teach me your paths.

Psalm 25:4

brings other sins to the surface. Sins of the spirit once thought to be mere peccadilloes—small, seemingly unimportant offenses—are revealed as ugly, ruinous attitudes and actions. Sins like pride, self-pity, complaining, pettiness, prejudice, spite, self-serving indulgence.

God reveals each sin so He can cast it aside. He reveals to heal. When harmful hidden attitudes come to the surface, we can pray as the psalmist David did, "For the sake of your name, LORD, forgive my iniquity, though it is great" (PSALM 25:11).

Humbling exposure, though painful, is good for the soul. It's one of the ways in which He "instructs sinners in his ways." He "guides the humble in what is right and teaches them his way" (VV. 8–9). 🌱   *DAVID H. ROPER*

Thank You, Lord, that You remember us according to Your love.
Instruct us and guide us. Teach us to live as those who have been
forgiven much.

Jesus takes us as we are and makes us what we should be.

Wonders in Focus

Some of us are inclined to look at the world and see only what's wrong. DeWitt Jones is a *National Geographic* photographer who has used his profession to celebrate what's right about the world. He waits and watches until a shaft of light or turn of perspective suddenly reveals a wonder that had been there all along. He uses his camera to find beauty in the most common faces of people and nature.

TODAY'S READING
Job 38:1–18

For from him and through him and for him are all things. Romans 11:36

If anyone had reason to focus on the wrongs of the world, Job did. After losing all that had given him joy, even his friends became his accusers. Together their voices taunted him for not admitting that he was suffering for sins he was hiding. When Job cried out to the heavens for help, God remained silent.

Finally, from within the chaos of a whirlwind and the darkness of a storm, God asked Job to consider wonders of nature that reflect a wisdom and power far beyond our own (JOB 38:2–4).

Would He now ask us? What about something as natural as the ways of a dog, cat, fluttering leaf, or blade of grass? Could a shaft of light, or a turn of perspective, reveal—even in our pain—the mind and heart of a Creator who has been with us and for us all along? ❧

MART DEHAAN

Father in heaven, we've spent too much time thinking only about
what is wrong and broken with our world. Please help us to see evidence
of Your presence in the wonder of what only You could have done.

In the faces of nature there are wonders that never cease.

Whispering Words

The young man fidgeted as he sat down for his flight. His eyes darted back and forth to the aircraft windows. Then he closed his eyes and breathed deeply, trying to calm himself—but it didn't work. As the plane took off, he slowly rocked back and forth. An older woman across the aisle from him put her hand on his arm and gently engaged him in conversation to divert his attention from his stress. "What's your name?" "Where are you from?" "We're going to be okay," and "You're doing well" were a few things she whispered. She could have been irritated with him or ignored him. But she chose a touch and a few words. Little things. When they landed three hours later, he said, "Thank you so much for helping me."

TODAY'S READING
Ephesians 4:22–32

[Build] others up according to their needs. Ephesians 4:29

Such beautiful pictures of tenderheartedness can be hard to find. Kindness does not come naturally to many of us; our primary concern is often ourselves. But when the apostle Paul urged, "Be kind and compassionate to one another" (EPHESIANS 4:32), he was not saying it all depends on us. After we've been given a new life by our faith in Jesus, the Spirit begins a transformation. Kindness is the ongoing work of the Spirit renewing our thoughts and attitudes (V. 23).

The God of compassion is at work in our hearts, allowing us in turn to touch others' lives by reaching out and whispering words of encouragement. 🌿

ANNE CETAS

Lord, use me today to bring someone hope, a lighter burden,
encouragement.

Compassion is understanding the troubles of others and reaching out.

Letters Home

Far from home and training for World War II, American recruits in basic training turned to humor and correspondence to cope with the challenges they faced. In one letter home a young man described the vaccination process with wonderful exaggeration: "Two medical officers chased us with harpoons. They grabbed us and pinned us to the floor and stuck one in each arm."

TODAY'S READING
Nehemiah 8:5-12

They read from the Book of the Law of God, making it clear and giving the meaning so that the people understood what was being read.

Nehemiah 8:8

Yet one soldier began to realize that humor could only take him so far. Then he received a Bible. "I enjoy it very much and I read it every night," he wrote. "I never realized you could learn so much from a Bible."

Long ago, the Jewish exiles returned home after years of slavery in Babylon to find their problems came with them. As they struggled to rebuild Jerusalem's walls, they faced opposition from enemies, famine, and their own sin. Amid their trouble, they turned to God's Word. They were surprised at what they learned. When the priests read from the Book of the Law of God, the people were moved to tears (NEHEMIAH 8:9). But they also found comfort. Nehemiah the governor told them, "Do not grieve, for the joy of the LORD is your strength" (V. 10).

We don't need to wait for trouble to hear from God. The Bible is where we learn about His character, His forgiveness, and His comfort. As we read it, we'll be surprised at what God's Spirit will show us in its pages. 🌼 *TIM GUSTAFSON*

The Bible helps us see ourselves as we really are, and also helps us see how much God loves us.

Our Daily Bread

A Good Season

Today is the first day of spring in the northern half of the world. If you live in Australia, it's the first day of autumn—the vernal equinox in the northern hemisphere and the autumnal equinox in the southern hemisphere. Today, the sun shines directly on the equator, and the hours of daylight and nighttime are nearly equal around the world.

New seasons are important for many people. Some count down the day because of what they hope the new season will bring. Perhaps you've been marking off a calendar for spring in Wisconsin to signal the end of another winter. Or maybe you live in Melbourne, and you can't wait for autumn to bring relief from the Australian sun.

> TODAY'S READING
> **Ecclesiastes 3:1–11**
>
> **There is a time for everything, and a season for every activity under the heavens.** Ecclesiastes 3:1

We also go through seasons of life that don't have to do with the weather. The author of Ecclesiastes told us there is a season for every activity under the sun—a time appointed by God during which we live our lives (3:1–11).

Moses spoke of a new season in his life after he led the people of Israel through the wilderness (DEUTERONOMY 31:2), and he had to give up his leadership role to Joshua. And Paul faced a lonely season while he was under house arrest in Rome—asking for visitors but realizing that God was "at my side" (2 TIMOTHY 4:17).

Regardless of the season of life, let's give thanks to God for His greatness, His help, and His companionship. 🏵 *DAVE BRANON*

Thank You, Father, for the promise of Your care during this season of my life. You have allowed this circumstance for a good reason. Help me to use this time appointed by You in a way that deepens my trust in You.

Every season brings a reason to rejoice.

The Art of a Grateful Heart

On our wedding day, Martie and I gladly vowed to be faithful "in good times as well as in bad, in sickness as well as in health, for richer or for poorer." In a way it may seem strange to include vows about the bleak reality of bad times, sickness, and poverty on a cheerful wedding day. But it underscores the fact that life often has "bad" times.

So what are we to do when we face life's inevitable difficulties? Paul urges us on behalf of Christ to "give thanks in all circumstances" (1 THESSALONIANS 5:18). As difficult as that may sound, there is good reason why God encourages us to embrace a spirit of gratitude. Gratitude is grounded in the truth that our Lord "is good" and "his love endures forever" (PSALM 118:1). He is present with us and strengthens us in the midst of trouble (HEBREWS 13:5–6), and He lovingly uses our trials to grow our character into His likeness (ROMANS 5:3–4).

When life hits us with hard times, choosing to be grateful focuses our attention on the goodness of God and gives us the strength to make it through our struggles. With the psalmist, we can sing, "Give thanks to the LORD, for he is good; his love endures forever" (PSALM 118:29). 🌾

JOE STOWELL

> **TODAY'S READING**
> **Psalm 118:1–14, 26–29**
>
> **Give thanks to the LORD, for he is good; his love endures forever.**
>
> Psalm 118:1

Lord, I realize that focusing on my troubles causes me to forget
that even in the midst of trials You are good.
Teach me the art of a grateful heart.

Thanksgiving is a virtue that grows through practice.

Our Daily Bread

Walking on Water

During an especially cold winter, I ventured out to Lake Michigan, the fifth largest lake in the world, to see it frozen over. Bundled up on the beach where I usually enjoy soaking up the sun, the view was breathtaking. The water was actually frozen in waves creating an icy masterpiece.

TODAY'S READING
Matthew 14:25–33

Jesus immediately said to them: "Take courage! It is I. Don't be afraid."
Matthew 14:27

Because the water was frozen solid next to the shore, I had the opportunity to "walk on water." Even with the knowledge that the ice was thick enough to support me, I took the first few steps tentatively. I was fearful the ice wouldn't continue to hold me. As I cautiously explored this unfamiliar terrain, I couldn't help but think of Jesus calling Peter out of the boat onto the Sea of Galilee.

When the disciples saw Jesus walking on the water, their response was also fear. But Jesus responded, "Take courage! It is I. Don't be afraid" (MATTHEW 14:26–27). Peter was able to overcome his fear and step out onto the water because he knew Jesus was present. When his courageous steps faltered because of the wind and waves, Peter cried out to Jesus. Jesus was still there, near enough to simply reach out His hand to rescue him.

If you are facing a situation today where Jesus is calling you to do something that may seem as impossible as walking on water, take courage. The one who calls you will be present with you. 🌱

LISA SAMRA

Dear Lord, thank You for the assurance that You are always with us.

When we call out to God, He hears.

Passing on the Legacy

My phone beeped, indicating an incoming text. My daughter wanted my grandmother's recipe for Peppermint Ice Cream Pie. As I thumbed through the yellowed cards in my aged recipe box, my eyes spotted the unique handwriting of my grandmother—and several jotted notes in the small cursive of my mother. It occurred to me that with my daughter's request, Peppermint Ice Cream Pie would make its entrance into a fourth generation within my family.

I wondered, *What other family heirlooms might be handed down generation to generation? What about choices regarding faith? Besides the pie, would the faith of my grandmother—and my own—play out in the lives of my daughter and her offspring?*

In Psalm 79, the psalmist bemoans a wayward Israel, which has lost its faith moorings. He begs God to rescue His people from the ungodly and to restore Jerusalem to safety. This done, he promises a restored—and ongoing—commitment to God's ways. "Then we your people, the sheep of your pasture, will praise you forever; from generation to generation we will proclaim your praise" (V. 13).

I eagerly shared the recipe, knowing my grandmother's dessert legacy would enjoy a new layer in our family. And I prayed sincerely for the most lasting hand-me-down of all: the influence of our family's faith on one generation to the next. 🌾

ELISA MORGAN

> TODAY'S READING
> **Psalm 79:8–13**
>
> **Then we your people, the sheep of your pasture, will praise you forever; from generation to generation we will proclaim your praise.** Psalm 79:13

Sharing and living out our faith is the best way to leave a legacy.

A Double Promise

Since she suffered with cancer several years ago, Ruth has been unable to eat, drink, or even swallow properly. She has also lost a lot of her physical strength, and numerous operations and treatments have left her a shadow of what she used to be.

Yet Ruth is still able to praise God; her faith remains strong, and her joy is infectious. She relies on God daily, and holds on to the hope that she will recover fully one day. She prays for healing and is confident that God will answer—sooner or later. What an awesome faith!

Ruth explained that what keeps her faith strong is the secure knowledge that God will not only fulfill His promises in His time, but will also sustain her until that happens. This was the same hope that God's people had as they waited for Him to complete His plans (ISAIAH 25:1), deliver them from their enemies (V. 2), wipe away their tears, remove their disgrace, and "swallow up death forever" (V. 8).

TODAY'S READING
Isaiah 25:1–9

In perfect faithfulness you have done wonderful things, things planned long ago. Isaiah 25:1

In the meantime, God gave His people refuge and shelter (V. 4) as they waited. He comforted them in their ordeals, gave them strength to endure, and gave them assurance that He was there with them.

This is the double promise we have—the hope of deliverance one day, plus the provision of His comfort, strength, and shelter throughout our lives. ❧

LESLIE KOH

Thank You, Lord, for Your wonderful gift of hope.
You have promised to save me and to walk with me every day of my life.

Trusting God's faithfulness can dispel our fearfulness.

The Power of Demonstration

My attempts at fixing things around the house usually lead to paying someone else to undo the damage I caused while trying to fix the original problem. But recently I successfully repaired a home appliance by watching a YouTube video where a person demonstrated step by step how to do it.

Paul was a powerful example to his young protégé Timothy who traveled with him and watched him in action. From prison in Rome, Paul wrote, "You . . . know all about my teaching, my way of life, my purpose, faith, patience, love, endurance, persecutions, sufferings" (2 TIMOTHY 3:10–11). In addition, he urged Timothy to "continue in what you have learned and have become convinced of, because you know those from whom you learned it, and how from infancy you have known the Holy Scriptures" (VV. 14–15).

> TODAY'S READING
> **2 Timothy 3:10–17**
>
> **All Scripture is God-breathed and is useful for teaching, rebuking, correcting and training in righteousness.**
> 2 Timothy 3:16

Paul's life demonstrated the necessity of building our lives on the bedrock of God's Word. He reminded Timothy that the Bible is the powerful, God-given source that we need to teach and to demonstrate to others who want to be Christ-followers.

As we thank the Lord for the people who helped us grow in faith, we are challenged to follow their example of living out the truth as we teach and encourage others.

That's the power of demonstration. ❀   *DAVID C. MCCASLAND*

Lord, as others have demonstrated Your truth to us,
may we in turn show it to others.

We are called to live out God's Word as we teach and encourage others.

What We Want to Hear

As human beings, we are prone to seek out information that supports the opinions we hold. Research shows that we're actually *twice* as likely to look for information that supports our position. When we're deeply committed to our own way of thinking, we avoid having that thinking challenged by opposing positions.

Such was the case in King Ahab's rule over Israel. When he and Jehoshaphat, the king of Judah, discussed whether to go to war against Ramoth Gilead, Ahab gathered 400 prophets—men he'd appointed to that role himself and would therefore tell him what he wanted to hear—to help them decide. Each replied he should go, saying "God will give it into the king's

TODAY'S READING
2 Chronicles 18:5–27

I hate him because he never prophesies anything good about me, but always bad.

2 Chronicles 18:7

hand" (2 CHRONICLES 18:5). Jehoshaphat asked whether there was a prophet who had been chosen by God through whom they could inquire of the Lord. Ahab responded reluctantly because God's prophet, Micaiah, "never prophesies anything good about [him], but always bad" (V. 7). Indeed, Micaiah indicated they *wouldn't* be victorious, and the people would be "scattered on the hills" (V. 16).

In reading their story, I see how I too tend to avoid wise advice if it isn't what I want to hear. In Ahab's case, the result of listening to his "yes men"—400 prophets—was disastrous (V. 34). May we be willing to seek and listen to the voice of truth, God's words in the Bible, even when it contradicts our personal preferences. ❧

KIRSTEN HOLMBERG

Lord, help me to seek and heed Your counsel
even when it's against my desires or popular thought.

God's counsel is trustworthy and wise.

The Point of Being Alive

Lately, as I've been skimming financial advice books, I've noticed an interesting trend. While almost all such books have good advice, many imply that the primary reason to cut costs is to live like millionaires later. But one book offered a refreshingly different perspective, arguing that living *simply* is essential for a rich life. If you need more or fancier stuff to feel joy, the book suggested, "You're missing the point of being alive."

TODAY'S READING
Luke 12:22–34

Watch out! Be on your guard against all kinds of greed; life does not consist in an abundance of possessions. Luke 12:15

Those insightful words brought to mind Jesus's response when a man asked Him to urge his brother to divide an inheritance with him. Instead of sympathizing, Jesus dismissed him abruptly before warning sternly about "all kinds of greed"—because "life does not consist in an abundance of possessions" (LUKE 12:14–15). He then described a wealthy person's plans to store his crops and enjoy a luxurious lifestyle—the first-century version of retirement planning—with a blistering conclusion. His wealth did him no good, since he died that night (VV. 16–20).

Although we *are* responsible to use our resources wisely, Jesus's words remind us to check our motivation. Our hearts should be focused on pursuing God's kingdom—knowing Him and serving others—not on securing our own futures (VV. 29–31). As we live for Him and freely share with others, we can fully enjoy a rich life with Him *now*—in the kingdom that gives meaning to all of life (VV. 32–34). 🌱

MONICA BRANDS

Lord, thank You for all You've so generously provided. Teach us how to enjoy what You've given and to share it with others. Help us to rest in You.

We don't need to wait to enjoy a rich life in God's kingdom.

Glory to the Grower

One day, I noticed an unexpected splash of yellow to the right of our driveway. Six stalks of daffodils, sandwiched between two large stones, bloomed bright and tall. Because I hadn't planted, fertilized, or intentionally watered the bulbs, I couldn't figure out how or why the flowers had sprouted in our yard.

Jesus illustrated a mystery of spiritual growth in the parable of the growing seed. He compares the kingdom of God to a farmer scattering seed on the ground (MARK 4:26). The one who scattered the seed may have done what he could to care for the soil. But Jesus said the seed sprouted whether or not that man slept in, woke up, or even understood the growth process (VV. 27–28). The land owner benefited

> **TODAY'S READING**
> **Mark 4:26–29**
>
> **So neither the one who plants nor the one who waters is anything, but only God, who makes things grow.**
>
> 1 Corinthians 3:7

from the harvest (V. 29), though its development didn't depend on what he did or his understanding of the workings beneath the surface of the soil.

The maturing of the seeds in Jesus's parable, like the blooming of my daffodils, occurred in God's time and because of God's growing power. Whether we're considering personal spiritual growth or God's plan to expand the church until Jesus returns, the Lord's mysterious ways aren't dependent on our abilities or understanding of His works. Still, God invites us to know, serve, and praise the Grower, reaping the benefits of the spiritual maturity He cultivates in and through us. ❦   XOCHITL DIXON

Lord, thank You for growing us spiritually and using us to
serve Your people, as You grow Your kingdom.

God deserves the glory for the growth of His people and His kingdom.

Strength in Suffering

When eighteen-year-old Sammy received Jesus as Savior, his family rejected him because their tradition was of a different faith. But the Christian community welcomed him, offering encouragement and financial resources for his education. Later, when his testimony was published in a magazine, his persecution intensified.

> **TODAY'S READING**
> 1 Peter 2:11–23
>
> **Christ suffered for you, leaving you an example, that you should follow in his steps.** 1 Peter 2:21

But Sammy did not stop seeing his family. He visited whenever he could and talked with his father, even though his siblings cruelly prevented him from participating in family affairs. When his father fell ill, Sammy overlooked his family's slighting and attended to him, praying his father would get well. When God healed him, the family began to warm up toward Sammy. Over time, his loving witness softened their attitude toward him—and some of his family members became willing to hear about Jesus.

Our decision to follow Christ may cause us difficulties. Peter wrote, "It is commendable if someone bears up under the pain of unjust suffering because they are conscious of God" (1 PETER 2:19). When we undergo discomfort or suffering because of our faith, we do so because "Christ suffered for [us], leaving [us] an example, that [we] should follow in his steps" (V. 21).

Even when others hurled insults at Jesus, "he did not retaliate; when he suffered, he made no threats. Instead, he entrusted himself to him who judges justly" (V. 23). Jesus is our example in suffering. We can turn to Him for strength. 🌼 *LAWRENCE DARMANI*

Dear Lord Jesus, help me to follow Your example in my conduct and in suffering for You.

When we suffer for Jesus, He comes to walk us through it.

Leaving a Legacy

ome years ago our sons and I spent a week on an abandoned backcountry ranch on the Salmon River, Idaho's "River of No Return."

One day, exploring the ranch, I came across an ancient grave with a wooden marker. Whatever inscription the marker may have borne had long since been weathered away. Someone lived and died—now was forgotten. The gravesite seemed tragic to me. After we got home I spent several hours reading about the history of the old ranch and that area, but could find no information about the person buried there.

> TODAY'S READING
> Isaiah 49:14–16
>
> **A scroll of remembrance was written in his presence concerning those who feared the LORD and honored his name.** Malachi 3:16

They say that the best among us is remembered for 100 years or so. The rest of us are soon forgotten. The memory of past generations, like our markers, soon fades away. Yet our legacy has been passed on through the family of God. How we've loved God and others in our lifetime lives on. Malachi 3:16–17 tells us, "a book of remembrance was written before Him for those who fear the LORD and who esteem His name. 'They will be Mine,' says the LORD of hosts, 'on the day that I prepare My own possession' " (NASB).

Paul said of David that he "served God's purpose in his own generation" and departed (ACTS 13:36). Like him, may we love the Lord and serve Him in *our* generation and leave the remembering to Him. "They will be Mine," says the Lord. 🌿

DAVID H. ROPER

May I be faithful to You today, Lord, as I spend my time loving others with Your love. Help me to trust You with the legacy I'm leaving behind.

Living for the Lord leaves a lasting legacy.

Only by Prayer

My friend called me late one night during her cancer treatment. Grieved by her uncontrollable sobs, I soon added my own tears and a silent prayer. *What am I supposed to do, Lord?*

Her wails squeezed my heart. I couldn't stop her pain, fix her situation, or find one intelligible word of encouragement. But I knew who could help. As I wept with my friend, stumbling through a prayer, I whispered repeatedly, "Jesus. Jesus. Jesus."

Her cries quieted to sniffs and whimpers, until her breathing slowed. Her husband's voice startled me. "She's asleep," he said. "We'll call tomorrow."

I hung up, weeping prayers into my pillow.

The gospel of Mark shares a story of another person who wanted to help his loved one. A desperate father brought his suffering son to Jesus (MARK 9:17). Doubt

TODAY'S READING
Mark 9:14–29

Everything is possible for one who believes. Mark 9:23

clung to his plea, as he reiterated the impossibility of their circumstances (VV. 20–22) and acknowledged his need for Jesus to empower his belief (V. 24). The father and son experienced freedom, hope, and peace when Jesus stepped in and took control (VV. 25–27).

When loved ones are hurting, it's natural to want to do the right things and say the perfect words. But Christ is the only One who can truly help us. When we call on the name of Jesus, He can enable us to believe and rely on the power of His presence. 🌾

XOCHITL DIXON

Jesus. Jesus. Jesus. Oh, how we need You, Jesus.

***The name of Jesus is the powerful prayer that leads us
into His mighty presence.***

Our Daily Bread

How Long?

n Lewis Carroll's classic *Alice in Wonderland,* Alice asks, "How long is forever?" The White Rabbit responds, "Sometimes, just one second."

That's how time felt when my brother David suddenly died. The days leading to his memorial dragged on, intensifying the sense of loss and grief we felt. Every second seemed to last forever.

TODAY'S READING
Psalm 13

How long, LORD? Will you forget me forever? How long will you hide your face from me?

Psalm 13:1

Another David echoed this sentiment, singing, "How long, LORD? Will you forget me forever? How long will you hide your face from me? How long must I wrestle with my thoughts and day after day have sorrow in my heart? How long will my enemy triumph over me?" (PSALM 13:1–2). Four times in just two verses he asks God, "How long?" Sometimes the pains of life seem as though they will never end.

Into this heartache steps the presence and care of our heavenly Father. Like King David, we can honestly go to Him with our pain and loss, knowing that He will never leave us or forsake us (HEBREWS 13:5). The psalmist discovered this as well, allowing his lament to move from a mournful minor key to a triumphant declaration: "But I trust in your unfailing love; my heart rejoices in your salvation" (PSALM 13:5).

In our seemingly endless moments of struggle, His unfailing love will carry us. We can rejoice in His salvation. 🌿

BILL CROWDER

In times of pain and loss, the timeless God is our greatest comfort.

Faith, Love, and Hope

For ten years, my Aunt Kathy cared for her father (my grandfather) in her home. She cooked and cleaned for him when he was independent, and then took on the role of nurse when his health declined.

Her service is one modern example of the words of Paul who wrote to the Thessalonians that he thanked God for "your work produced by faith, your labor prompted by love, and your endurance inspired by hope in our Lord Jesus Christ" (1 THESSALONIANS 1:3).

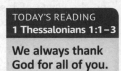

TODAY'S READING
1 Thessalonians 1:1–3

We always thank God for all of you.
1 Thessalonians 1:2

My aunt served in faith and love. Her daily, consistent care was the result of her belief that God called her to this important work. Her labor was borne out of love for God and her father.

She also endured in hope. My grandfather was a very kind man, but it was difficult to watch him decline. She gave up time with family and friends, and limited travel to care for him. She was able to endure because of the hope that God would strengthen her each day, along with the hope of heaven that awaited my grandfather.

Whether it is caring for a relative, helping a neighbor or volunteering your time, be encouraged as you do the work God has called you to do. Your labor can be a powerful testimony of faith, hope, and love. 🌿

LISA SAMRA

Lord, may I this day have eyes to see others' needs, direction from You on any ways I might help, and the Spirit's power to obey. May I live out the faith, love, and hope You've given to me.

The glory of life is to love, not to be loved; to give, not to get; to serve, not to be served.

Anonymous Kindness

When I first graduated from college, I found myself needing to adopt a strict grocery budget—twenty-five dollars a week, to be exact. One day, while entering the checkout line, I suspected the groceries I'd selected cost slightly more than my remaining money. "Just stop when we reach twenty dollars," I told the cashier, and I was able to purchase everything I'd selected but a bag of peppers.

As I was about to drive home, a man stopped by my car. "Here's your peppers, ma'am," he said, handing the bag to me. Before I had time to thank him, he was already walking away.

Remembering the simple goodness of this act of kindness still warms my

> **TODAY'S READING**
> **Matthew 6:1–4**
>
> When you give to the needy, do not let your left hand know what your right hand is doing.
>
> Matthew 6:3

heart and brings to mind Jesus's words in Matthew 6. Criticizing those who made a show of giving to the needy (V. 2), Jesus taught His disciples a different way. Instead of making giving all about them and their generosity, He urged that giving should be done so secretly it's like their left hand isn't even aware their right is giving (V. 3)!

As one person's anonymous kindness reminded me, giving should never be about us. We give only because of what our generous God has so lavishly given us (2 CORINTHIANS 9:6–11). As we give quietly and generously, we reflect who He is—and God receives the thanksgiving only He deserves (V. 11). 🌺 *MONICA BRANDS*

Giving quietly and generously reflects God's generosity.

Sweet and Bitter

Some people like bitter chocolate and some prefer sweet. Ancient Mayans in Central America enjoyed chocolate as a beverage and seasoned it with chili peppers. They liked this "bitter water," as they called it. Many years later it was introduced in Spain, but the Spaniards preferred chocolate sweet, so they added sugar and honey to counteract its natural bitterness.

Like chocolate, days can be bitter or sweet as well. A seventeenth-century French monk named Brother Lawrence wrote, "If we knew how much [God] loves us, we would always be ready to receive equally . . . from His hand the sweet and

> **TODAY'S READING**
> **Psalm 119:65–72**
>
> **You are good, and what you do is good.** Psalm 119:68

the bitter." Accept the sweet and the bitter equally? This is difficult! What is Brother Lawrence talking about? The key lies in God's character. The psalmist said of God, "You are good, and what you do is good" (PSALM 119:68).

Mayans also valued bitter chocolate for its healing and medicinal properties. Bitter days have value too. They make us aware of our weaknesses and they help us depend more on God. The psalmist wrote, "It was good for me to be afflicted so that I might learn your decrees" (V. 71). Let us embrace life today, with its different flavors—reassured of God's goodness. Let us say, "You have done many good things for me, LORD, just as you promised" (V. 65 NLT).

KEILA OCHOA

> Father, help me to see Your goodness
> even in times of trouble.

God is good.

Front-Porch Relief

O n a particularly hot day, eight-year-old Carmine McDaniel wanted to make sure his neighborhood mail carrier stayed cool and hydrated. So he left a cooler filled with a sports drink and water bottles on their front step. The family security camera recorded the mail carrier's reaction: "Oh man, water and Gatorade. Thank God; thank you!"

TODAY'S READING
Philippians 4:10–20

I have learned the secret of being content in any and every situation.

Philippians 4:12

Carmine's mom says, "Carmine feels that it's his 'duty' to supply the mailman with a cool beverage even if they're not home."

This story warms our hearts, but it also reminds us that there is One who will "meet all your needs," as the apostle Paul phrased it. Though Paul was languishing in jail and uncertain about his future, he expressed joy for the Christians in Philippi because God had met his needs through their financial gift to him. The Philippian church was not wealthy, but they were generous, giving to Paul and others out of their poverty (SEE 2 CORINTHIANS 8:1–4). As the Philippians had met Paul's needs, so God would meet theirs, "according to the riches of his glory in Christ Jesus" (PHILIPPIANS 4:19).

God often sends vertical help through horizontal means. Put another way, He sends us what we need through the help of others. When we trust Him for what we need, we learn, as Paul did, the secret of true contentment (VV. 12–13). 🌿 MARVIN WILLIAMS

How might God be prompting you to meet the needs of others?
In what ways and through whom has God met your needs?
Spend time thanking God for His provision.

God's provisions are always greater than our problems.

Who Is This?

magine standing shoulder to shoulder with onlookers by a
dirt road. The woman behind you is on her tiptoes, trying to
see who is coming. In the distance, you glimpse a man riding
a donkey. As He approaches, people toss their coats onto the
road. Suddenly, you hear a tree crack behind you. A man is cutting down palm branches, and people are
spreading them out ahead of the donkey.

Jesus's followers zealously honored
Him as He entered Jerusalem a few days
before His crucifixion. The multitude
rejoiced and praised God for "all the
miracles they had seen" (LUKE 19:37). Jesus's
devotees surrounded Him, calling out,

> TODAY'S READING
> **Luke 19:28–40**
>
> **Blessed is the king
> who comes in the
> name of the Lord!**
> Luke 19:38

"Blessed is the king who comes in the name of the LORD!" (V. 38).
Their enthusiastic honor affected the people of Jerusalem. When
Jesus finally arrived, "the whole city was stirred and asked, 'Who
is this?'" (MATTHEW 21:10).

Today, people are still curious about Jesus. Although we
can't pave His way with palm branches or shout praises to Him
in person, we can still honor Him. We can discuss His remarkable works, assist people in need, patiently bear insults, and
love each other deeply. Then we must be ready to answer the
onlookers who ask, "Who is Jesus?"   *JENNIFER BENSON SCHULDT*

Lord, may my life and my words express what I know about who You are.
I want others to see You in me and to know You too.

We honor God's name when we live like His children.

Comfort Shared

"**G**od sent you to me tonight!"

Those were the parting words from the woman standing in front of me as we exited our flight to Chicago. She had sat across the aisle from me, where I learned she was headed home after several flights in a round-trip that day. "Do you mind if I ask why you had such a quick turn-around?" I inquired. She glanced downward: "I just put my daughter in rehab for drug abuse today."

In the moments that followed I gently shared the story of my son's struggle with heroin addiction and how Jesus had set him free. As she listened, a smile broke through her tears. After the plane landed we prayed together before parting, asking God to break her daughter's chains.

> TODAY'S READING
> **2 Corinthians 1:1–10**
>
> **Peace be with you! As the Father has sent me, I am sending you.** John 20:21

Later that evening I thought of Paul's words in 2 Corinthians 1:3–4: "Praise be to the God and Father of our Lord Jesus Christ, the Father of compassion and the God of all comfort, who comforts us in all our troubles, so that we can comfort those in any trouble with the comfort we ourselves receive from God."

All around us are people who need to be encouraged with the comfort only God can give. He wants us to reach out to them with tenderhearted compassion, to share the love He has shared with us. May God send us to those who need His comfort today!

JAMES BANKS

I praise You for Your compassion for us at the cross, Lord! Help me to comfort others with Your kindness and love today.

God's kindness meets our deepest need.

Fair Play

When Singaporean runner **Ashley Liew** found himself at the head of the pack during a marathon at the Southeast Asian Games, he knew something was wrong. He quickly realized that the lead runners had taken a wrong turn and were now behind. Ashley could have taken advantage of their mistake, but a strong sense of sportsmanship told him it would not be a genuine victory. He wanted to win because he was faster—not because those ahead of him had made a mistake. Acting on his convictions, he slowed down to let them catch up.

TODAY'S READING
Titus 2:7–8, 11–14

In everything set them an example by doing what is good. Titus 2:7

In the end, Ashley lost the race and missed out on a medal. But he won the hearts of his country-men—and an international award for his act of fair play. It spoke well of his faith as a Christian, and must have prompted some to ask, "What made him do that?"

Ashley's act challenges me to share my faith through my actions. Little acts of thoughtfulness, kindness, or forgiveness can glorify God. As Paul put it simply, "Show integrity, seri-ousness and soundness of speech that cannot be condemned" (TITUS 2:7–8).

Our positive actions toward others can show the world that we are able to live differently because of the Holy Spirit's work in us. He will give us the grace to reject ungodliness and wrong passions, and to live upright lives that point people to God (VV. 11–12).    *LESLIE KOH*

Heavenly Father, may our behavior today cause others to ask us why we are different. We ask that we follow Your Holy Spirit's leading as we explain to them the hope that is in us.

Live so that others will want to know Jesus.

Look and Be Quiet

I n the song "Look at Him," Mexican composer Rubén Sotelo describes Jesus at the cross. He invites us to look at Jesus and be quiet, because there is really nothing to say before the type of love Jesus demonstrated at the cross. By faith we can imagine the scene described in the Gospels. We can imagine the cross and the blood, the nails, and the pain.

When Jesus breathed His last, those who "had gathered to witness this sight... beat their breasts and went away" (LUKE 23:48). Others "stood at a distance, watching these things" (V. 49). They looked and were quiet. Only one spoke, a centurion, who said, "Surely this was a righteous man" (V. 47).

> TODAY'S READING
> **Luke 23:44–49**
>
> **Look around and see. Is any suffering like my suffering...?**
> Lamentations 1:12

Songs and poems have been written to describe this great love. Many years before, Jeremiah wrote about Jerusalem's pain after its devastation. "Is it nothing to you, all you who pass by?" (LAMENTATIONS 1:12). He was asking people to look and see; he thought there was no greater suffering than Jerusalem's. However, has there been any suffering like Jesus's suffering?

All of us are passing by the road of the cross. Will we look and see His love? This Easter, when words and poems are not enough to express our gratitude and describe God's love, let us take a moment to ponder Jesus's death; and in the quietness of our hearts, may we whisper to Him our deepest devotion. 🕊

KEILA OCHOA

Dear Jesus, as I look at Your cross, I have no words to express my gratitude for Your perfect sacrifice. But I thank You for Your love.

Look at the cross and worship.

Basin of Love

One day in physics class many years ago, our teacher asked us to tell him—without turning around—what color the back wall of the classroom was. None of us could answer, for we hadn't noticed.

Sometimes we miss or overlook the "stuff" of life simply because we can't take it all in. And sometimes we don't see what's been there all along.

It was like that for me as I recently read again the account of Jesus washing His disciples' feet. The story is a familiar one, for it is often read during Passion Week. That our Savior and King would stoop to cleanse the feet of His disciples awes us. In Jesus's day, even Jewish servants were spared this task because it was seen as beneath them. But what I

> TODAY'S READING
> **John 13:1–17**
>
> **After that, he poured water into a basin and began to wash his disciples' feet.**
>
> John 13:5

hadn't noticed before was that Jesus, who was both man and God, washed the feet of Judas. Even though He knew Judas would betray Him, as we see in John 13:11, Jesus still humbled Himself and washed Judas's feet.

Love poured out in a basin of water—love that He shared even with the one who would betray Him. As we ponder the events of this week leading up to the celebration of Jesus's resurrection, may we too be given the gift of humility so that we can extend Jesus's love to our friends and any enemies. ❧

AMY BOUCHER PYE

Lord Jesus Christ, fill my heart with love that I might roll up my sleeves and wash the feet of others for Your glory.

Because of love, Jesus humbled Himself and washed His disciples' feet.

Our Daily Bread

The Via Dolorosa

During Holy Week, we remember the final days before Jesus's crucifixion. The road Jesus traveled to the cross through the streets of Jerusalem is known today as the Via Dolorosa, the way of sorrows.

But the writer of Hebrews viewed the path Jesus took as more than just a path of sorrows. The way of suffering that Jesus willingly walked to Golgotha made a "new and living way" into the presence of God for us (HEBREWS 10:20).

For centuries the Jewish people had sought to come into God's presence through animal sacrifices and by seeking to keep the law. But the law was "only a shadow of the good things that are coming," for "it is impossible for the blood of bulls and goats to take away sins" (VV. 1, 4).

TODAY'S READING
Hebrews 10:1–10

We have been made holy through the sacrifice of the body of Jesus Christ once for all.

Hebrews 10:10

Jesus's journey down the Via Dolorosa led to His death and resurrection. Because of His sacrifice, we can be made holy when we trust in Him for the forgiveness of our sins. Even though we aren't able to keep the law perfectly, we can draw near to God without fear, fully confident that we are welcomed and loved (VV. 10, 22).

Christ's way of sorrow opened for us a new and living way to God. 🏵

AMY PETERSON

Jesus, thank You for walking the way of sorrow
and making a way for us to be reconciled to God.

Christ's sacrifice was what God desired and what our sin required.

The King's Crown

We sat around the table, each person adding a toothpick to the foam disc before us. At our evening meal in the weeks leading up to Easter, we created a crown of thorns—with each toothpick signifying something we had done that day for which we were sorry and for which Christ had paid the penalty. The exercise brought home to us, night after night, how through our wrongdoing we were guilty and how we needed a Savior. And how Jesus freed us through His death on the cross.

TODAY'S READING
Matthew 27:27–31

They . . . twisted together a crown of thorns and set it on his head.

Matthew 27:28–29

The crown of thorns that Jesus was made to wear was part of a cruel game the Roman soldiers played before He was crucified. They also dressed Him in a royal robe and gave Him a staff as a king's scepter, which they then used to beat Him. They mocked Him, calling Him "king of the Jews" (MATTHEW 27:29), not realizing that their actions would be remembered thousands of years later. This was no ordinary king. He was the King of Kings whose death, followed by His resurrection, gives us eternal life.

On Easter morning, we celebrated the gift of forgiveness and new life by replacing the toothpicks with flowers. What joy we felt, knowing that God had erased our sins and given us freedom and life forever in Him! 🌿   *AMY BOUCHER PYE*

Lord Jesus Christ, my heart hurts to think of all of the pain and suffering You endured for me. Thank You for Your gift of love that sets me free.

The crown of thorns has become a crown of life.

Despised for All of This

Susannah Cibber gained fame in the eighteenth century for her talent as a singer. However, she was equally well known for her scandalous marital problems. That's why when Handel's *Messiah* was first performed in Dublin in April 1742, many in the audience did not approve of her role as a featured soloist.

During that inaugural performance, Cibber sang of the Messiah: "He is despised and rejected of men; a man of sorrows, and acquainted with grief" (ISAIAH 53:3 KJV). Those words so moved Rev. Patrick Delany that he jumped to his feet and said, "Woman, for this be all thy sins forgiven thee!"

> TODAY'S READING
> **Isaiah 53:3–12**
>
> **He bore the sin of many, and made intercession for the transgressors.**
>
> Isaiah 53:12

The connection between Susannah Cibber and the theme of Handel's *Messiah* is evident. The "man of sorrows"—Jesus the Messiah—was "despised and rejected" because of *sin*. The prophet Isaiah said, "My righteous servant will justify many, and he will bear their iniquities" (V. 11).

The connection between Messiah and us is no less apparent. Whether we stand with the judgmental audience members, with Susannah Cibber, or somewhere in between, we all need to repent and receive God's forgiveness. Jesus, by His life, death, and resurrection, restored our relationship with God our Father.

For this—for all *Jesus* did—be all our sins forgiven. 🌱

TIM GUSTAFSON

Father in heaven, we all stand in need of Your forgiveness. We stand too in awe of Your Son Jesus, who was despised and rejected for our sins. Thank You for coming to us in Jesus 2,000 years ago so that we might know You now.

Alleluia: for the Lord God omnipotent reigneth. REVELATION 19:6 KJV

When One Hurts, All Hurt

When a coworker called in sick due to extreme pain, everyone at the office was concerned. After a trip to the hospital and a day of bed rest, he returned to work and showed us the source of that pain—a kidney stone. He'd asked his doctor to give him the stone as a souvenir. Looking at that stone, I winced in sympathy, remembering the gallstone I had passed years ago. The pain had been excruciating.

Isn't it interesting that something so small can cause a whole body so much agony? But in a way, that's what the apostle Paul alludes to in 1 Corinthians 12:26: "If one part suffers, every part suffers with it." Throughout chapter 12, Paul used the metaphor of a body to describe Christians around the world. When Paul said, "God has put the body together" (V. 24), he was referring to the entire body of Christ—all Christians. We all have different gifts and roles. But since we're all part of the same body, if one person hurts, we all hurt. When a fellow Christian faces persecution, grief, or trials, we hurt as if we're experiencing that pain.

> TODAY'S READING
> **1 Corinthians 12:14–26**
>
> **If one part suffers, every part suffers with it; if one part is honored, every part rejoices with it.** 1 Corinthians 12:26

My coworker's pain drove him to get the help his body needed. In the body of Christ, someone's pain ignites our compassion and moves us toward action. We might pray, offer a word of encouragement, or do whatever it takes to aid the healing process. That's how the body works together.   *LINDA WASHINGTON*

Lord, please give peace to those who are persecuted or in pain.
Your family is my family too.

We're in this together.

Into Our Storms

Wind howled, lightning flashed, waves crashed. I thought I was going to die. My grandparents and I were fishing on a lake, but we'd stayed out too long. As the sun set, a fast-moving squall swept over our small boat. My grandfather instructed me to sit in front to keep it from capsizing. Terror flooded my heart. But then, somehow, I began to pray. I was fourteen.

I asked God for His reassurance and protection. The storm didn't weaken, but we made it to shore. To this day, I don't know if I've experienced a deeper certainty of God's presence than that night in the storm.

Jesus is no stranger to storms. In Mark 4:35-41, He told His disciples to head across a lake that would soon turn windy and wild. The storm that night tested and bested these rugged fisher-

> **TODAY'S READING**
> **Mark 4:35-41**
>
> **He got up, rebuked the wind and said to the waves, "Quiet! Be still!" Then the wind died down and it was completely calm.** Mark 4:39

men. They too thought they were going to die. But Jesus calmed the water and then led His disciples to deeper faith.

Likewise, Jesus invites us to trust Him in our storms. Sometimes He miraculously stills the winds and the waves. Sometimes He does something equally miraculous: He steadies our hearts and helps us to trust Him. He asks us to rest in the belief that He has the power to say to the waves, "Quiet! Be still!" ❧

ADAM HOLZ

Lord, the storms of our lives sometimes seem like they will swamp us.
Help us trust that You are the Master of the storm, to place our faith in
You when life's winds blow fiercely.

No danger can come so near that God is not nearer still.

Reason to Sing

When I was thirteen, my school required students to take four exploratory courses, including home economics, art, choir, and woodworking. On my first day in choir, the instructor called each student to the piano individually to hear their voices and place them in the room according to their vocal range. During my turn at the piano, I sang the notes she played multiple times, but wasn't directed to a section in the room. Instead, after repeated tries, she sent me to the counseling office to find a different class to take. From that moment on, I felt I shouldn't sing at all, that my voice shouldn't be heard in song.

TODAY'S READING
Psalm 98

Sing to the LORD a new song, for he has done marvelous things.

Psalm 98:1

I carried that thought with me for more than a decade until I read Psalm 98 as a young adult. The writer opens with an invitation to "sing to the LORD" (PSALM 98:1). The reason offered has nothing to do with the quality of our voices; He delights in all His children's songs of thanksgiving and praise. Instead, we are invited to sing because God "has done marvelous things" (V. 1).

The psalmist points out two wonderful reasons to joyfully praise God in song and in attitude: His saving work in our lives and His ongoing faithfulness toward us. In God's choir, we each have a place to sing of the marvelous things He has done. 🌱

KIRSTEN HOLMBERG

Lord, You have done great things in my life. Even if my voice isn't one
that would be heard on stage, I want to join the choir in thanking You
for the amazing things You've done.

God loves to hear the voices of His children.

Just a Second

Scientists are pretty fussy about time. At the end of 2016, the folks at Goddard Space Flight Center in Maryland added an extra second to the year. So if you felt that year dragged on a bit longer than normal, you were right.

Why did they do that? Because the rotation of the earth slows down over time, the years get just a tiny bit longer.
When scientists track manmade objects launched into space, they must have accuracy down to the millisecond. This is "to make sure our collision avoidance programs are accurate," according to one scientist.

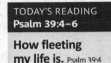

TODAY'S READING
Psalm 39:4–6

How fleeting my life is. Psalm 39:4

For most of us, a second gained or lost doesn't make much difference. Yet according to Scripture, our time and how we use it *is* important. For instance, Paul reminded us in 1 Corinthians 7:29 that "time is short." The time we have to do God's work is limited, so we must use it wisely. He urged us to "[make] the best use of the time, because the days are evil" (EPHESIANS 5:16 ESV).

This doesn't mean we have to count each second as do the scientists, but when we consider the fleeting nature of life (PSALM 39:4), we can be reminded of the importance of using our time wisely. 🌱

DAVE BRANON

Lord, thank You for each moment You give us.
May we strive to honor You with this gift by using our time
wisely for Your honor and glory.

Don't just spend time—invest it.

Learning to Know God

For as long as I can remember, I've wanted to be a mother. I dreamed about getting married, getting pregnant, and holding my baby in my arms for the first time. When I finally got married, my husband and I never even considered waiting to expand our family. But with each negative pregnancy test, we realized we were struggling with infertility. Months of doctors' visits, tests, and tears followed. We were in the middle of a storm. Infertility was a bitter pill to swallow and left me wondering about God's goodness and faithfulness.

> **TODAY'S READING**
> **John 6:16–21**
>
> **But he said to them, "It is I; don't be afraid."** John 6:20

When I reflect on our journey, I think about the story of the disciples caught in the storm on the sea in John 6. As they struggled against the waves in the dark of the storm, Jesus unexpectedly came to them walking on the stormy waves. He calmed them with His presence, saying, "It is I; don't be afraid" (V. 20).

Like the disciples, my husband and I had no idea what was coming in our storm; but we found comfort as we learned to know God more deeply as the One who is always faithful and true. Although we would not have the child we had dreamed of, we learned that in all our struggles we can experience the power of His calming presence. Because He is there powerfully working in our lives, we need not be anxious. ❧

KAREN WOLFE

Dear Lord, thank You that I do not have to face the storms in this life without You. Thank You for Your calming presence and power carrying me through whatever I face.

We can experience God's powerful presence even in the storms of our lives.

Our Daily Bread

Judging Origins

"**W**here are you from?**"** We often use that question to get to know someone better. But for many of us, the answer is complicated. Sometimes we don't want to share all the details.

In the book of Judges, Jephthah might not have wanted to answer that question at all. His half-brothers had chased him out of his hometown of Gilead for his "questionable" origins. "You are the son of another woman," they declared (JUDGES 11:2). The text says starkly, "His mother was a prostitute" (V. 1).

TODAY'S READING
Judges 11:1–8, 29

The Spirit of the LORD came on Jephthah. Judges 11:29

But Jephthah was a natural leader, and when a hostile tribe picked a fight with Gilead, the people who had sent him packing suddenly wanted him back. "Be our commander," they said (V. 6). Jephthah asked, "Didn't you hate me and drive me from my father's house?" (V. 7). After getting assurances that things would be different, he agreed to lead them. The Scripture tells us, "Then the Spirit of the LORD came on Jephthah" (V. 29). Through faith, he led them to a great victory. The New Testament mentions him in its list of heroes of the faith (HEBREWS 11:32).

God so often seems to choose the unlikeliest people to do His work, doesn't He? It doesn't matter where we're from, how we got here, or what we've done. What matters is that we respond in faith to His love. 🌻

TIM GUSTAFSON

Lord, we take great comfort knowing that You don't show favoritism based on where we're from. Our heritage is found in You. Thank You for adopting us into Your family.

Many who are first will be last, and many who are last will be first.

MATTHEW 19:30

Hurry Not

"**R**uthlessly eliminate hurry." When two friends repeated that adage by the wise Dallas Willard to me, I knew I needed to consider it. Where was I spinning my wheels, wasting time and energy? More important, where was I rushing ahead and not looking to God for guidance and help? In the weeks and months that followed, I remembered those words and reoriented myself back to the Lord and His wisdom. I reminded myself to trust in Him, rather than leaning on my own ways.

TODAY'S READING
Isaiah 26:1–4

You will keep in perfect peace those whose minds are steadfast, because they trust in you. Isaiah 26:3

After all, rushing around frantically seems to be the opposite of the "perfect peace" the prophet Isaiah speaks of. The Lord gives this gift to "those whose minds are steadfast," because they trust in Him (v. 3). And He is worthy of being trusted today, tomorrow, and forever, for "the LORD, the LORD himself, is the Rock eternal" (v. 4). Trusting God with our minds fixed on Him is the antidote to a hurried life.

How about us? Do we sense that we're hurried or even hasty? Maybe, in contrast, we often experience a sense of peace. Or perhaps we're somewhere in between the two extremes.

Wherever we may be, I pray today that we'll be able to put aside any hurry as we trust the Lord, who will never fail us and who gives us His peace.   *AMY BOUCHER PYE*

> Lord God, You give the peace that passes all understanding,
> which is a gift I don't want to take for granted. Thank You.

God's peace helps us not to hurry.

The Art of Forgiveness

One afternoon I spent two hours at an art exhibit—*The Father & His Two Sons: The Art of Forgiveness*—in which all of the pieces were focused on Jesus's parable of the prodigal son (SEE LUKE 15:11–31). I found Edward Riojas's painting *The Prodigal Son* especially powerful. The painting portrays the once wayward son returning home, wearing rags and walking with his head down. With a land of death behind him, he steps onto a pathway where his father is already running toward him. At the bottom of the painting are Jesus's words, "But when he was yet a great way off, his father saw him, and had compassion" (V. 20 KJV).

TODAY'S READING
Luke 15:11–24

While he was still a long way off, his father saw him and was filled with compassion for him; he ran to his son, threw his arms around him and kissed him.

Luke 15:20

I was deeply moved by realizing once more how God's unchanging love has altered my life. When I walked away from Him, He didn't turn His back, but kept looking, watching, and waiting. His love is undeserved yet unchanging; often ignored yet never withdrawn.

We all are guilty, yet our heavenly Father reaches out to welcome us, just as the father in this story embraced his wayward son. "Let's have a feast and celebrate," the father told the servants. "For this son of mine was dead and is alive again; he was lost and is found" (VV. 23–24).

The Lord still rejoices over those who return to Him today—and that is worth celebrating! 🌱

DAVID C. MCCASLAND

Father, as we receive Your love and forgiveness,
may we also extend it to others in Your name.
God's love for us is undeserved yet unchanging.

Anywhere

TODAY'S READING
Jeremiah 2:1–8; 3:14–15

As I flipped through a box of my old wedding photographs, my fingers stopped at a picture of my husband and me, newly christened "Mr. and Mrs." My dedication to him was obvious in my expression. I would go *anywhere* with him.

Nearly four decades later, our marriage is tightly threaded with love and a commitment that has carried us through both hard and good times. Year after year, I've recommitted my dedication to go *anywhere* with him.

In Jeremiah 2:2, God yearns for His beloved but wayward Israel, "I remember the devotion of your youth, how as a bride you loved me and followed me."

> **I remember the devotion of your youth, how as a bride you loved me and followed me through the wilderness.** Jeremiah 2:2

The Hebrew word for *devotion* conveys the highest loyalty and commitment possible. At first, Israel expressed this unwavering devotion to God, but gradually she turned away.

Despite the undeniably powerful feelings in the early stages of commitment, complacency can dull the sharp edge of love and a lack of zeal can lead to unfaithfulness. We know the importance of fighting against such a lag in our marriages. What about the fervor of our love relationship with God? Are we as devoted to Him now as we were when we first came to faith?

God faithfully allows His people to return (3:14–15). Today we can renew our vows to follow Him—anywhere. 🌿   *ELISA MORGAN*

Dear God, help me to keep the promises I've made to You.
I will follow You anywhere.

You don't need to know where you're going if you know God is leading.

God in the Details

When my "chocolate" Labrador retriever puppy was three months old, I took him to the veterinarian's office for his shots and checkup. As our vet carefully looked him over, she noticed a small white marking in his fur on his left hind paw. She smiled and said to him, "That's where God held you when He dipped you in chocolate."

I couldn't help but laugh. But she had unintentionally made a meaningful point about the deep and personal interest God takes in His creation.

Jesus tells us in Matthew 10:30 that "even the very hairs of your head are all numbered." God is so great that He is able to take infinite interest in the most intimate details of our lives. There is nothing so small that it escapes His notice, and there is no concern too trivial to bring before Him. He simply cares that much.

> TODAY'S READING
> **Matthew 10:29–31**
>
> **The LORD is good to all; he has compassion on all he has made.**
> Psalm 145:9

God not only created us; He sustains and keeps us through every moment. It's sometimes said that "the devil is in the details." But it's better by far to understand that God is in them, watching over even the things that escape our notice. How comforting it is to know that our perfectly wise and caring heavenly Father holds us—along with all of creation—in His strong and loving hands.

JAMES BANKS

Loving Lord, I praise You for the wonder of Your creation.
Help me to reflect Your compassion by taking care of
what You have made.

God attends to our every need.

The Secret of Peace

Grace is a very special lady. One word comes to mind when I think of her: *peace*. The quiet and restful expression on her face has seldom changed in the six months I have known her, even though her husband was diagnosed with a rare disease and then hospitalized.

When I asked Grace the secret of her peace, she said, "It's not a secret, it's a person. It's Jesus in me. There is no other way I can explain the quietness I feel in the midst of this storm."

The secret of peace is our relationship to Jesus Christ. He is our peace. When Jesus is our Savior and Lord, and as we become more like Him, peace becomes real. Things like sickness, financial difficulties, or danger may be present, but peace reassures us that God holds our lives in His hands (DANIEL 5:23), and we can trust that things will work together for good.

> TODAY'S READING
> **2 Thessalonians 3:16–18**
>
> **The Lord of peace himself give you peace.** 2 Thessalonians 3:16

Have we experienced this peace that goes beyond logic and understanding? Do we have the inner confidence that God is in control? My wish for all of us today echoes the words of the apostle Paul: "May the Lord of peace himself give you peace." And may we feel this peace "at all times and in every way" (2 THESSALONIANS 3:16).    *KEILA OCHOA*

Dear Lord, please give us Your peace at all times
and in every situation.

To trust in Jesus is peace.

Our Daily Bread

The Waiting Place

"**W**aiting for the fish to bite** or waiting for wind to fly a kite. Or waiting around for Friday night . . . . Everyone is just waiting"—or so Dr. Seuss, author of many children's books, says.

So much of life is about waiting, but God is never in a hurry—or so it seems. "God has His hour and delay," suggests an old, reliable saying. Thus we wait.

> **TODAY'S READING**
> **Psalm 70**
>
> **Be still before the LORD and wait patiently for him.**
> Psalm 37:7

Waiting is hard. We twiddle our thumbs, shuffle our feet, stifle our yawns, heave long sighs, and fret inwardly in frustration. Why must I live with this awkward person, this tedious job, this embarrassing behavior, this health issue that will not go away? Why doesn't God come through?

God's answer: "Wait awhile and see what I will do."

Waiting is one of life's best teachers for in it we learn the virtue of . . . well, waiting—waiting while God works in us and for us. It's in waiting that we develop endurance, the ability to trust God's love and goodness, even when things aren't going our way (PSALM 70:5).

But waiting is not dreary, teeth-clenched resignation. We can "rejoice and be glad in [Him]" while we wait (v. 4). We wait in hope, knowing that God will deliver us in due time—in this world or in the next. God is never in a hurry, but He's always on time. 🌿

DAVID H. ROPER

Dear Lord, thank You for Your loving presence.
Help us to make the most of our waiting through trust in
and service for You.

God is with us in our waiting.

Amnesia

Emergency Services in Carlsbad, California, came to the rescue of a woman with an Australian accent who couldn't recall who she was. Because she was suffering from amnesia and had no ID with her, she was unable to provide her name or where she had come from. It took the help of doctors and international media to restore her health, tell her story, and reunite her with her family.

Nebuchadnezzar, king of Babylon, also lost sight of who he was and where he had come from. His "amnesia," though, was spiritual. In taking credit for the kingdom he'd been given, he forgot that God is the King of Kings, and everything he had was from Him (DANIEL 4:17, 28–30).

> **TODAY'S READING**
> **Daniel 4:28–37**
>
> **My understanding returned to me; and I blessed the Most High.**
>
> Daniel 4:34 NKJV

God dramatized the king's state of mind by driving him into the fields to live with wild animals and graze like a cow (VV. 32–33). Finally, after seven years Nebuchadnezzar looked up to the skies, and his memory of who he was and who had given him his kingdom returned. With his senses restored, he declared, "I, Nebuchadnezzar, praise and exalt and glorify the King of heaven" (V. 37).

What about us? Who do we think we are? Where did we come from? Since we are inclined to forget, who can we count on to help us remember but the King of Kings? 🖋 *MART DEHAAN*

Father, we are so inclined to forget who we are, where we've come from, and that we belong to You. Help us to remember that in Christ we are Your children—known, loved, gifted, and cared for— now and forever.

When we forget who we are, our Father cares.

The Widow's Faith

t is pitch dark when Ah-pi starts her day. Others in the village will wake up soon to make their way to the rubber plantation. Harvesting latex is one of the main sources of income for people living in Hongzhuang Village, China. To collect as much latex as possible, the trees must be tapped very early in the morning, before daybreak. Ah-pi will be among the rubber tappers, but first she will spend time communing with God.

Ah-pi's father, husband, and only son have passed away, and she—with her daughter-in-law—is providing for an elderly mother and two young grandsons. Her story reminds me of another widow in the Bible who trusted God.

TODAY'S READING
2 Kings 4:1–7

The pagans run after all these things, and your heavenly Father knows that you need them.

Matthew 6:32

The widow's husband had died and left her in debt (2 KINGS 4:1). In her distress, she looked to God for help by turning to His servant Elisha. She believed that God cared and that He could do something about her situation. And God did. He provided miraculously for the dire needs of this widow (VV. 5–6). This same God also provided for Ah-pi—though less miraculously—through the toil of her hands, the produce from the ground, and gifts from His people.

Though life can make various demands on us, we can always draw strength from God. We can entrust our cares to Him, do all we can, and let Him amaze us with what He can do with our situation. 🌱

POH FANG CHIA

Father, thank You for Your patience when I trust in my own resources and turn to You only as a last resort. Teach me to seek Your help before I do anything at all.

*We may face situations beyond our reserves,
but never beyond God's resources.*

Wisdom's Call

Malcolm Muggeridge, the noted British journalist and social critic, came to faith in Christ at the age of sixty. On his seventy-fifth birthday he offered twenty-five insightful observations about life. One said, "I never met a rich man who was happy, but I have only very occasionally met a poor man who did not want to become a rich man."

Most of us would agree that money can't make us happy, but we might like to have more so we can be sure.

King Solomon's net worth has been estimated at more than two trillion US dollars. Although he was very wealthy, he knew that money had great limitations. Proverbs 8 is based on his experience and offers "Wisdom's Call" to all people. "I raise my voice to all mankind. . . . My mouth speaks what is true" (VV. 4–7). "Choose my instruction instead of silver, knowledge rather than choice gold, for wisdom is more precious than rubies, and nothing you desire can compare with her" (VV. 10–11).

> TODAY'S READING
> **Proverbs 8:10–21**
>
> **Wisdom is more precious than rubies, and nothing you desire can compare with her.** Proverbs 8:11

Wisdom says, "My fruit is better than fine gold; what I yield surpasses choice silver. I walk in the way of righteousness, along the paths of justice, bestowing a rich inheritance on those who love me and making their treasuries full" (VV. 19–21).

These are true riches indeed! 🌱

DAVID C. MCCASLAND

Lord, thank You for the riches of Your wisdom
that guide our steps today.

God offers the true riches of wisdom to all who seek and follow Him.

On-the-Job Training

When my son's teacher asked me to serve as a chaperone for their science camp, I hesitated. How could I be a role model when mistakes littered my past, when I still struggled, stumbled, and slipped into old bad habits? God helped me love and raise my son, but I often doubted He could use me to serve others.

Sometimes I still fail to recognize that God—the only perfect One, the only One who can change hearts and lives—transforms us over time. Then the Holy Spirit reminds me how Paul encouraged Timothy to embrace his on-the-job training, persevere in faith, and use the

TODAY'S READING
2 Timothy 1:6–14

Of this gospel I was appointed a herald and an apostle and a teacher. 2 Timothy 1:11

gifts God had given him (2 TIMOTHY 1:6). Timothy could be courageous because God, his power source, would help him love and be disciplined as he continued to grow and serve those within his sphere of influence (v. 7).

Christ saves and empowers us to honor Him with our lives, not because we have special qualifications but because we're each valuable members of His family (v. 9).

We can persevere with confidence when we know our role is to simply love God and others. Christ's role is to save us and give us a purpose that extends beyond our small vision of the world. As we follow Jesus daily, He transforms us *while* using us to encourage others as we share His love and truth wherever He sends us. ✿

XOCHITL DIXON

Lord, thanks for affirming we can depend on You completely as we share You cheerfully, confidently, and courageously.

Knowing our power-source personally gives us confidence in our role as servants to the King.

Take Another Look at Jesus!

I f there ever was a faithful person, it was Brother Justice. He was committed to his marriage, dedicated to his job as a postal worker, and each Sunday stood at his post as a leader in our local church. I visited my childhood church recently, and perched on the upright piano was the same bell that Brother Justice rang to notify us that the time for Bible study was about to end. The bell has endured the test of time. And although Brother Justice has been with the Lord for years, his legacy of faithfulness also endures.

> **TODAY'S READING**
> **Hebrews 3:1–6**
>
> **But Christ is faithful as the Son over God's house. And we are his house, if indeed we hold firmly to our confidence and the hope in which we glory.** Hebrews 3:6

Hebrews 3 brings a faithful servant and a faithful Son to the readers' attention. Though the faithfulness of Moses as God's "servant" is undeniable, Jesus is the one believers are taught to focus on. "Therefore, holy brothers and sisters . . . fix your thoughts on Jesus" (v. 1). Such was the encouragement to all who face temptation (2:18). Their legacy could come only from following Jesus, the faithful One.

What do you do when the winds of temptation are swirling all around you? When you are weary and worn and want to quit? The text invites us to, as one paraphrase renders it, "Take a good hard look at Jesus" (3:1 THE MESSAGE). Look at Him again—and again and again. As we reexamine Jesus, we find the trustworthy Son of God who gives us courage to live in His family. ❧

ARTHUR JACKSON

Father, through Your Spirit, empower us to courageously love, honor, and follow the Lord Jesus Christ.

Looking to Jesus can give us courage to face the challenges in our lives.

Breaking the Chains

We found our visit to Christ Church Cathedral in Stone Town, Zanzibar, deeply moving, for it sits on the site of what was formerly the largest slave market in East Africa. The designers of this cathedral wanted to show through a physical symbol how the gospel breaks the chains of slavery. No longer would the location be a place of evil deeds and horrible atrocities, but of God's embodied grace.

> **TODAY'S READING**
> **Ephesians 1:3–14**
>
> **In him we have redemption through his blood, the forgiveness of sins.** Ephesians 1:7

Those who built the cathedral wanted to express how Jesus's death on the cross provides freedom from sin—that which the apostle Paul speaks of in his letter to the church at Ephesus: "In him we have redemption through his blood" (EPHESIANS 1:7). Here the word *redemption* points to the Old Testament's notion of the marketplace, with someone buying back a person or item. Jesus buys back a person from a life of slavery to sin and wrongdoing.

In Paul's opening words in this letter (VV. 3–14), he bubbles over with joy at the thought of his freedom in Christ. He points, in layer after layer of praise, to God's work of grace for us through Jesus's death, which sets us free from the cords of sin. No longer do we need to be slaves to sin, for we are set free to live for God and His glory. 🖋

AMY BOUCHER PYE

Lord God, through the death of Your Son, You have given us life forever.
Help me to share this gift of grace with someone today.

Jesus redeems us from the slavery of sin.

Waiting in Anticipation

Every May Day (MAY 1) in Oxford, England, an early morning crowd gathers to welcome spring. At 6:00, the Magdalen College Choir sings from the top of Magdalen Tower. Thousands wait in anticipation for the dark night to be broken by song and the ringing of bells.

Like the revelers, I often wait. I wait for answers to prayers or guidance from the Lord. Although I don't know the exact time my wait will end, I'm learning to wait expectantly. In Psalm 130 the psalmist writes of being in deep distress facing a situation that feels like the blackest of nights. In the midst of his troubles, he chooses to trust God and stay alert like a guard on duty charged

> TODAY'S READING
> **Psalm 130:1–6**
>
> **I wait for the LORD more than watchmen wait for the morning, more than watchmen wait for the morning.** Psalm 130:6

with announcing daybreak. "I wait for the LORD more than watchmen wait for the morning, more than watchmen wait for the morning" (V. 6).

The anticipation of God's faithfulness breaking through the darkness gives the psalmist hope to endure even in the midst of his suffering. Based on the promises of God found throughout Scripture, that hope allows him to keep waiting even though he has not yet seen the first rays of light.

Be encouraged if you are in the middle of a dark night. The dawn is coming—either in this life or in heaven! In the meantime, don't give up hope but keep watching for the deliverance of the Lord. He will be faithful. ❧   LISA SAMRA

Please bring light to my darkness. Open my eyes to see You at work and to trust You. I'm grateful that You are faithful, Father.

God can be trusted in the light and in the dark.

Longing for God

One day my daughter was visiting with our one-year-old grandson. I was getting ready to leave the house on an errand, but as soon as I walked out of the room my grandson began to cry. It happened twice, and each time I went back and spent a moment with him. As I headed out the door the third time, his little lip began to quiver again. At that point my daughter said, "Dad, why don't you just take him with you?"

> TODAY'S READING
> **1 John 4:13–16**
>
> **My heart and my flesh cry out for the living God.**
>
> Psalm 84:2

Any grandparent could tell you what happened next. My grandson went along for the ride, just because I love him.

How good it is to know that the longings of our hearts for God are also met with love. The Bible assures us that we can "know and rely on the love God has for us" (1 JOHN 4:16). God doesn't love us because of anything we have or haven't done. His love isn't based on our worthiness at all, but on His goodness and faithfulness. When the world around us is unloving and unkind, we can rely on God's unchanging love as our source of hope and peace.

Our heavenly Father's heart has gone out to us through the gift of His Son and His Spirit. How comforting is the assurance that God loves us with love that never ends! ❧   *JAMES BANKS*

Loving Lord, thank You for Your compassion for me, proven at the cross.
Please help me to obey and love You today.

God longs for us to long for Him.

A Change in Perspective

My hometown had experienced its heaviest winter in thirty years. My muscles ached from hours of shoveling the unrelenting snow. When I stepped inside after what felt like a fruitless effort, weary as I kicked off my boots, I was greeted by the warmth of a fire and my children gathered around it. As I gazed out the window from the shelter of my home, my perspective of the weather shifted completely. Instead of seeing more work to do, I savored the beauty of frosted tree branches and the way the snow blanketed the colorless landscape of winter.

TODAY'S READING
Psalm 73:12–28

It troubled me deeply till I entered the sanctuary of God.

Psalm 73:16–17

I see a similar, but much more poignant, shift in Asaph when I read his words in Psalm 73. In the beginning, he laments the way the world seems to work, how wrongs seem to be rewarded. He doubts the value of being different than the crowd and living for the good of others (V. 13). But when he enters the sanctuary of God, his outlook changes (VV. 16–17): he remembers that God will deal with the world and its troubles perfectly and, more importantly, that it is good to be with God (V. 28).

When we're chilled by the seemingly ceaseless problems in our world, we can enter God's sanctuary in prayer and be warmed through by the life-altering, perspective-changing truth that His judgment is better than ours. Though our circumstances may not change, our perspective can. 🌱   *KIRSTEN HOLMBERG*

Lord, I admit I quickly become frustrated with the way things appear.
Help me to see the way You do.

God gives us the right perspective.

Before the Beginning

"**B**ut if God has no beginning and no end, and has always existed, what was He doing before He created us? How did He spend His time?" Some precocious Sunday school student always asks this question when we talk about God's eternal nature. I used to respond that this was a bit of a mystery. But recently I learned that the Bible gives us an answer to this question.

TODAY'S READING
Matthew 3:13–17

You loved me before the creation of the world.
John 17:24

When Jesus prays to His Father in John 17, He says "Father, . . . you loved me before the creation of the world" (V. 24). This is God as revealed to us by Jesus: Before the world was ever created, God was a trinity (Father, Son, and Holy Spirit)—all loving each other and being loved. When Jesus was baptized, God sent His Spirit in the form of a dove and said, "This is my Son, whom I love" (MATTHEW 3:17). The most foundational aspect of God's identity is this outgoing, life-giving love.

What a lovely and encouraging truth this is about our God! The mutual, outgoing love expressed by each member of the Trinity—Father, Son, and Holy Spirit—is key to understanding the nature of God. What was God doing before the beginning of time? What He always does: He was loving because He is love (1 JOHN 4:8). 🌱

AMY PETERSON

God, thank You for Your overflowing, self-giving love.

We are created in the image of a God who is loving and relational.

Keeping Close

My mile-long walk home from dropping off my daughter at her school gives me the opportunity to memorize some verses from the Bible—if I'm intentional about doing so. When I take those minutes to turn over God's Word in my mind, I often find them coming back to me later in the day, bringing me comfort and wisdom.

> **TODAY'S READING**
> **Deuteronomy 6:1–9**
>
> **Tie them as symbols on your hands and bind them on your foreheads.**
>
> Deuteronomy 6:8

When Moses prepared the Israelites to enter the Promised Land, he urged them to hold close to God's commands and decrees (DEUTERONOMY 6:1–2). Wanting them to flourish, he said they should turn these instructions over in their minds and discuss them with their children (VV. 6–7). He even said to tie them to their wrists and bind them to their foreheads (V. 8). He didn't want them to forget God's instructions to live as people who honored the Lord and enjoyed His blessings.

How might you consider God's words today? One idea is to write out a verse from Scripture, and every time you wash your hands or take a drink, read the words and turn them over in your mind. Or before you go to sleep, consider a short passage from the Bible as the last act of the day. Many are the ways of keeping God's Word close to our hearts!

AMY BOUCHER PYE

Lord God, thank You for giving us the Bible, which is a wellspring for life.
Help us to read and digest it today.

Surround yourself with God's Word.

Standing on the Promises

My friend's brother (when they were both children) assured his sister an umbrella had enough lift to hold her up if she would only "believe." So "by faith" she jumped off a barn roof and knocked herself out, suffering a minor concussion.

What God has promised, He will do. But we must be sure we stand on God's *actual* word when we claim a promise, for only then do we have the assurance that God will do or give what He's promised. Faith has no power in itself. It only counts when it's based on a clear and unambiguous promise from God. Anything else is just wishful thinking.

TODAY'S READING
John 15:5–8

Ask whatever you wish, and it will be done for you.

John 15:7

Here's a case in point: God has promised, "Ask whatever you wish, and it will be done for you. This is to my Father's glory, that you bear much fruit" (JOHN 15:7–8). These verses are not a promise that God will answer every prayer we utter, but rather a promise that He will respond to every longing for personal righteousness—what Paul calls "the fruit of the Spirit" (GALATIANS 5:22–23). If we hunger and thirst for holiness and ask God for it, He will begin to satisfy us. It will take time; for spiritual growth, like human growth, is gradual. Don't give up. Keep asking God to make you holy. In His time and at His pace "it will be done for you." God doesn't make promises He doesn't keep. 🖋 *DAVID H. ROPER*

Dear Lord, thank You for Your many promises to us in Your Word.
And thank You for sending Your Holy Spirit who gives discernment.

We have a promise-keeping God.

The Fingerprint of God

Lygon Stevens loved to climb mountains with her brother Nick. They were experienced climbers and both had summitted Mt. McKinley (Denali), the highest point in North America. Then, in January 2008, they were swept off a Colorado mountain by an avalanche, injuring Nick and killing twenty-year-old Lygon. When Nick later discovered his sister's journal in one of her satchels, he was deeply comforted by its contents. It was filled with reflections, prayers, and praise to God as seen in this entry: "I am a work of art, signed by God. But He's not done; in fact, He has just begun. . . . I have on me the fingerprint of God. Never will there ever be another person like me. . . . I have a job to do in this life that no other can do."

> TODAY'S READING
> **Ephesians 2:1–10**
>
> **For we are God's handiwork, created in Christ Jesus to do good works, which God prepared in advance for us to do.** Ephesians 2:10

Although Lygon is no longer physically present on earth, through the legacy of her life and her journal she inspires and challenges those she left behind.

Because we are made in God's image (GENESIS 1:26), each person is a "work of art, signed by God." As the apostle Paul says, "We are God's handiwork, created in Christ Jesus to do good works, which God prepared in advance for us to do" (EPHESIANS 2:10).

Praise God that He uses each of us, in His own time and way, to help others. 🌱

DENNIS FISHER

How would You like to use me, Lord?
I am open and willing.

Each person is a unique expression of God's loving design.

Responding to God's Leading

n August 2015, when I was preparing to attend a university a couple of hours from home, I realized I probably wouldn't move back home after graduation. My mind raced. *How can I leave home? My family? My church? What if God later calls me to another state or country?*

Like Moses, when God told him to go "to Pharaoh to bring [His] people the Israelites out of Egypt" (EXODUS 3:10), I was afraid. I didn't want to leave my comfort zone. Yes, Moses obeyed and followed God, but not before questioning Him and requesting that someone else go instead (VV. 11–13; 4:13).

TODAY'S READING
Exodus 3:7–14

At once they left their nets and followed him.

Matthew 4:20

In Moses's example, we can see what we shouldn't do when we sense a clear calling. We can instead strive to be more like the disciples. When Jesus called them, they left everything and followed Him (MATTHEW 4:20–22; LUKE 5:28). Fear is natural, but we can trust God's plan.

Being so far from home is still difficult. But as I continually seek God, He opens doors for me that confirm I am where I'm supposed to be.

When we are led out of our comfort zone, we can either go reluctantly, like Moses, or willingly like the disciples—who followed Jesus wherever He led them. Sometimes this means leaving our comfortable life hundreds or even thousands of miles behind us. But no matter how difficult it may be, following Jesus is worth it. ❧

JULIE SCHWAB

Lord, help me to follow You wherever You lead.

We are not called to be comfortable.

The Point of No Return

I t wasn't as simple as just crossing another river. By law, no Roman general could lead armed troops into Rome. So when Julius Caesar led his Thirteenth Legion across the Rubicon River and into Italy in 49 BC, it was an act of treason. The impact of Caesar's decision was irreversible, generating years of civil war before Rome's great general became absolute ruler. Still today, the phrase "crossing the Rubicon" is a metaphor for "passing the point of no return."

Sometimes we can cross a relational Rubicon with the words we say to others. Once spoken, words can't be taken back. They can either offer help and comfort or do damage that feels just as irreversible as Caesar's march on Rome. James gave us another word picture about words when he said, "The tongue also is a fire, a world of evil among the parts of the body. It corrupts the whole body, sets the whole course of one's life on fire, and is itself set on fire by hell" (JAMES 3:6).

> TODAY'S READING
> James 3:1–12
>
> **The tongue also is a fire, a world of evil among the parts of the body. It corrupts the whole body.** James 3:6

When we fear we have crossed a Rubicon with someone, we can seek their forgiveness—and God's (MATTHEW 5:23–24; 1 JOHN 1:9). But even better is to daily rest in God's Spirit, hearing Paul's challenge, "Let your conversation be always full of grace" (COLOSSIANS 4:6), so that our words will not only honor our Lord, but lift up and encourage those around us. 🕊️   BILL CROWDER

Lord, please guard my heart and my words today. May I speak only words that please You and bring health and healing to others.

When words become weapons, our relationships soon become casualties.

The Land of Far Distances

Amy Carmichael (1867–1951) is known for her work of rescuing orphaned girls in India and giving them a new life. In the midst of this exhausting work there were times she called "moments of vision." In her book *Gold by Moonlight,* she wrote, "In the midst of a crowded day we are given almost a glimpse of 'the land of far distances,' and we stand still, arrested on the road."

> TODAY'S READING
> **Isaiah 33:17–22**
>
> **Your eyes will see the king in his beauty and view a land that stretches afar.** Isaiah 33:17

The prophet Isaiah spoke of a time when God's rebellious people would turn back to Him. "Your eyes will see the king in his beauty and view a land that stretches afar" (ISAIAH 33:17). To view this "land of far distances" is to be lifted above the circumstances of the immediate present and to gain an eternal perspective. During difficult times, the Lord enables us to see our lives from His viewpoint and regain hope. "For the LORD is our judge, the LORD is our lawgiver, the LORD is our king; it is he who will save us" (V. 22).

Each day, we can choose to look down in discouragement or lift our eyes to "the land of far distances," to the Lord who is "our Mighty One" (V. 21).

Amy Carmichael spent more than fifty years in India helping young women in great need. How did she do it? Each day she fixed her eyes on Jesus and placed her life in His care. And so can we. ❧

DAVID C. MCCASLAND

Lord, today we lift our eyes from the circumstances that discourage us
to see You in Your splendor, and find peace.

Fix your eyes on Jesus.

Persevering with Peace

As I continue trusting God through my struggles with chronic pain, even the simplest setback can feel like a fierce enemy attacker. Problem One jabs me from the right. Problem Two shoves me from behind. Problem Three punches me square in the nose. During these times, when my strength wanes and immediate relief evades me, running and hiding can seem like a good idea. But since I can't escape my pain, change my circumstances, or ignore my emotions, I'm learning slowly to rely on God to carry me through.

TODAY'S READING
Psalm 3

I lie down and sleep; I wake again, because the LORD sustains me. Psalm 3:5

When I need encouragement, comfort, and courage, I prayerfully read through the songs of the psalmists, who honestly bring their situations to God. In one of my favorite psalms, King David flees from Absalom, his son who wanted to kill him and take his kingdom. Though David lamented his painful situation (PSALM 3:1–2), he trusted God's protection and expected Him to answer his prayers (VV. 3–4). The king didn't lose sleep worrying or fearing what could happen, because he trusted God to sustain and save him (VV. 5–8).

Physical and emotional pain can often feel like aggressive adversaries. We may be tempted to give up or wish we could escape when we're weary and can't see the end of our current battle. But, like David, we can learn to trust that God will hold us up and help us rest in His constant and loving presence. ❧

XOCHITL DIXON

Lord, thanks for giving us rest in the peace of Your constant presence
and assuring us of the victory You've already won.

God offers us peace as He holds us up and carries us through every trial.

Take the Time

Rima, a Syrian woman who had recently moved to the United States, tried to explain to her tutor with hand motions and limited English why she was upset. Tears trickled down her cheeks as she held up a beautifully arranged platter of *fatayer* (meat, cheese, and spinach pies) that she had made. Then she said, "One man," and made a swishing sound as she pointed from the door to the living room and then back to the door. The tutor pieced together that several people from a nearby church were supposed to visit Rima and her family and bring some gifts. But only one man had shown up. He had hurried in, dropped off a box of items, and rushed out. He was busy taking care of a responsibility, while she and her family were lonely and longed for community and to share their *fatayer* with new friends.

TODAY'S READING
Luke 19:1–10

Come down immediately. I must stay at your house today. Luke 19:5

Taking time for people is what Jesus was all about. He attended dinner parties, taught crowds, and took time for interaction with individuals. He even invited Himself to one man's house. Zacchaeus, a tax collector, climbed a tree to see Him, and when Jesus looked up, He said, "Come down immediately. I must stay at your house today" (LUKE 19:1–9). And Zacchaeus's life was changed forever.

Because of other responsibilities, we won't always be able to take the time. But when we do, we have a wonderful privilege of being with others and watching the Lord work through us. 🌱

ANNE CETAS

How have others taken time for you? How might you show Jesus's love to someone this week?

The best gift you can give to others may be your time.

Treasure in Heaven

When I was growing up, my two sisters and I liked to sit side-by-side on top of my mother's large cedar-lined chest. My mom kept our wool sweaters in it and handiwork that was embroidered or crocheted by my grandmother. She valued the contents of the chest and relied on the pungent odor of the cedar wood to discourage moths from destroying what was inside.

> **TODAY'S READING**
> **Matthew 6:19–21**
>
> **For where your treasure is, there your heart will be also.** Matthew 6:21

Most earthly possessions can easily be destroyed by insects or rust, or can even be stolen. Matthew 6 encourages us to place a special focus—not on things that have a limited lifespan but on those that have *eternal* value. When my mom died at fifty-seven, she had not accumulated a lot of earthly possessions, but I like to think about the treasure she stored up in heaven (VV. 19–20).

I recall how much she loved God and served Him in quiet ways: caring faithfully for her family, teaching children in Sunday school, befriending a woman abandoned by her husband, comforting a young mother who had lost her baby. And she *prayed.* . . . Even after she lost her sight and became confined to a wheelchair, she continued to love and pray for others.

Our real treasure isn't measured in what we accumulate—but in what or whom we invest our time and our passions. What "treasures" are we storing up in heaven by serving and following Jesus?   *CINDY HESS KASPER*

Dear Father, help me to choose to invest my life
in things that are eternal.

Our real wealth is what we invest for eternity.

Not What It Seems

Listen!" my wife said to me over the phone. "There's a monkey in our yard!" She held up the phone so I could hear. And yes, it sounded just like a monkey. Which is weird, because the nearest wild monkey was 2,000 miles away.

Later, my father-in-law burst our bubble. "That's a barred owl," he explained. Reality was not what it had seemed.

TODAY'S READING
2 Kings 19:29-37

Do not believe every spirit, but test the spirits to see whether they are from God. 1 John 4:1

When King Sennacherib's armies had Judah's King Hezekiah trapped inside Jerusalem's walls, the Assyrians thought victory was theirs. Reality proved different. Although the Assyrian field commander used smooth words and pretended to speak for God, the Lord had His hand on His people.

"Have I come to attack and destroy this place without word from the LORD?" the commander asked (2 KINGS 18:25). As he tried to entice Jerusalem to surrender, he even said, "Choose life and not death!" (V. 32).

That *sounds* like something God would say. But the prophet Isaiah told the Israelites the true words of the Lord. "[Sennacherib] will not enter this city or shoot an arrow here," God said. "I will defend this city and save it" (19:32-34; ISAIAH 37:35). That very night "the angel of the LORD" destroyed the Assyrians (V. 35).

From time to time, we'll encounter smooth-talking people who "advise" us while denying God's power. That isn't God's voice. He speaks to us through His Word. He guides us with His Spirit. His hand is on those who follow Him, and He will never abandon us. 🌿

TIM GUSTAFSON

Teach us to discern Your voice, Lord.

God is always trustworthy.

God at Work

"**H**ow have you** seen God at work lately?" I asked some friends. One replied, "I see Him at work as I read the Scriptures each morning; I see Him at work as He helps me face each new day; I see Him at work when I know that He has been with me every step of the way—I realize how He has helped me to face challenges while giving me joy." I love his answer because it reflects how through God's Word and the indwelling presence of the Holy Spirit, God stays near to, and works in, those who love Him.

TODAY'S READING
Hebrews 13:20–21

May he work in us what is pleasing to him, through Jesus Christ. Hebrews 13:21

God working in His followers is a wonderful mystery that the writer to the Hebrews refers to as he draws his letter to a close in what's known as a benediction: ". . . and may he work in us what is pleasing to him, through Jesus Christ" (HEBREWS 13:21). With this conclusion, the writer reinforces the essential message of his letter—that God will equip His people to follow Him and that God will work in and through them for His glory.

The gift of God working in us can take us by surprise; perhaps we forgive someone who wrongs us or show patience to someone we find difficult. Our "God of peace" (V. 20) spreads His love and peace in and through us. How have you seen God at work lately? ✿

AMY BOUCHER PYE

Lord Jesus Christ, You equip me to do Your works for Your glory.
Open my eyes today, that I might understand how You are
calling me to follow You.

God works in and through His followers.

Free to Follow

My high school cross-country coach once advised me before a race, "Don't try to be in the lead. The leaders almost always burn out too quickly." Instead, he suggested I stay close behind the fastest runners. By letting them set the pace, I could conserve the mental and physical strength I'd need to finish the race well.

Leading can be exhausting; following can be freeing. Knowing this improved my running, but it took me a lot longer to realize how this applies to Christian discipleship. In my own life, I was prone to think being a believer in Jesus meant trying *really hard.* By pursuing my own exhausting expectations for what a Christian should be, I was inadvertently missing the joy and freedom found in simply following Him (JOHN 8:32, 36).

> **TODAY'S READING**
> **Matthew 11:25–30**
>
> **Take my yoke upon you and learn from me, for I am gentle and humble in heart, and you will find rest for your souls.** Matthew 11:29

But we weren't meant to direct our own lives, and Jesus didn't start a self-improvement program. Instead, He promised that in seeking Him we will find the rest we long for (MATTHEW 11:25–28). Unlike many other religious teachers' emphasis on rigorous study of Scripture or an elaborate set of rules, Jesus taught that it's simply through knowing Him that we know God (V. 27). In seeking Him, we find our heavy burdens lifted (VV. 28–30) and our lives transformed.

Because following Him, our gentle and humble Leader (V. 29), is never burdensome—it's the way of hope and healing. Resting in His love, we are free. 🌿

MONICA BRANDS

Lord, I'm so thankful I don't have to be in charge of my own life.
Help me rest in You.

True freedom is found in following Christ.

Praising God's Goodness

Someone in our Bible-study group suggested, "Let's write our own psalms!" Initially, some protested that they didn't have the flair for writing, but after some encouragement everyone wrote a moving poetic song narrating how God had been working in their lives. Out of trials, protection, provision, and even pain and tears came enduring messages that gave our psalms fascinating themes. Like Psalm 136, each psalm revealed the truth that *God's love endures forever*.

> **TODAY'S READING**
> **Psalm 136:1–15**
>
> **Give thanks to the LORD, for he is good.** *His love endures forever.*
>
> Psalm 136:1

We all have a story to tell about God's love—whether we write or sing or tell it. For some, our experiences may be dramatic or intense—like the writer of Psalm 136 who recounted how God delivered His people from captivity and conquered His enemies (VV. 10–15). Others may simply describe God's marvelous creation: "who by his understanding made the heavens . . . spread out the earth upon the waters . . . made the great lights—. . . the sun to govern the day . . . the moon and stars to govern the night" (VV. 5–9).

Remembering who God is and what He has done brings out praise and thanksgiving that glorifies Him. We can then "[speak] to one another with psalms, hymns, and songs from the Spirit" (EPHESIANS 5:19) about the goodness of the Lord whose *love endures forever*! Turn your experience of God's love into a praise song of your own and enjoy an overflow of His never-ending goodness. 🌿

LAWRENCE DARMANI

Lord, thank You for the world You made and for the blessings on my life. Fill my heart with gratitude and put words in my mouth to acknowledge and appreciate You.

For all eternity, God's love endures forever.

Our Daily Bread

Overflowing

"No! No! No! NO!" I screamed. It didn't help. Not one bit. My brilliant solution for our plugged problem—flushing again—accomplished exactly the opposite of what I'd intended. I knew I had made a mistake the second I pushed the lever down. And I stood helplessly as water overflowed.

TODAY'S READING
Romans 15:4–13

May the God of hope fill you with all joy and peace as you trust in him.

Romans 15:13

How many times have our kids tried to pour milk and misjudged the process, with white liquid flowing everywhere. Or maybe we failed to remember that a two-liter bottle of soda just rolled around in the trunk . . . with explosively startling results.

No, spills are almost never a good thing. But there might be just *one* exception. The apostle Paul uses that image, *overflowing*, to describe a people so full of God's Spirit that what naturally spills out of them is *hope* (ROMANS 15:13). I love that picture, of being filled to the brim with joy, peace, and faith because of His powerful presence in our lives. So much so, in fact, that we can't help but exude and express winsome confidence in our heavenly Father. That might be during the beautiful, sunny seasons of our lives. Or when the proverbial cup of our lives gets jostled. Either way, what sloshes out over the top is life-giving hope to those around us who are "drenched" by it. 🍃

ADAM HOLZ

Lord, spills happen in life. But when they do, help us to be
so full of Your Spirit that what pours out of us is the kind of hope
that others can't help but notice and be blessed by.

The Father gave us the Spirit to make us like the Son.

Even If

Sometimes life deals us a tremendous blow. Other times the miraculous happens.

Three young men, captives in Babylon, stood in front of the fearsome king of that land and boldly proclaimed that under no circumstances would they worship the giant image of gold towering above them. Together they declared: "If we are thrown into the blazing furnace, the God we serve is able to deliver us from it, and he will deliver us from Your Majesty's hand. But even if he does not, we want you to know… we will not… worship the image" (DANIEL 3:17–18).

> **TODAY'S READING**
> **Daniel 3:8–18**
>
> **The God we serve is able to deliver us from [the fire].... But even if he does not, we want you to know, Your Majesty, that we will not serve your gods.** Daniel 3:17–18

These three men—Shadrach, Meshach, and Abednego—were hurled into the fiery furnace; and God miraculously delivered them so that not a hair of their head was singed and their clothing was smoke-free (VV. 19–27). They had been prepared to die but their trust in God was unwavering—"even if" He had not saved them.

God desires that we cling to Him—*even if* our loved one isn't healed, *even if* we lose our job, *even if* we are persecuted. Sometimes God rescues us from danger in this life, and sometimes He doesn't. But the truth we can hold firmly is this: "The God we serve is able," loves us, and is with us in every fiery trial, every *even if.* 🌿

ALYSON KIEDA

Dear Lord, we love You! Please give us unwavering faith—
and strength and hope for each day—no matter the circumstance.

God is able.

A New Community

My friend Carrie's five-year-old daughter, Maija, has an interesting approach to playtime. She loves mixing together dolls from different playsets to come up with a new community. In the world of her imagination, everything belongs together. These are her people. She believes they are happiest when they're together, despite being different sizes and shapes.

TODAY'S READING
Acts 2:1–12, 42–47

All the believers were together and had everything in common. Acts 2:44

Her creativity reminds me of God's purpose for the church. On the day of Pentecost, Luke tells us, "Now there were staying in Jerusalem God-fearing Jews from every nation under heaven" (ACTS 2:5). Though these people were from different cultures and spoke different languages, the Holy Spirit's arrival made them a new community: the church. From then on, they would be considered one body, unified by the death and resurrection of Jesus.

The leaders of this new body were a group of men Jesus brought together during His time on earth—His disciples. If Jesus hadn't united them, more than likely they would never have come together. And now more people—"about three thousand" (2:41)—had become Christ-followers. Thanks to the Holy Spirit, this once divided group "had everything in common" (V. 44). They were willing to share what they had with each other.

The Holy Spirit continues to bridge the gaps between people groups. We might not always get along, nor readily understand one another. But as believers in Christ, we belong together. 🌱   *LINDA WASHINGTON*

Jesus, thank You for dying for us and uniting us as one people in the church.
The Holy Spirit turns "us" and "them" into "we."

A Prayer of Forgiveness

n 1960, **six-year-old Ruby Bridges** was the first African-American child to integrate an all-white public elementary school in the American South. Every day for months, federal marshals escorted Ruby past a mob of angry parents shouting curses, threats, and insults at her. Safely inside, she sat in a classroom alone with Barbara Henry, the only teacher willing to instruct her while parents kept their children from attending school with Ruby.

Noted child psychiatrist Robert Coles met with Ruby for several months to help her cope with the fear and stress she experienced. He was amazed by the prayer Ruby said every day as she walked to school and back home. "Please, God, forgive them because they don't know what they're doing" (SEE LUKE 23:34).

The words of Jesus spoken from the cross were stronger than the hatred and insults hurled at Him. In the most agonizing hours of His life, our Lord demonstrated the radical response He taught His followers: "Love your enemies, do good to those who hate you, bless those who curse you, pray for those who mistreat you . . . . Be merciful, just as your Father is merciful" (LUKE 6:27–28, 36).

TODAY'S READING
Luke 6:27–36

Love your enemies, do good to those who hate you, bless those who curse you, pray for those who mistreat you. Luke 6:27–28

This remarkable approach is possible only as we consider the powerful love Jesus has given us—love stronger than even the deepest hatred.

Ruby Bridges helped show us the way. 🌿   *DAVID C. MCCASLAND*

Father, You have so graciously forgiven us. Help us today to forgive others who have wronged us.

Bless those who curse you and pray for those who mistreat you.

Our Daily Bread

Up a Tree

My mother discovered my kitten Velvet atop the kitchen counter, devouring homemade bread. With a huff of frustration, she scooted her out the door. Hours later, we searched our yard for the missing cat without success. A faint meow whistled on the wind, and I looked up to the peak of a poplar tree where a black smudge tilted a branch.

In her haste to flee my mother's frustration over her behavior, Velvet chose a more precarious predicament. Is it possible that we sometimes do something similar—running from our errors and putting ourselves in danger? And even then God comes to our rescue.

TODAY'S READING
Jonah 2:1–10

In my distress I called to the LORD, and he answered me. Jonah 2:2

The prophet Jonah fled in disobedience from God's call to preach to Nineveh, and was swallowed up by a great fish. "From inside the fish Jonah prayed to the LORD his God. He said: 'In my distress I called to the LORD, and he answered me' " (JONAH 2:1-2). God heard Jonah's plea and, "commanded the fish, and it vomited Jonah onto dry land" (V. 10). Then God gave Jonah another chance (3:1).

After exhausting our efforts to woo Velvet down, we summoned the local fire department. With the longest ladder fully extended, a kind man climbed high, plucked my kitten from her perch, and returned to place her safely in my arms.

Oh the heights—and in the depths—God goes to in rescuing us from our disobedience with His redeeming love! 🌿

ELISA MORGAN

Dear God, how we need Your rescue today!

Jesus's death on the cross rescued us from our sins.

The Babushka Lady

The "Babushka Lady" is one of the mysteries surrounding the 1963 assassination of US President John F. Kennedy. Captured on film recording the events with a movie camera, she has proven to be elusive. This mystery woman, wearing an overcoat and scarf (resembling a Russian *babushka*), has never been identified and her film has never been seen. For decades, historians and scholars have speculated that fear has prevented the "Babushka Lady" from telling her story of that dark November day.

TODAY'S READING
Acts 2:22–36

Let all Israel be assured of this: God has made this Jesus, whom you crucified, both Lord and Messiah.

Acts 2:36

No speculation is needed to understand why Jesus's disciples hid. They cowered in fear because of the authorities who had killed their Master (JOHN 20:19)—reluctant to come forward and declare their experience. But then Jesus rose from the grave. The Holy Spirit soon arrived and you couldn't keep those once-timid followers of Christ quiet! On the day of Pentecost, a Spirit-empowered Simon Peter declared, "Let all Israel be assured of this: God has made this Jesus, whom you crucified, both Lord and Messiah" (ACTS 2:36).

The opportunity to boldly speak in Jesus's name is not limited to those with daring personalities or career ministry training. It is the indwelling Spirit who enables us to tell the good news of Jesus. By His strength, we can experience the courage to share our Savior with others. 🌀   *BILL CROWDER*

Lord, please give me the strength and boldness to
talk to others about You.

Speak of the matchless love of Christ to those who need to hear.

Tossing and Turning

What keeps you awake at night? Lately I've been losing sleep, tossing and turning on my bed, trying to work out a solution to an issue. Eventually I begin fretting about not getting enough rest to handle the challenges of the next day!

Sound familiar? Troubled relationships, an uncertain future, whatever it is—we all give in to worry at one point or another.

King David was clearly in distress when he penned Psalm 4. People were ruining his reputation with groundless accusations (V. 2). And some were questioning his competency to rule (V. 6). David probably felt angry for being treated so unfairly. Surely he could have spent nights stewing about it. Yet we read these remarkable words: "In peace I will lie down and sleep" (V. 8).

TODAY'S READING
Psalm 4

In peace I will lie down and sleep, for you alone, LORD, make me dwell in safety. Psalm 4:8

Charles Spurgeon explains verse 8 beautifully: "In thus lying down, . . . [David] resigned himself into the hands of another; he did so completely, for in the absence of all care, he slept; there was here a perfect trust." What inspired this trust? From the start, David was confident that God would answer his prayers (V. 3). And he was sure that since God had chosen to love him, He would lovingly meet his needs.

May God help us to rest in His power and presence when worries threaten. In His sovereign and loving arms, we can "lie down and sleep." 🌾

POH FANG CHIA

Dear Father, thank You for hearing me when I call.
I surrender my worries to You and rest in Your power and presence.

We can entrust our cares to a wholly trustworthy God.

Accidental Wisdom

A **few years ago,** a woman shared with me a story about finding her preteen son watching news coverage of a violent event. Instinctively, she reached for the remote and changed the channel. "You don't need to be watching that stuff," she told him rather abruptly. An argument followed, and eventually she shared that he needed to fill his mind with "whatever is right, whatever is pure, whatever is lovely . . ." (PHILIPPIANS 4:8). After dinner, she and her husband were watching the news when suddenly their five-year-old daughter burst in and turned off the television. "You don't need to be watching that stuff," she declared in her best "mom" voice. "Now, think about those Bible things!"

> TODAY'S READING
> **Philippians 4:4–9**
>
> **Whatever is true, whatever is noble, whatever is right, whatever is pure, whatever is lovely, whatever is admirable . . . think about such things.** Philippians 4:8

As adults, we can better absorb and process the news than our children. Still, the couple's daughter was both amusing and wise when she echoed her mother's earlier instructions. Even well-adjusted adults can be affected by a steady diet of the darker side of life. Meditating on the kind of things Paul lists in Philippians 4:8 is a powerful antidote to the gloom that sometimes settles on us as we see the condition of our world.

Making careful decisions about what fills our minds is an excellent way to honor God and guard our hearts as well. 🍂

RANDY KILGORE

Father, open our eyes today to what's beautiful.
Teach us to meditate on You.

What we let into our minds shapes the state of our souls.

Nobody Likes Me

As a child, when I felt lonely, rejected, or sorry for myself, my mother would sometimes attempt to cheer me up by singing a popular ditty: "Nobody likes me, everybody hates me. I think I'll go eat worms." After a smile came from my downcast face, she'd help me see the many special relationships and reasons for gratitude I truly did have.

When I read that David felt no one cared for him, that ditty rings in my ears. Yet David's pain wasn't at all exaggerated. Where I had feelings of loneliness typical for my age, David actually had good reason to feel abandoned. He wrote these words in the dark depths of a cave

TODAY'S READING
Psalm 142

No one is concerned for me. I have no refuge; no one cares for my life. Psalm 142:4

where he hid from Saul, who pursued him with murderous plans (1 Samuel 22:1; 24:3–10). David had been anointed as Israel's future king (16:13), had spent years in Saul's service, but now he lived "on the move," always fearing for his life. In the midst of the loneliness David felt, he cried out to God as his "refuge" and "portion in the land of the living" (PSALM 142:5).

Like David, we can cry out to God when we feel alone, giving voice to our feelings in the safety of His love. God never minimizes our loneliness. He wants to be our companion in the dark caves of our lives. Even when we think no one cares for our life, God cares! ❀

KIRSTEN HOLMBERG

Lord, You are my friend when I feel alone. Thank You for being with me in the dark caves of life.

God is our friend in seasons of loneliness.

God with Skin On

My husband left for a month-long trip, and almost immediately I was overwhelmed by the needs of my job, our house, and our children. A writing deadline loomed. The lawn mower broke. My children were on school break and bored. How would I take care of all of these things on my own?

I soon realized I wasn't on my own. Friends from church showed up to help. Josh came over to fix my lawn mower. John brought me lunch. Cassidy helped with the laundry. Abi invited my kids over to play with hers so I could get my work done. God worked through each of these friends to provide for me. They

> **TODAY'S READING**
> **Romans 12:9–18**
>
> **Share with the Lord's people who are in need. Practice hospitality.**
> Romans 12:13

were a living picture of the kind of community Paul describes in Romans 12. They loved sincerely (V. 9), considered the needs of others rather than just their own (V. 10), shared with me when I was in need, and showed hospitality (V. 13).

Because of the love my friends showed to me, I remained "joyful in hope" and "patient in affliction" (V. 12), even the mild affliction of solo parenting for a month. My brothers and sisters in Christ became what one friend calls "God with skin on" for me. They showed me the kind of sincere love we ought to show to everyone, especially those in our community of faith (GALATIANS 6:10). I hope to be more like them. 🌱 *AMY PETERSON*

God, thank You for placing us in communities. Help me to look out for others' needs and to show hospitality.

To whom do I need to be "God with skin on" today?

Our Daily Bread

The Last Call

After serving his country for two decades as a helicopter pilot, James returned home to serve his community as a teacher. But he missed helicopters, so he took a job flying medical evacuations for a local hospital. He flew until late in his life.

Now it was time to say goodbye to him. As friends, family, and uniformed co-workers stood vigil at the cemetery, a colleague called in one last mission over the radio. Soon the distinctive sound of rotors beating the air could be heard. A

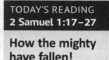

TODAY'S READING
2 Samuel 1:17–27

How the mighty have fallen!
2 Samuel 1:27

helicopter circled over the memorial garden, hovered briefly to pay its respects, then headed back to the hospital. Not even the military personnel who were present could hold back the tears.

When King Saul and his son Jonathan were killed in battle, David wrote an elegy for the ages called "the lament of the bow" (2 SAMUEL 1:18). "A gazelle lies slain on your heights," he sang. "How the mighty have fallen!" (V. 19). Jonathan was David's closest friend and brother-in-arms. And although David and Saul had been enemies, David honored them both. "Weep for Saul," he wrote. "I grieve for you, Jonathan my brother" (VV. 24, 26).

Even the best goodbyes are oh-so-difficult. But for those who trust in the Lord, the memory is much more sweet than bitter, for it is never forever. How good it is when we can honor those who have served others! 🌿   *TIM GUSTAFSON*

Lord, we thank You for those who serve their communities as
First Responders. We humbly ask You for their safety.

We honor the Creator when we honor the memory of His creatures.

Gazing at the Horizon

Almost as soon as the ferryboat started to move, my little daughter said she felt ill. Seasickness had already begun to affect her. Soon I was feeling queasy myself. "Just stare at the horizon," I reminded myself. Sailors say this helps to regain a sense of perspective.

The Maker of the horizon (JOB 26:10) knows that sometimes in life we may become fearful and restless. We can regain perspective by focusing on the distant but steady point of our destiny.

TODAY'S READING
Hebrews 11:8–16

We are looking for the city that is to come. Hebrews 13:14

The writer of Hebrews understood this. He sensed discouragement in his readers. Persecution had driven many of them from their homes. So he reminded them that other people of faith had endured extreme trials and had been left homeless. They endured it all because they anticipated something better.

As exiles, these readers could look forward to the city whose architect is God, the heavenly country, the city God prepared for them (HEBREWS 11:10, 14, 16). So in his final exhortations, the writer asked his readers to focus on God's promises. "For here we do not have an enduring city, but we are looking for the city that is to come" (13:14).

Our present troubles are temporary. We are "foreigners and strangers on earth" (11:13), but gazing at the horizon of God's promises provides the point of reference we need. ❧ *KEILA OCHOA*

Father, in the midst of troubles,
help me to focus on Your promises.

Focus on God and regain perspective.

Our Daily Bread

When Words Fail

Not long ago I sent my wife, Cari, a text message using only voice prompts. I was on my way out the door to give her a ride home from work and intended to send the words, "Where would you like me to pick you up, old gal?"

Cari doesn't mind my calling her "old gal"—it's one of the affectionate nicknames we use around the house. But my cell phone didn't "understand" the phrase, and sent the words "old cow" instead.

Fortunately for me, Cari immediately understood what had happened and found it funny. She later posted my text message on social media and asked, "Should I be offended?" We were both able to laugh about it.

> TODAY'S READING
> **Romans 8:22–27**
>
> **May your unfailing love be with us, LORD, even as we put our hope in you.** Psalm 33:22

My wife's loving response to my awkward words that day makes me think about God's loving understanding of our prayers. We may not know what to say when we pray or even what to ask for, but when we belong to Christ, His Spirit within "intercedes for us through wordless groans" (ROMANS 8:26) and lovingly helps us articulate our deepest needs before Him.

Our heavenly Father doesn't stand at a distance waiting for us to get our words right. We can come to Him with every need, assured that He understands and receives us with love.

JAMES BANKS

Abba, Father, thank You that I can come to You
without fear of having to get my words just right.
Help me to keep company with You today.

God's love is beyond words.

Interrupted Fellowship

The loud, sorrowful cry pierced the dark afternoon air. I imagine it drowning out the sound of mourning from friends and loved ones gathered at Jesus's feet. It must have overwhelmed the moans of the dying criminals who flanked Jesus on both sides. And surely startled all who heard it.

TODAY'S READING
Matthew 27:32–50

My God, my God, why have you forsaken me?

Matthew 27:46

"*Eli, Eli, lema sabachthani!*" Jesus cried out in agony and in utter despondency as He hung on that cross of shame on Golgotha (MATTHEW 27:45–46).

"My God," He said, "my God, why have you forsaken me?"

I cannot think of more heart-wrenching words. Since eternity, Jesus had been in perfect fellowship with God the Father. Together they had created the universe, had fashioned mankind in their image, and planned salvation. Never in the eons past had they not been in total fellowship with each other.

And now, as the anguish of the cross continued to bring devastating pain on Jesus—He for the first time lost the awareness of God's presence as He carried the burden of the sins of the world.

It was the only way. Only through this time of interrupted fellowship could our salvation be provided for. And it was only because Jesus was willing to experience this sense of being forsaken on the cross that we humans can gain fellowship with God.

Thank You, Jesus, for experiencing such pain so we could be forgiven. 🕊 *DAVE BRANON*

Jesus, we again stand in awe at Your sacrifice. We kneel in Your presence and with gratitude acknowledge what You did for us on the cross. Thank You for making it possible to have fellowship with the Father forever.

The cross reveals God's heart for the lost.

Stop

My friend and I sat in the sand, near the ever-rhythmic ocean. As the sun sank in the distance, wave after wave curled, paused and then rippled toward our extended toes, stopping just short each time. "I love the ocean," she smiled. "It moves so I don't have to."

What a thought! So many of us struggle to *stop*. We do, do, do and go, go, go, somehow afraid that if we cease our efforts we will cease to be. Or that by stopping we will expose ourselves to the ever-present realities we work to keep at bay.

TODAY'S READING
Psalm 46

Be still, and know that I am God.

Psalm 46:10

In Psalm 46:8–9, God flexes His omnipotent muscles, putting His power on display. "Come and see what the LORD has done . . . . He makes wars cease to the ends of the earth. He breaks the bow and shatters the spear; he burns the shields with fire." God is a busy God, who works to create calm within the chaos of our days.

And then in verse 10 we read, "Be still, and know that I am God."

Of course it's possible to know God while running here and there. But the psalmist's invitation to cease striving beckons us into a different kind of knowing. A knowing that we can stop—and still be—because God never stops. A knowing that it is God's power that gives us ultimate value, protection, and peace. 🌿

ELISA MORGAN

Dear God, help me to find my rest in You.

We rest well when we're in the loving arms and perfect will of God.

The "Chewing" Years

My wife recently gave me a Labrador retriever puppy we named Max. One day when Max was spending time with me in my study, I was concentrating at my desk and heard the sound of paper ripping behind me. I turned to find a guilty-looking puppy with a book wide open and a page dangling from his mouth.

Our veterinarian tells us that Max is going through his "chewing years." As puppies lose their milk teeth and permanent ones grow, they soothe their gums by chewing almost anything. We have to watch Max carefully to ensure he isn't gnawing on something that could harm him, and we point him to healthy alternatives.

TODAY'S READING
1 Peter 2:1–11

Blessed are those who hunger and thirst for righteousness, for they will be filled.
Matthew 5:6

Max's urge to chew—and my responsibility to watch him—cause me to think about what we "chew on" in our minds and hearts. Do we carefully consider what we are feeding our eternal souls when we read or surf the web or watch TV? The Bible encourages us, "Like newborn babies, crave pure spiritual milk, so that by it you may grow up in your salvation, now that you have tasted that the Lord is good" (1 PETER 2:2–3). We need to fill ourselves daily with God's Word and truth if we are to thrive as followers of Christ. Only then can we grow to maturity in Him.

JAMES BANKS

Loving Lord, help me to hunger for You and Your Word and to stay away from that which harms me. Fill me with Your goodness today.

When Christ returns, what will He find us craving?

Clocks and Calendars

My father died at 58 years of age. Ever since then, I pause on the date he died to remember Dad and reflect on his influence in my life. When I realized I had lived more of life *without* my dad than *with* him, I began pondering the brevity of my own life.

On reflection, we may wrestle with both an event in time and the feelings it stirs within us. Though we *measure* time with clocks and calendars, we *remember* times because of events. In the moments of life that trigger our deepest emotions, we can experience joy, loss, blessing, pain, success, failure.

TODAY'S READING
Psalm 62

Trust in him at all times, you people; pour out your hearts to him, for God is our refuge.

Psalm 62:8

The Scriptures encourage us: "Trust in him at all times, you people; pour out your hearts to him, for God is our refuge" (PSALM 62:8). This confident statement did not occur in a time of ease. David wrote these words while surrounded by enemies (VV. 3–4). Still, he waited quietly before God (vv. 1, 5) reminding us that God's unfailing love (V. 12) is greater than any of the times of struggle we may face.

In every event, we have this confidence: Our God stands with us, and He is more than adequate to carry us through all of life's moments. When the times of life threaten to overwhelm us, His help will be right on time. 🌑 *BILL CROWDER*

We're grateful that You are always and will always be faithful to us, Father.

Our God is ready to be with us in all the times of life.

Open My Eyes

The first time I went to the gorgeous Chora Church in Istanbul, I was able to figure out some Bible stories from the Byzantine frescos and mosaics on the ceiling. But there was much I missed. The second time, however, I had a guide. He pointed to all the details I had previously missed, and suddenly everything made perfect sense! The first aisle, for instance, depicted the life of Jesus as recorded in the gospel of Luke.

Sometimes when we read the Bible we understand the basic stories, but what about the connections—those details that weave Scripture into the one perfect story? We have Bible commentaries and study tools, yes, but we also need a guide—someone to open our eyes and help us see the wonders of God's written revelation. Our guide is the Holy Spirit who teaches us "all things" (JOHN 14:26). Paul wrote that He explains "spiritual realities with Spirit-taught words" (1 CORINTHIANS 2:13).

> **TODAY'S READING**
> **John 14:23-31**
>
> **The Holy Spirit, whom the Father will send in my name, will teach you all things.**
> John 14:26

How wonderful to have the Author of the Book to show us the wonders of it! God has not only given us His written Word and His revelation but He also helps us to understand it and learn from it. So let us pray with the psalmist, saying, "Open my eyes that I may see wonderful things in your law" (PSALM 119:18).

KEILA OCHOA

Dear Lord, as I read Your Word, open my eyes that I may discover the wonders of Your revelation.

We need God in order to understand Scripture.

A Blind Man's Plea

Some years ago a traveling companion noticed I was straining to see objects at a distance. What he did next was simple but life changing. He took off his glasses and said, "Try these." When I put his glasses on, surprisingly my blurred vision cleared up. Eventually I went to an optometrist who prescribed glasses to correct my vision problem.

Today's reading in Luke 18 features a man with no vision at all, and living in total darkness had forced him to beg for a living. News about Jesus, the popular teacher and miracle worker, had reached the blind beggar's ears. So when Jesus's travel route took Him by where the blind

TODAY'S READING
Luke 18:35–43

Jesus, Son of David, have mercy on me! Luke 18:38

man was sitting, hope was ignited in his heart. "Jesus, Son of David, have mercy on me!" (v. 38) he called. Though without sight physically, the man possessed spiritual insight into Jesus's true identity and faith in Him to meet his need. Compelled by this faith, "He shouted all the more, 'Son of David, have mercy on me!'" (v. 39). The result? His blindness was banished, and he went from begging for his living to blessing God because he could see (v. 43).

In moments or seasons of darkness, where do you turn? Upon what or to whom do you call? Eyeglass prescriptions help improve vision, but it's the merciful touch of Jesus, God's Son, that brings people from spiritual darkness to light. ❧

ARTHUR JACKSON

Father, open the eyes of my heart to clearly see
who Jesus is and what He can do.

The Father's delight is to give sight to those who ask Him.

Side by Side

I n ancient times, a city with broken walls revealed a defeated people, exposed to danger and shame. That is why the Jews rebuilt the walls of Jerusalem. How? By working side by side, an expression that can well describe Nehemiah 3.

At first glance, chapter 3 might appear to be a boring account of who did what in the recon-struction. However, a closer look high-lights how people worked together. Priests were working alongside rulers. Perfume-makers were helping as well as goldsmiths. There were some who lived in nearby towns and came to give a hand. Others made repairs opposite their houses. Shallum's daughters, for example, worked alongside the men (3:12), and some people repaired two sections, like the men of Tekoa (vv. 5, 27).

> TODAY'S READING
> **Nehemiah 3:1–12**
>
> **Two are better than one, because they have a good return for their labor.** Ecclesiastes 4:9

Two things stand out from this chapter. First, they all worked together for a common goal. Second, all of them are commended for being part of the work, not for how much or little they did as compared to others.

Today we see damaged families and a broken society. But Jesus came to build the kingdom of God through the transfor-mation of lives. We can help to rebuild our neighborhoods by showing others they can find hope and new life in Jesus. All of us have something to do. So let us work side by side and do our part—whether big or small—to create a community of love where people can find Jesus.

KEILA OCHOA

Dear Lord, help me to work with others, side by side, by showing love and pointing others to Jesus.

Let's work together to build the kingdom of God.

And in Truth

Years ago, I attended a wedding where two people from different countries got married. Such a blending of cultures can be beautiful, but this ceremony included Christian traditions mixed with rituals from a faith that worshiped many gods.

Zephaniah the prophet pointedly condemned the mixing of other religions with faith in the one true God (sometimes called syncretism). Judah had become a people who bowed in worship to the true God but who *also* relied on the god Molek (ZEPHANIAH 1:5). Zephaniah described their adoption of pagan culture (V. 8) and warned

TODAY'S READING
Zephaniah 1:1–6; 2:1–3

In his love he will no longer rebuke you, but will rejoice over you with singing. Zephaniah 3:17

that as a result God would drive the people of Judah from their homeland.

Yet God never stopped loving His people. His judgment was to show them their need to turn to Him. So Zephaniah encouraged Judah to "Seek righteousness, seek humility" (2:3). Then the Lord gave them tender words promising future restoration: "At that time I will gather you; at that time I will bring you home" (3:20).

It's easy to condemn examples of obvious syncretism like the wedding I attended. But in reality, *all* of us easily blend God's truth with the assumptions of our culture. We need the Holy Spirit's guidance to test our beliefs against the truth of God's Word and then to stand for that truth confidently and lovingly. Our Father warmly embraces anyone who worships Him in the Spirit and in truth (SEE JOHN 4:23–24). 🌱   *TIM GUSTAFSON*

When I am in trouble, where do I turn? A crisis reveals where I put my trust. Is my faith completely in God? What do I need to give over to Him today?

God is always ready to forgive and restore.

Faces

When our granddaughter Sarah was very young, she explained to me what happens when you die: "Only your face goes to heaven, not your body. You get a new body, but keep the same face."

Sarah's concept of our eternal state was a child's understanding, of course, but she did grasp an essential truth. In a sense, our faces are a visible reflection of the invisible soul.

My mother used to say that an angry look might someday freeze on my face. She was wiser than she knew. A worried brow, an angry set to our mouths, a sly look in our eyes may reveal a miserable soul. On the other hand, kind eyes, a gentle look, a warm and welcoming smile—despite wrinkles, blemishes, and other disfigurements—become the marks of inner transformation.

> **TODAY'S READING**
> **Galatians 5:22–26**
>
> **We all, who with unveiled faces contemplate the Lord's glory, are being transformed into his image with ever-increasing glory.** 2 Corinthians 3:18

We can't do much about the faces we were born with, but we can do something about the kind of person we're growing into. We can pray for humility, patience, kindness, tolerance, gratefulness, forgiveness, peace, and love (GALATIANS 5:22-26).

By God's grace, and in His time, may you and I grow toward an inner resemblance to our Lord, a likeness reflected in a kind, old face. Thus, as English poet John Donne (1572–1631) said, age becomes "loveliest at the latest day."   *DAVID H. ROPER*

Lord Jesus, I want to be more like You each day. Help me to cooperate
with the work You want to do in my heart.

There's nothing like the beauty of a loving heart.

The Perfect Father

Standing in the crowded store aisle, I struggled to find the perfect Father's Day card. Although we had reconciled after years of a strained connection, I had never felt close to my dad.

The woman next to me groaned and shoved the card she'd been reading back into the display. "Why can't they make cards for people who don't have good relationships with their fathers, but are trying to do the right thing?"

She stormed off before I could respond, so I prayed for her. Thanking God for affirming only He could be a perfect Father, I asked Him to strengthen my relationship with my dad.

I long for deeper intimacy with my heavenly Father too. I want David's confidence in God's constant presence, power, and protection (PSALM 27:1–6).

> TODAY'S READING
> **Psalm 27**
>
> **Though my father and mother forsake me, the LORD will receive me.** Psalm 27:10

When David cried out for help, he expected God's answers (VV. 7–9). Though earthly parents could reject, abandon, or neglect their children, David declared God's unconditional acceptance (V. 10). He lived with assurance in the Lord's goodness (VV. 11–13). Like most of us, David sometimes struggled, but the Holy Spirit helped him persevere in trust and dependence on the Lord (V. 14).

We will encounter difficult relationships on this side of eternity. But even when people fall short, fail us, or hurt us, we're still completely loved and protected by the only Perfect Father.

XOCHITL DIXON

Lord, thank You for being a Father we can always count on.

God—the Perfect Father—will never let us down, leave us, or stop loving us.

A Warm Welcome

"**W**ho will hug everybody?"

That was one of the questions our friend Steve asked after he got the news that he had cancer and realized he would be away from our church for a while. Steve is the kind of man who makes everyone feel welcome—with a friendly greeting, a warm handshake, and even a "holy hug" for some—to adapt an application from Romans 16:16, which says, "Greet one another with a holy kiss."

TODAY'S READING
1 Peter 4:7–11

Offer hospitality to one another without grumbling.

1 Peter 4:9

And now, as we pray for Steve that God will heal him, he is concerned that as he goes through surgery and treatment—and is away from our church for a time—we will miss out on those welcoming greetings.

Perhaps not all of us are cut out to greet one another as openly as Steve does, but his example of caring for people is a good reminder to us. Notice that Peter says to "offer hospitality to one another without grumbling," or in a way that centers on love (1 PETER 4:9; SEE PHILIPPIANS 2:14). While first-century hospitality included offering accommodations to travelers—even that always starts with a welcoming greeting.

As we interact with others in love, whether with a hug or just a friendly smile, we do so "that in all things God may be praised through Jesus Christ" (1 PETER 4:11). 🌱   *DAVE BRANON*

Lord, help us to represent You to others. Guide us to show hospitality in a way that will show others Your love.

When we practice hospitality, we share God's goodness.

Advice from My Father

After being laid off from an editorial job, I prayed, asking for God to help me find a new one. But when weeks went by and nothing came of my attempts at networking and filling out applications, I began to pout. "Don't You know how important it is that I have a job?" I asked God, my arms folded in protest at my seemingly unanswered prayer.

When I talked to my father, who had often reminded me about believing God's promises, about my job situation, he said, "I want you to get to the point where you trust what God says."

My father's advice reminds me of Proverbs 3, which includes wise advice from a parent to a beloved child. This familiar passage was especially applicable to my situation: "Trust in the LORD with all your heart and lean not on your own understanding; in all your ways submit to him, and he will make your paths straight" (PROVERBS 3:5–6). To "make . . . paths straight" means God will guide us toward His goals for our growth. His ultimate goal is that I become more like Him.

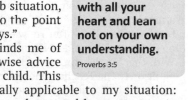

TODAY'S READING
Proverbs 3:1–7

Trust in the LORD with all your heart and lean not on your own understanding.

Proverbs 3:5

This does not mean that the paths He chooses will be easy. But I can choose to trust that His direction and timing are ultimately for my good.

Are you waiting on God for an answer? Choose to draw near to Him and trust that He will guide you. 🌿

LINDA WASHINGTON

Lord, thank You for guiding and caring for us every step of the way.
Help us to trust in You daily.

Your Father in heaven knows what's best for you.

Called by Name

Advertisers have concluded that the most attention-grabbing word that viewers react to is their own name. Thus a television channel in the UK has introduced personalized advertisements with their online streaming services.

We might enjoy hearing our name on television, but it doesn't mean much without the intimacy that comes when someone who loves us says our name.

Mary Magdalene's attention was arrested when, at the tomb where Jesus's body had been laid after He was crucified on the cross, He spoke her name (JOHN 20:16). With that single word, she turned in recognition to the Teacher whom she loved and followed, I imagine with a rush of disbelief and joy. The familiarity with which He spoke her name confirmed for her beyond a doubt that the One who'd known her perfectly was alive and not dead.

> **TODAY'S READING**
> John 20:11–18
>
> **Jesus said to her, "Mary." She turned toward him and cried out in Aramaic, "Rabboni!"** John 20:16

Although Mary shared a unique and special moment with Jesus, we too are personally loved by God. Jesus told Mary that He would ascend to His Father (V. 17), but He had also told His disciples that He would not leave them alone (JOHN 14:15–18). God would send the Holy Spirit to live and dwell in His children (SEE ACTS 2:1–13).

God's story doesn't change. Whether then or now, He knows those whom He loves (SEE JOHN 10:14–15). He calls us by name. 🌿

AMY BOUCHER PYE

Loving Father, living Jesus, comforting Holy Spirit, thank You that You know me completely, and that You love me unceasingly.

The God who created the cosmos also made you, and He calls you by name.

Humble Love

When Benjamin Franklin was a young man he made a list of twelve virtues he desired to grow in over the course of his life. He showed it to a friend, who suggested he add "humility" to it. Franklin liked the idea. He then added some guidelines to help him with each item on the list. Among Franklin's thoughts about humility, he held up Jesus as an example to emulate.

TODAY'S READING
Philippians 2:1–11

The greatest among you will be your servant.
Matthew 23:11

Jesus shows us the ultimate example of humility. God's Word tells us, "In your relationships with one another, have the same mindset as Christ Jesus: Who, being in very nature God, did not consider equality with God something to be used to his own advantage; rather, he made himself nothing by taking the very nature of a servant" (PHILIPPIANS 2:5–7).

Jesus demonstrated the greatest humility of all. Though eternally with the Father, He chose to bend beneath a cross in love so that through His death He might lift any who receive Him into the joy of His presence.

We imitate Jesus's humility when we seek to serve our heavenly Father by serving others. Jesus's kindness helps us catch a breathtaking glimpse of the beauty of setting ourselves aside to attend to others' needs. Aiming for humility isn't easy in our "me first" world. But as we rest securely in our Savior's love, He will give us everything we need to follow Him. ❧   *JAMES BANKS*

Beautiful Savior, I am Your servant. Please help me to live in Your love and be a blessing to someone today.

We can serve because we are loved.

Quieting the Critic

work with a team to put on an annual community event. We spend eleven months plotting many details to ensure the event's success. We choose the date and venue. We set ticket prices. We select everything from food vendors to sound technicians. As the event approaches, we answer public questions and provide directions. Afterward we collect feedback. Some good. Some that is hard to hear. Our team hears excitement from attendees and also fields complaints. The negative feedback can be discouraging and sometimes tempts us to give up.

TODAY'S READING
Nehemiah 4:1–6

Hear us, our God, for we are despised. Turn their insults back on their own heads. Nehemiah 4:4

Nehemiah had critics too as he led a team to rebuild the wall of Jerusalem. They actually mocked Nehemiah and those working alongside him saying, "Even a fox climbing up on it would break down [your] wall of stones" (NEHEMIAH 4:3). His response to the critics helps me handle my own: Instead of feeling dejected or trying to refute their comments, he turned to God for help. Instead of responding directly, he asked God to hear the way His people were being treated and to defend them (V. 4). After entrusting those concerns to God, he and his co-laborers continued to work steadily on the wall "with all their heart" (V. 6).

We can learn from Nehemiah not to be distracted by criticism of our work. When we're criticized or mocked, instead of responding to our critics out of hurt or anger, we can prayerfully ask God to defend us from discouragement so we can continue with a whole heart. 🌱 KIRSTEN HOLMBERG

Help me to evaluate the good and bad in the criticism, to trust You, and to continue in my work wholeheartedly.

God is our best defense against criticism.

"Lovable!"

Lovable!"

That exclamation came from my daughter as she got ready one morning. I didn't know what she meant. Then she tapped her shirt, a hand-me-down from a cousin. Across the front was that word: "Lovable." I gave her a big hug, and she smiled with pure joy. "You are lovable!" I echoed. Her smile grew even bigger, if that was possible, as she skipped away, repeating the word over and over again.

TODAY'S READING
Jeremiah 31:1–6

**I have loved you
with an everlasting
love; I have drawn
you with unfailing
kindness.** Jeremiah 31:3

I'm hardly a perfect father. But that moment was perfect. In that spontaneous, beautiful interaction, I glimpsed in my girl's radiant face what receiving unconditional love looked like: It was a portrait of delight. She knew the word on her shirt corresponded completely with how her daddy felt about her.

How many of us know in our hearts that we are loved by a Father whose affection for us is limitless? Sometimes we struggle with this truth. The Israelites did. They wondered if their trials meant God no longer loved them. But in Jeremiah 31:3, the prophet reminds them of what God said in the past: "I have loved you with an everlasting love." We too long for such unconditional love. Yet the wounds, disappointments, and mistakes we experience can make us feel anything but lovable. But God opens His arms—the arms of a perfect Father—and invites us to experience and rest in His love. 🌱   *ADAM HOLZ*

Lord, hard things in our lives can tempt us to believe we are unlovable.
But You say otherwise. Please help us to receive the life-transforming gift
of Your everlasting love for us.

No one loves us like our Father.

As Advertised

During a vacation, my husband and I signed up for a leisurely rafting tour down Georgia's Chattahoochee River. Dressed in sandals, a sundress, and a wide brimmed hat, I groaned when we discovered—contrary to the advertisement—that the trip included light rapids. Thankfully, we rode with a couple experienced in whitewater rafting. They taught my husband the basics of paddling and promised to navigate us safely to our destination. Grateful for my life jacket, I screamed and gripped the plastic handle on the raft until we reached the muddy bank downriver. I stepped onto the shore and dumped water from my purse as my husband helped me wring out the hem of my soaked dress. We enjoyed a good laugh, even though the trip had not turned out as advertised.

TODAY'S READING
John 16:25–33

In this world you will have trouble. But take heart! I have overcome the world. John 16:33

Unlike the tour brochure, which clearly left out a key detail about the trip, Jesus explicitly warned His disciples that rough waters were ahead. He told them that they'd be persecuted and martyred and that He would die and be resurrected. He also guaranteed His trustworthiness, affirming that He would guide them toward undeniable triumph and everlasting hope (JOHN 16:16–33).

Although it would be nice if life were easier when we follow Jesus, He made it clear that His disciples would have troubles. But He promised to be with us. Trials won't define, limit, or destroy God's plan for us, because Jesus's resurrection has already propelled us to eternal victory. 🌿   *XOCHITL DIXON*

Lord, thank You for the promises in Your Word that assure us You've planned our path and remain with us and for us, no matter what comes.

Jesus promises to be with us through the roughest waters.

Our Safe Place

My very first job was at a fast-food restaurant. One Saturday evening, a guy kept hanging around, asking when I got out of work. It made me feel uneasy. As the hour grew later, he ordered fries, then a drink, so the manager wouldn't kick him out. Though I didn't live far, I was scared to walk home alone through a couple of dark parking lots and a stretch through a sandy field. Finally, at midnight, I went in the office to make a phone call.

> **TODAY'S READING**
> **Psalm 91**
>
> **I will say of the LORD, "He is my refuge and my fortress, my God, in whom I trust."**
>
> Psalm 91:2

And the person who answered—my dad—without a second thought got out of a warm bed and five minutes later was there to take me home.

The kind of certainty I had that my dad would come to help me that night reminds me of the assurance we read about in Psalm 91. Our Father in heaven is always with us, protecting and caring for us when we are confused or afraid or in need. He declares: "When they call on me, I will answer" (PSALM 91:15 NLT). He is not just a *place* we can run to for safety. He *is* our shelter (V. 1). He is the Rock we can cling to for refuge (V. 2).

In times of fear, danger, or uncertainty, we can trust God's promise that when we call on Him, He will hear and be with us in our trouble (VV. 14–15). God is our safe place. 🌱   *CINDY HESS KASPER*

Dear Father, thank You for being my Rock and my safe place.

The living God will always be our shelter.

Blessing in the Mess

I got myself into this mess, so I'd better get myself out, I sometimes find myself thinking. Although I believe in a God of grace, I'm still prone to act as if His help is available only when I deserve it.

God's first encounter with Jacob is a beautiful illustration of how untrue this is.

Jacob had spent a lifetime trying to alter his destiny. He'd been born second at a time when firstborn sons typically received their father's blessing—believed to guarantee future prosperity.

> TODAY'S READING
> **Genesis 28:10–22**
>
> **He who began a good work in you will carry it on to completion until the day of Christ Jesus.** Philippians 1:6

So Jacob decided to do whatever it would take to get his father's blessing anyway. Eventually, he succeeded—through deceit—obtaining the blessing intended for his brother (GENESIS 27:19–29).

But the price was a divided family, as Jacob fled from his furious brother (VV. 41–43). As night descended (28:11), Jacob must have felt as far from a life of blessing as ever.

But it was there, leaving behind a trail of deception, that Jacob met God. God showed him he didn't need desperate schemes to be blessed; he *already was.* His destiny—a purpose far greater than material prosperity (V. 14)—was held securely by the One who would never leave him (V. 15).

It was a lesson Jacob would spend his whole life learning.

And so will we. No matter how many regrets we carry or how distant God seems, He is still there—gently guiding us out of our mess into *His* blessing. 🕊 MONICA BRANDS

Lord, so often we feel trapped by our mistakes, thinking there's no future left for us. Remind us that you are the God of Jacob, the God who will never give up on Your purposes for us.

God never gives up on His love and purposes for our lives.

Impaired Judgment

've been quick to judge anyone I saw walking in the street while staring at a phone. *How could they be so oblivious to the cars about to hit them?* I've told myself. *Don't they care about their own safety?* But one day, while crossing the entrance to an alleyway, I was so engrossed in a text message, that I missed seeing a car at my left. Thankfully, the driver saw me and came to an abrupt stop. But I felt ashamed. All of my self-righteous finger-pointing came back to haunt me. I had judged others, only to do the same thing myself.

TODAY'S READING
Matthew 7:1–6

Do not judge, or you too will be judged. Matthew 7:1

My hypocrisy is the kind of thinking that Jesus addressed in the Sermon on the Mount: "First take the plank out of your own eye, and then you will see clearly to remove the speck from your brother's eye" (MATTHEW 7:5). I had a huge "plank"—a blind spot through which I judged others with my own impaired judgment.

"For in the same way you judge others, you will be judged," Jesus also said (7:2). Recalling the disgusted look on the driver's face that day, after having to make an abrupt stop when I walked in front of the car, I'm reminded of the disgusted looks I gave others engrossed in their phones.

None of us is perfect. But sometimes I forget that in my haste to judge others. We're all in need of God's grace. 🕊

LINDA WASHINGTON

Heavenly Father, please help me be quicker to console or encourage, and slower to judge someone else.

Be slow to judge others.

Every Moment Matters

When I met Ada, she had outlived her entire group of friends and family and was living in a nursing home. "It's the hardest part of getting old," she told me, "watching everyone else move on and leave you behind." One day I asked Ada what kept her interest and how she spent her time. She answered me with a Scripture passage from the apostle Paul (PHILIPPIANS 1:21): "For to me, to live is Christ and to die is gain." Then she said, "While I'm still around, I have work to do. On my good days, I get to talk to the people here about Jesus; on the hard days, I can still pray."

Significantly, Paul wrote Philippians while in prison. And he acknowledged a reality many Christians understand as they face their mortality: Even though heaven seems so inviting, the time we have left on Earth matters to God.

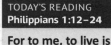

TODAY'S READING
Philippians 1:12–24

For to me, to live is Christ and to die is gain. Philippians 1:21

Like Paul, Ada recognized that every breath she took was an opportunity to serve and glorify God. So Ada spent her days loving others and introducing them to her Savior.

Even in our darkest moments, Christians can hold on to the promise of permanent joy in the company of God. And while we live, we enjoy relationship with Him. He fills all our moments with significance. 🌱

RANDY KILGORE

Lord, grant me the strength to serve You with every breath I take, so that every moment of my remaining days matters to Your Kingdom.

When God comes to call us home, may He find us serving Him.

Telling Time

"**W**esterners have watches. Africans have time." So said Os Guinness, quoting an African proverb in his book *Impossible People*. That caused me to ponder the times I have responded to a request with, "I don't have time." I thought about the tyranny of the urgent and how schedules and deadlines dominate my life.

Moses prayed in Psalm 90, "Teach us to number our days, that we may gain a heart of wisdom" (V. 12). And Paul wrote, "Be very careful, then, how you live . . . making the most of every opportunity, because the days are evil" (EPHESIANS 5:15-16).

TODAY'S READING
Psalm 90:9-17

[Make] the most of every opportunity, because the days are evil. Ephesians 5:16

I suspect that Paul and Moses would agree that our wise use of time isn't just a matter of clock-watching. The situation may call for us to keep a tight schedule—or it may compel us to give someone an extended gift of our time.

We have but a brief moment to make a difference for Christ in our world, and we need to maximize that opportunity. That may mean ignoring our watches and planners for a while as we show Christ's patient love to those He brings into our lives.

As we live in the strength and grace of the timeless Christ, we impact our time for eternity. 🍃

BILL CROWDER

Father, You have given us all the time we need to accomplish what You have given us to do. May we use our time in ways that honor You.

Time management is not about clock-watching, it's about making the most of the time we have.

Fellowship with Jesus

'll **never forget** the time I had the privilege of sitting next to Billy Graham at a dinner. I was honored but also somewhat nervous about what would be appropriate to say. I thought it would be an interesting conversation starter to ask what he loved most about his years of ministry. Then I awkwardly started to suggest possible answers. Was it knowing presidents, kings, and queens? Or preaching the gospel to millions of people around the world?

TODAY'S READING
Philippians 3:7–14

I consider everything a loss because of the surpassing worth of knowing Christ Jesus my Lord.

Philippians 3:8

Before I had finished offering suggestions, Rev. Graham stopped me. Without hesitation he said, "It has been my fellowship with Jesus. To sense His presence, to glean His wisdom, to have Him guide and direct me—that has been my greatest joy." I was instantly convicted and challenged. Convicted because I'm not sure that his answer would have been my answer, and challenged because I wanted it to be.

That's what Paul had in mind when he counted his greatest achievements to be of no worth compared to the "surpassing worth of knowing Christ Jesus my Lord" (PHILIPPIANS 3:8). Think of how rich life would be if Jesus and our fellowship with Him was our highest pursuit.

JOE STOWELL

Lord, forgive me for chasing after things that matter far less than my fellowship with You. Thank You that You stand ready to enrich my life with Your presence and power.

To remain faithful where God has placed you,
give Christ first place in your heart.

Our Daily Bread

Belonging

'd been out late the night before, just as I was every Saturday night. Just twenty years old, I was running from God as fast as I could. But suddenly, strangely, I felt compelled to attend the church my dad pastored. I put on my faded jeans, well-worn T-shirt, and unlaced high-tops and drove across town.

I don't recall the sermon Dad preached that day, but I can't forget how delighted he was to see me. With his arm over my shoulder, he introduced me to everyone he saw. "This is my son!" he proudly declared. His joy became a picture of God's love that has stuck with me all these decades.

> **TODAY'S READING**
> Isaiah 44:1–5
>
> **The LORD who made you and helps you says: "Do not be afraid . . . my chosen one."** Isaiah 44:2 NLT

The imagery of God as loving Father occurs throughout the Bible. In Isaiah 44, the prophet interrupts a series of warnings to proclaim God's message of family love. "Dear Israel, my chosen one," he said. "I will pour out my Spirit on your descendants, and my blessing on your children" (VV. 2–3 NLT). Isaiah noted how the response of those descendants would demonstrate family pride. "Some will proudly claim, 'I belong to the LORD,'" he wrote. "Some will write the LORD's name on their hands" (V. 5 NLT).

Wayward Israel belonged to God, just as I belonged to my adoptive father. Nothing I could do would ever make him lose his love for me. He gave me a glimpse of our heavenly Father's love for us. 🕮

TIM GUSTAFSON

Heavenly Father, we all come from families that are broken in one way or another. Thank You for loving us in that brokenness and for showing us what real love looks like.

God's love for us offers us the sense of belonging and identity we all crave.

A Friend's Comfort

I **read about a mom** who was surprised to see her daughter muddy from the waist down when she walked in the door after school. Her daughter explained that a friend had slipped and fallen into a mud puddle. While another classmate ran to get help, the little girl felt sorry for her friend sitting by herself and holding her hurt leg. So, the daughter went over and sat in the mud puddle with her friend until a teacher arrived.

When Job experienced the devastating loss of his children and became afflicted with painful sores on his entire body, his suffering was overwhelming. The Bible tells us that three of his friends wanted to comfort him. When they found Job, "they began to weep aloud, and they tore their robes and sprinkled dust on their heads. Then they sat on the ground with him for seven days and seven nights. No one said a word to him, because they saw how great his suffering was" (JOB 2:12–13).

> TODAY'S READING
> **Job 2:7–13**
>
> **No one said a word to him, because they saw how great his suffering was.**
> Job 2:13

Job's friends initially showed remarkable understanding. They sensed that Job simply needed someone to sit and mourn with him. The three men will begin to speak in the next few chapters. The irony is that when the friends do begin to speak, they end up giving Job poor advice (16:1–4).

Often the best thing we can do when comforting a hurting friend is to sit with them in their suffering.   *LISA SAMRA*

Heavenly Father, help me to be a good friend to those who are hurting.
Thank You that You promise to be near to those who are suffering and
provide encouragement through Your Holy Spirit.

A friend's presence in the midst of suffering provides great comfort.

Saying Grace

For many years, I've enjoyed the writings of British author G. K. Chesterton. His humor and insight often cause me to chuckle and then pause for more serious contemplation. For example, he wrote, "You say grace before meals. All right. But I say grace before the play and the opera, and grace before the concert and panto-mime, and grace before I open a book, and grace before sketching, painting, swimming, fencing, boxing, walking, playing, dancing; and grace before I dip the pen in the ink."

> TODAY'S READING
> **Colossians 3:12–17**
>
> **Whatever you do, whether in word or deed, do it all in the name of the Lord Jesus, giving thanks to God the Father through him.** Colossians 3:17

It's good for us to thank the Lord before every meal, but it shouldn't stop there. The apostle Paul saw every activity, every endeavor as something for which we should thank God and that we should do for His glory. "And whatever you do, whether in word or deed, do it all in the name of the Lord Jesus, giving thanks to God the Father through him" (COLOSSIANS 3:17). Recreation, occupation, and education are all avenues through which we can honor the Lord and express our gratefulness to Him.

Paul also encouraged the believers in Colossae to "let the peace of Christ rule in your hearts, since as members of one body you were called to peace. And be thankful" (V. 15).

The best place to "say grace" is anywhere and anytime we want to give thanks to the Lord and honor Him. 🍂

DAVID C. MCCASLAND

Thank You for Your gift of life eternal. May we acknowledge and honor You throughout this day.

In all we do, let's give thanks to God and honor Him.

Set Free

When I was a boy in the village, something about chickens fascinated me. Whenever I caught one, I held it down for a few moments and then gently released it. Thinking I was still holding it, the chicken remained down; even though it was free to dash away, it felt trapped.

When we put our faith in Jesus, He graciously delivers us from sin and the hold that Satan had on us. However, because it may take time to change our sinful habits and behavior, Satan can make us feel trapped. But God's Spirit has set us free; He doesn't enslave us. Paul told the Romans, "Therefore, there is now no condemnation for those who are in Christ Jesus, because through Christ Jesus the law of the Spirit who gives life has set you free from the law of sin and death" (ROMANS 8:1-2).

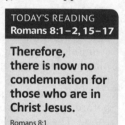

TODAY'S READING
Romans 8:1-2, 15-17

Therefore, there is now no condemnation for those who are in Christ Jesus.

Romans 8:1

Through our Bible reading, prayer, and the power of the Holy Spirit, God works in us to cleanse us and to help us live for Him. The Bible encourages us to be confident in our walk with Jesus without feeling as if we are not set free.

Jesus said, "If the Son sets you free, you will be free indeed" (JOHN 8:36). May the freedom we have in Christ spur us on to love Him and serve Him. 🍃

LAWRENCE DARMANI

Lord, forgive me for sometimes revisiting my past and forgetting that You have washed away my sins. Thank You for taking my burden and setting me free to enjoy living for You.

My chains fell off, my heart was free, I rose, went forth, and followed Thee.

CHARLES WESLEY

Unlocked

A **boy born with** cerebral palsy was unable to speak or communicate. But his mother, Chantal Bryan, never gave up, and when he was ten years old she figured out how to communicate with him through his eyes and a letter board. After this breakthrough, she said, "He was unlocked and we could ask him anything." Now Jonathan reads and writes, including poetry, by communicating through his eyes. When asked what it's like to "talk" with his family and friends, he said, "It is wonderful to tell them I love them."

TODAY'S READING
Colossians 1:13–23

Once you were alienated from God .... But now he has reconciled you. Colossians 1:21–22

Jonathan's story is profoundly moving and leads me to consider how God unlocks us from the prison of sin. As the apostle Paul wrote to the Christians at Colossae, once we were "alienated from God" (COLOSSIANS 1:21), our evil behavior making us His enemy, but through Christ's death on the cross we are now presented to God as "holy in his sight" (V. 22). We may now "live a life worthy of the Lord" as we bear fruit, grow in the knowledge of God, and are strengthened in His power (VV. 10–11).

We can use our unlocked voices to praise God and share His good news that we are no longer bound to a life of sin. As we continue in our faith, we can hold firm to our hope in Christ. 🍂

AMY BOUCHER PYE

Lord God, You have released us from our chains of unbelief
and given us words to praise You. May we share this freedom
with others for Your glory.

The Lord unlocks us from our prison of sin.

Ring in a Dumpster

n college, I woke up one morning to find Carol, my room-mate, in a panic. Her signet ring was missing. We searched everywhere. The next morning we found ourselves picking through a dumpster.

I ripped open a trash bag. "You're so dedicated to finding this!"

"I'm not losing a two-hundred-dollar ring!" she exclaimed.

Carol's determination reminds me of the parable Jesus told about the king-dom of heaven, which "is like treasure hidden in a field. When a man found it,

> TODAY'S READING
> **Matthew 13:44–46**
>
> **Seek and you will find; knock and the door will be opened to you.**
> Matthew 7:7

he hid it again, and then in his joy went and sold all he had and bought that field" (MATTHEW 13:44). Certain things are worth going great lengths to find.

Throughout the Bible, God promises that those who seek Him will find Him. In Deuteronomy, He explained to the Israelites that they would find Him when they turned from their sin and sought Him with all their hearts (4:28-29). In the book of 2 Chronicles, King Asa gained encouragement from a similar promise (15:2). And in Jeremiah, God gave the same promise to the exiles, saying He would bring them back from captivity (29:13-14).

If we seek God, through His Word, worship, and in our daily lives, we will find Him. Over time, we'll know Him on a deeper level. That will be even better than the sweet moment when Carol pulled her ring out of that trash bag! ❧

JULIE SCHWAB

Lord, help me to seek You with all my heart.

To find God, we must be willing to seek Him.

Pictures of Love

My children and I have started a new daily practice. Every night at bedtime, we gather colored pencils and light a candle. Asking God to light our way, we get out our journals and draw or write answers to two questions: *When did I show love today?* and *When did I withhold love today?*

Loving our neighbors has been an important part of the Christian life "from the beginning" (2 JOHN 1:5). That's what John writes in his second letter to his congregation, asking them to love one another in obedience to God (2 JOHN 1:5–6). Love is one of John's favorite topics throughout his letters. He says that practicing real love is one way to know that we "belong to the truth," that we're liv-

> **TODAY'S READING**
> **2 John 1:1–6**
>
> I am not writing you a new command but one we have had from the beginning. I ask that we love one another. 2 John 1:5

ing in God's presence (1 JOHN 3:18-19). When my kids and I reflect, we find that in our lives love takes shape in simple actions: sharing an umbrella, encouraging someone who is sad, or cooking a favorite meal. The moments when we're withholding love are equally practical: we gossip, refuse to share, or satisfy our own desires without thinking of others' needs.

Paying attention each night helps us be more aware each day, more tuned in to what the Spirit might be showing us as we walk through our lives. With the Spirit's help, we're learning to walk in love (2 JOHN 1:6). 🌱   *AMY PETERSON*

Lord, let us not love just in words, but in actions and in truth.
Teach us to be obedient to Your call to love.

How can I show love today?

Light of the World

One of my favorite pieces of art hangs in the Keble College chapel in Oxford, England. The painting, *The Light of the World* by English artist William Holman Hunt, shows Jesus holding a lantern in His hand and knocking on a door to a home.

One of the intriguing aspects of the painting is that the door doesn't have a handle. When questioned about the lack of a way to open the door, Hunt explained that he wanted to represent the imagery of Revelation 3:20, "Here I am! I stand at the door and knock. If anyone hears my voice and opens the door, I will come in."

> **TODAY'S READING**
> **Revelation 3:14–22**
>
> **Here I am! I stand at the door and knock. If anyone hears my voice and opens the door, I will come in.**
>
> Revelation 3:20

The apostle John's words and the painting illustrate the kindness of Jesus. He gently knocks on the door of our souls with His offer of peace. Jesus stands and patiently waits for us to respond. He does not open the door Himself and force His way into our lives. He does not impose His will on ours. Instead, He offers to all people the gift of salvation and light to guide us.

To anyone who opens the door, He promises to enter. There are no other requirements or prerequisites.

If you hear the voice of Jesus and His gentle knock on the door of your soul, be encouraged that He patiently waits for you and will enter if you welcome Him in.   LISA SAMRA

Lord, thank You for the gift of salvation and Your promise to enter
when we open the door. Please help me to respond to this gift
and open the door for You today.

Open the door to Jesus; He is patiently waiting for you.

Intended for the Good Life

Feature Article

Several years ago, my wife and I, along with my sister and brother-in-law, began a rim-to-rim hike of the Grand Canyon in Arizona. This was my second hike across the canyon, a spectacularly beautiful and rugged landscape that is 277 miles (446 km) long and a mile (1.6 km) deep. The rim-to-rim hike across the canyon is 21 miles (34 km).

Early on our trek I realized we had made several serious miscalculations. We were doing the hike too late in the summer, the hottest time of year. We began our hike too late in the morning. And a couple of us drank too little water during the first miles on the trail.

After only a few hours, my sister grew ill, faint, and disoriented. Insistent we must move forward, I hoisted her 50-pound pack atop my shoulders (adding this weight onto my 70-pound pack). The day wore on, and the temperature skyrocketed. When we finally limped onto the desert canyon floor, the thermometer on a pole beside the trail read 129 degrees. However, this was the maximum temperature the thermometer could record, so I have no idea how scorching it truly was.

> Early on our trek I realized we had made several serious miscalculations.

For the remainder of the afternoon, we soaked in Phantom Creek, debating our options. My sister was sick, and I was now dehydrated with severe exhaustion and dry heaves. Our plan was to hike two more days and emerge on the North Rim, but the chances of us successfully traversing the sizzling, rugged terrain in our condition were slim. It was clear we had to alter the plan. We needed to head back out of the canyon, retracing the brutal miles we had just endured.

But deciding to do that wasn't easy. I had dreamed of having this adventure with my wife, and arranging our travel schedule had required intricate planning and maneuvering. If we quit now, would we ever have another opportunity to do this? Furthermore, in the shape I was in, I could not climb out of the canyon lugging two packs; I would have to leave one of my backpacks behind. However, my sister had borrowed my equipment, so one pack represented an investment and the other had sentimental value. I didn't want to leave either behind. In order to make the right decision (the *good* decision), I would have to relinquish my expectations as well as my "stuff." I would have to turn around and leave a few things behind. I would have to remember what was truly good: the people I loved (and me) making it out safely.

> In order to make the right decision (the *good* decision), I would have to relinquish my expectations as well as my "stuff."

What do we hang onto that keeps us from pursuing what is good for us? What expectations do we have to let go of as we face the realities around us? Do we need to head in a different direction? And if we do, what "stuff' do we need to abandon?

As we look at the realities of life around us, some of our biggest questions have to do with God. *If we believe God is real, how do we deal with evil, war, and violence?* The world we know seems at odds with the notion of a loving God. A number of years ago, I endured an extended dark season when a relentless battle with fear threatened to unravel me. One night, in the wee hours, I sat on a cold leather couch while my family slept. My prayers erupted with tears and anger: *Will this ever end? Is God anywhere? What is wrong with me?* Is there really a God who will do anything to save us, to rescue us? Because we do need rescuing.

Most of us are achingly and sorrowfully aware that something has gone terribly wrong in our world. We know that the injustices, loneliness, and social fractures are evils we ought to rail against. Many of us might not even know what we think about God or eternity, but we know that we encounter evil all around us—in refugee camps, in acts of horrific terror, in urban centers where neighborhoods are torn apart and young girls are forced to peddle their bodies on the streets.

And we know—somehow we simply know—it was not meant to be this way. But how do we know? My hunch is that we have this basic intuition because we are humans created in God's image. We were created for a perfect world like Eden, that stunning landscape where God breathed life into Adam and Eve. If we were intended for a world infused with love, goodness, and God, then it makes sense that we would gasp at beauty and be furious at evil. Perhaps Jesus's story—God becoming human, dying as an act of sacrificial love, and then walking out of His tomb as the signal of God's intention to resurrect everything death has ruined—tells us what our heart already knows: We are meant to be people of life, not death.

> Most of us are achingly and sorrowfully aware that something has gone terribly wrong in our world.

Vanity Fair magazine has a regular feature, the "Proust Questionnaire," where they ask a celebrity twenty-one questions on a variety of topics. In one issue they interviewed actor and filmmaker Dennis Hopper. "What is your greatest fear?" they asked Hopper. He replied with a single word: "Death." When they asked him to name his deepest regret,

Hopper answered: "Mortality—that you don't live forever." This somber theme reappeared at the conclusion of the interview, though it took a more humorous tone: **How would you like to die?** *With my boots on.* **What is your life motto?** *Never wear boots.*

Whether we want to acknowledge it or not, the gloomy fact is that someday each of us will breathe our last. A headstone will mark the spot where our family and friends lay our body to rest. And many wonder if that will be the end. We do not need to wait for the grave, however, to contend with death's menacing grip. The violence that scrolls across the news ticker 24 hours a day reminds us that all is not well. There is much joy in this world, to be sure. But we also live many of our days on edge, threatened by the possibility of chaos, aware of the frailness of our lives. And one of our piercing questions is simply this: *Is there really a God who will do anything to change our lives?*

> One of our piercing questions is simply this: *Is there really a God who will do anything to change our lives?*

The Bible's resounding answer, from its first pages to its final word, is yes! Creation itself was God's insistence that we are designed for abundance, beauty, and life. In the Genesis story, after each day when God finished crafting lush hillsides or colorful finches or a marvelous scattering of stars, God sat back and with a deep sigh of contentment exhaled a simple word: *good.* Day one: *good.* Day two: *good.* Days three, four, five: *good, good, good.* Finally, when God fashioned His pinnacle work, humanity, His exuberant exclamation was *very good!* In other words, good humans were intended for a good world, a good life. This truth is woven into our being and emerges alongside our longings for love and hope.

Our Daily Bread

Of course, the human story took a disastrous turn. When God created Adam and Eve, He created them with the ability to choose, so there was always the possibility that they might walk away from Him, walk away from life—which they did. Adam and Eve believed the lie that God was not good and that God did not intend good for them. They rejected God, chose a renegade path, and now we live with the consequences of that choice, which is death. When we abandon God, only death remains—the death of everything.

Death opposes God's intentions for us. Death is contrary to the beauty and flourishing life God designed for His creation.

But God is a God of life, not death. God is a God of goodness, not destruction. God could not abandon the people He loves, the world He loves, any more than He could cease being God. God did not watch His world from afar, unmoved by our plight. God did not cover His ears or close His eyes to the ruin we had brought upon ourselves. God did not stay distant, smugly assured that we deserved whatever calamity we encountered. God acted. He came to us. Compelled by compassion and love for His creation, God came to us in human form. Jesus, the Son of God, came to rescue us.

> God did not stay distant, smugly assured that we deserved whatever calamity we encountered. God acted.

On the cross, Jesus took on himself all our evil and all our suffering. In the resurrection, Jesus conquered what we most fear: the vile reality that unleashes havoc in our world—death. Jesus walked out of the tomb, victor over death.

Jesus's resurrection does not promise that we will never have a grave, but it does assure us that death no longer holds power over us. One day we will be resurrected to life anew. Every remnant of death (war, disease, broken relationships, injustice) will, in the end, be dismantled. Death—and all the mayhem death inflicts—does not win. God wins! Life wins. God has acted. God has rescued us. We can have joy and confidence. In the end, all will be well.

When we encountered major difficulties in our Grand Canyon adventure, I had a choice. The wrong choice would lead to disaster. The right choice would lead us to safety and possibly save our lives. But to make that choice, I had to give up some things.

> **In Jesus, we encounter jaw-dropping good news.**

God offers us a choice too. Are we willing to let go of the things we hold onto so tightly, convinced they are our life? Are we willing to move toward God so we can receive the goodness He longs to give? Will we trust that God is generous, kind, and intent on our joy? Will we trust that God has acted (and will act) on our behalf?

Our questions about God and evil, about life and death, and about God's apparent silence amid unrelenting fear all reveal the same concern: Is the good life really possible and can God truly offer it to us?

In Jesus, we encounter jaw-dropping good news. Death might be everywhere, but death does not have the final word. Jesus has come, and death of every sort will one day be undone. As author Frederick Buechner writes, "What's lost is nothing to what's found, and all the death that ever was, set next to life, would scarcely fill a cup." This is the good life God intends for us, the good life God offers. 🕊️

WINN COLLIER, PASTOR AND AUTHOR

What Is God Like?

To celebrate a special occasion, my husband took me to a local art gallery and said I could choose a painting as a gift. I picked out a small picture of a brook flowing through a forest. The streambed took up most of the canvas, and because of this much of the sky was excluded from the picture. However, the stream's reflection revealed the location of the sun, the treetops, and the hazy atmosphere. The only way to "see" the sky was to look at the surface of the water.

> TODAY'S READING
> **Hebrews 1:1–10**
>
> **The Son is . . . the exact representation of [God's] being.**
> Hebrews 1:3

Jesus is like the stream, in a spiritual sense. When we want to see what God is like, we look at Jesus. The writer of Hebrews said He is "the exact representation of [God's] being" (1:3). Although we can learn facts about God through direct statements in the Bible such as "God is love," we can deepen our understanding by seeing the way God would act if He faced the same problems we have on earth. Being God in human flesh, this is what Jesus has shown us.

In temptation, Jesus revealed God's holiness. Confronting spiritual darkness, He demonstrated God's authority. Wrestling with people problems, He showed us God's wisdom. In His death, He illustrated God's love.

Although we cannot grasp everything about God—He is limitless and we are limited in our thinking—we can be certain of His character when we look at Christ.  *JENNIFER BENSON SCHULDT*

Dear God, thank You for making a way for us to know You.
Help us to grow closer to You by looking at Jesus.

Looking at Jesus shows us God's character.

Living Out Loud

While staying at a hotel in Austin, Texas, I noticed a card lying on the desk in my room. It said:

> *Welcome*
> *Our prayer is that your stay here will be restful*
> *and that your travels will be fruitful.*
> *May the Lord bless you and keep you, and make*
> *His face shine upon you.*

This card from the company that manages the hotel made me want to know more, so I accessed their website and read about their culture, strength, and values. In a winsome way, they seek to pursue excellence and live out their faith in the workplace.

TODAY'S READING
1 Peter 3:8–16

In your hearts revere Christ as Lord. 1 Peter 3:15

Their philosophy reminded me of Peter's words to the followers of Jesus scattered throughout Asia Minor. He encouraged them to demonstrate their faith in Christ in the society where they lived. Even as they faced threats and persecution, Peter told them not to be afraid, "But in your hearts revere Christ as Lord. Always be prepared to give an answer to everyone who asks you to give the reason for the hope that you have. But do this with gentleness and respect" (1 PETER 3:15).

A friend of mine calls this "living a lifestyle that demands an explanation." No matter where we live or work, may we in God's strength live out our faith today—always ready to reply gently and respectfully to everyone who asks the reason for our hope. 🍂 *DAVID C. MCCASLAND*

May our lives cause others to ask the reason we have hope.

I See You

When Xavier was two, he darted into one aisle after another in a small shoe store. Hiding behind stacks of shoeboxes, he giggled when my husband, Alan, said, "I see you."

Moments later, I saw Alan dash frantically from aisle to aisle, calling Xavier's name. We raced to the front of the store. Our child, still laughing, ran toward the open door leading to the busy street outside.

Within seconds, Alan scooped him up. We embraced as I thanked God, sobbed, and kissed our toddler's chubby cheeks.

A year before I became pregnant with Xavier, I'd lost our first child during the pregnancy. When God blessed us with our son, I became a fearful parent. Our shoe store experience proved I wouldn't always be able to see or protect our child. But I discovered peace as I learned to turn to my only sure source of help—God—when I struggled with worry and fear.

> TODAY'S READING
> **Psalm 121**
>
> **The LORD will watch over your coming and going both now and forevermore.**
> Psalm 121:8

Our heavenly Father never takes His eyes off His children (PSALM 121:1–4). While we can't prevent trials, heartache, or loss, we can live with confident faith, relying on an ever-present Helper and Protector who watches over our lives (VV. 5–8).

We may encounter days when we feel lost and helpless. We may also feel powerless when we can't shield loved ones. But we can trust that our all-knowing God never loses sight of us— His precious and beloved children. ❧

XOCHITL DIXON

Thank You for watching over our loved ones and us, Lord.

God always keeps His eye on His children.

A Perfect World

Katie was given a school assignment to write an essay entitled "My Perfect World." She wrote: "In my perfect world … ice cream is free, lollipops are everywhere, and the sky is blue all the time, with only a few clouds that have interesting shapes." Then her essay took a more serious turn. In that world, she continued, "No one will come home to bad news. And no one will have to be the one to deliver it."

No one will come home to bad news. Isn't that wonderful? Those words point powerfully to the confident hope we have in Jesus. He is "making everything new"—healing and transforming our world (REVELATION 21:5).

> **TODAY'S READING**
> **Revelation 21:1–5**
>
> **He who was seated on the throne said, "I am making everything new!"** Revelation 21:5

Paradise is the place of "no more"—no more evil, no more death, no more mourning, no more pain, no more tears (V. 4)! It is a place of perfect communion with God, who by His love has redeemed and claimed believers as His own (V. 3). What marvelous joy awaits us!

We can enjoy a foretaste of this perfect reality here and now. As we seek to fellowship with God daily, we experience the joy of His presence (COLOSSIANS 1:12–13). And even as we struggle against sin, we experience, in part, the victory that is ours in Christ (2:13–15), the One who fully conquered sin and death. 🌰

POH FANG CHIA

Lord, thank You that You are making all things new. Help us to live in the hope of the day we will live with You, pure and blameless, on a new earth in Your presence forever and ever.

God's perfect world is for all who believe in Jesus.

God's Great Creation

O n a recent visit with some of our grandchildren, we enjoyed watching a web cam that focused on an eagle family in Florida. Every day we would check in on the mom, the dad, and the baby as they went about their daily routine in their nest high off the ground. Each day the parent birds would keep a constant, protective vigil over the eaglet, bringing it fish from a nearby river for nourishment.

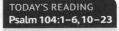
TODAY'S READING
Psalm 104:1–6, 10–23

The birds of the sky nest by the waters; they sing among the branches. Psalm 104:12

This little eagle family depicts for us one image the psalmist gave us of God's magnificent creation in Psalm 104—an array of creation images, of scenes from the work of God's creative hand.

We see the majesty of God's creation as it relates to the universe (VV. 2–4).

We experience the creation of the earth itself—waters, mountains, valleys (VV. 5–9).

We enjoy the glory of God's gift of animals, birds, and crops (VV. 10–18).

We marvel at the cycles God created in our world—morning/night, darkness/light, work/rest (VV. 19–23).

What a glorious world God has fashioned with His hands for our enjoyment—and for His glory! "Praise the LORD, my soul!" (V. 1). Each one of us can say thank You to God for all He has given us to appreciate and enjoy. 🌿   *DAVE BRANON*

Praise God! Praise You, Lord, for the wonder of the earth You created.

The beauty of creation reflects the beauty of our Creator.

Hidden Beauty

Our children needed a little coaxing to believe that it was worth putting on snorkeling gear to peer beneath the surface of the Caribbean Sea off the shore of the island of Tobago. But after they dove in, they resurfaced ecstatic, "There are thousands of fish of all different kinds! It's so beautiful! I've never seen such colorful fish!"

Because the surface of the water looked similar to freshwater lakes near our home, our children could have missed the beauty hidden just below the surface.

TODAY'S READING
1 Samuel 16:1–7

People look at the outward appearance, but the LORD looks at the heart. 1 Samuel 16:7

When the prophet Samuel went to Bethlehem to anoint one of Jesse's sons to be the next king, Samuel saw the oldest son, Eliab, and was impressed by his appearance. The prophet thought he had found the right man, but the Lord rejected Eliab. God reminded Samuel that He "does not look at the things people look at. People look at the outward appearance, but the LORD looks at the heart" (1 SAMUEL 16:7).

So Samuel asked if there were more sons. The youngest boy wasn't present but caring for the family's sheep. This son, David, was summoned and the Lord directed Samuel to anoint him.

Often we look at people only on a surface level and don't always take the time to see their inner, sometimes hidden, beauty. We don't always value what God values. But if we take the time to peer beneath the surface, we may find great treasure. 🌸
LISA SAMRA

Heavenly Father, thank You for not valuing people based on outward appearances but instead by looking at our hearts. Help me to take the time to see beyond simply what my eyes can see in order to discover true and lasting beauty.

God can help me to see the inner beauty in others.

Declaring Dependence

Laura's mom was battling cancer. One morning Laura prayed for her with a friend. Her friend, who had been disabled for years by cerebral palsy, prayed: "Lord, you do everything for me. Please do everything for Laura's mother."

Laura was deeply moved by her friend's "declaration of dependence" on God. Reflecting on the moment, she said, "How often do I acknowledge my need for God in everything? It's something I should do every day!"

> TODAY'S READING
> **John 5:16–23**
>
> **Apart from me you can do nothing.**
> John 15:5

During His days on earth Jesus demonstrated continual dependence on His heavenly Father. One might think that because Jesus is God in a human body, He would have the best of all reasons to be self-sufficient. But when the religious authorities asked Him to give a reason for "working" on a legally ordained day of rest because He healed someone on the Sabbath, He responded, "Very truly I tell you, the Son can do nothing by himself; he can do only what he sees his Father doing" (JOHN 5:19). Jesus declared His dependence as well!

Jesus's reliance on the Father sets the ultimate example of what it means to live in relationship with God. Every moment we draw breath is a gift from God, and He wants our lives to be filled with His strength. When we live to love and serve Him through our moment-by-moment prayer and reliance on His Word, we are declaring our dependence on Him.

JAMES BANKS

I need You for everything, Lord! Help me to live to serve You.
I praise You for being my Savior and my strength!

Prayerlessness is our declaration of independence from God.

DANIEL HENDERSON

Many Gifts, One Purpose

Corn, also called maize, is the staple food in my home country of Mexico. There are so many different types. You can find yellow, brown, red, and black cobs, even ones with a wonderful spotted pattern. But people in the cities usually won't eat the spotted cobs. Restaurateur and researcher Amado Ramírez explains that they believe uniformity is a synonym of quality. Yet the spotted cobs taste good, and they make excellent tortillas.

> **TODAY'S READING**
> **1 Corinthians 12:4–14**
>
> Just as a body, though one, has many parts, but all its many parts form one body, so it is with Christ.
> 1 Corinthians 12:12

The church of Christ is much more similar to a spotted ear of corn than to a cob of just one color. The apostle Paul used the imagery of a body to describe the church, because even though we are all one body, and we have the same God, each of us has been given a different gift. As Paul said, "There are different kinds of service, but the same Lord. There are different kinds of working, but in all of them and in everyone it is the same God at work" (1 CORINTHIANS 12:5-6). Our diversity in the ways we help each other shows God's generosity and creativity.

As we embrace our diversity, may we also make every effort to keep our unity in faith and purpose. Yes, we have different abilities and backgrounds. We speak different languages and come from different countries. But we have the same wonderful God, the Creator who delights in so much variety. 🌿

KEILA OCHOA

Father, may we make every effort to be one, respecting and valuing each other and our various gifts and talents.

We need one another in order to be what God wants us to be.

Be Still, My Soul!

Picture a parent poised lovingly over a child, finger gently placed in front of nose and lips softly speaking the words—"hush," "shhhh." The demeanor and simple words are meant to comfort and quiet anxious little ones in the midst of disappointment, discomfort, or pain. Scenes like this are universal and timeless and most of us have been on the giving or receiving end of such loving expressions. When I ponder Psalm 131:2, this is the picture that comes to mind.

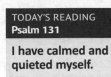

TODAY'S READING
Psalm 131

I have calmed and quieted myself.

Psalm 131:2

The language and flow of this psalm suggest that the writer, David, had experienced something that provoked serious reflection. Have you experienced a disappointment, defeat, or failure that prompted thoughtful, reflective prayer? What do you do when you are humbled by life's circumstances? When you fail a test or lose a job or experience the end of a relationship? David poured out his heart to the Lord and in the process did a bit of honest soul-searching and inventory (PSALM 131:1). In making peace with his circumstances, he found contentment like that of a young child who was satisfied with simply being with his or her mother (V. 2).

Life's circumstances change and sometimes we are humbled. Yet we can be hopeful and content knowing that there is One who has promised to never leave or forsake us. We can trust Him fully. 🌿

ARTHUR JACKSON

Father, when things change in my life, help me not to be anxious but to trust You and find contentment in You alone.

Contentment is found in Christ alone.

God of the Depths

"**W**hen you go to the deep sea, every time you take a sample, you'll find a new species," says marine biologist Ward Appeltans. In one recent year, scientists identified 1,451 new types of undersea life. We simply don't know the half of what's down there.

In Job 38–40, God reviewed His creation for Job's benefit. In three poetic chapters, God highlighted the wonders of weather, the vastness of the cosmos, and the variety of creatures in their habitats. These are things we can observe. Then God spoke of the mysterious Leviathan—for an entire chapter. Leviathan is a creature like no other, with harpoon-deflecting armor (JOB 41:7, 13), graceful power (V. 12), and "fearsome teeth" (V. 14). "Flames stream from its mouth . . . smoke pours from its nostrils" (VV. 19–20). "Nothing on earth is its equal" (V. 33).

> TODAY'S READING
> **Job 41:12–34**
>
> **There is the sea, vast and spacious, . . . and Leviathan, which you formed to frolic there.**
>
> Psalm 104:25–26

Okay, so God talks about a huge creature we haven't seen. Is that the point of Job 41?

No! Job 41 broadens our understanding of God's surprising character. The psalmist expanded on this when he wrote, "There is the sea, vast and spacious, . . . and Leviathan, which you formed to frolic there" (PSALM 104:25–26). After the terrifying description in Job, we learn that God created a playpen for this most fearsome of all creatures. Leviathan *frolics*.

We have the present to explore the ocean. We'll have eternity to explore the wonders of our magnificent, mysterious, playful God.

TIM GUSTAFSON

Our exploration of creation teaches us about the Creator.

Strangers Welcome Strangers

When my husband and I moved to Seattle to be near his sister, we didn't know where we would live or work. A local church helped us find a place: a rental house with many bedrooms. We could live in one bedroom, and rent the others to international students. For the next three years, we were strangers welcoming strangers: sharing our home and meals with people from all over the world. We and our housemates also welcomed dozens of international students into our home every Friday night for Bible study.

TODAY'S READING
Leviticus 19:1–9, 33–34

When a foreigner resides among you in your land, do not mistreat them. . . . Love them as yourself, for you were foreigners in Egypt. Leviticus 19:33–34

God's people know what it means to be far from home. For several hundred years, the Israelites were literal foreigners—and slaves—in Egypt. In Leviticus 19, alongside familiar instructions like "Respect your mother and father" and "Do not steal" (VV. 3, 11), God reminded His people to empathetically care for foreigners, because they knew what it was like to be foreigners and afraid (VV. 33–34).

While not all of us as followers of God today have experienced literal exile, we all know how it feels to be "foreigners" on earth (1 PETER 2:11)—people who feel like outsiders because our ultimate allegiance is to a heavenly kingdom. We are called to create a community of hospitality—strangers welcoming strangers into God's family. The hospitable welcome my husband and I experienced in Seattle taught us to extend welcome to others—and this is at the heart of being the family of God (ROMANS 12:13). 🌾

AMY PETERSON

To whom can I show hospitality?

An Anchor When We're Afraid

Are you a worrier? I am. I wrestle with anxiety almost daily. I worry about big things. I worry about small things. Sometimes, it seems like I worry about everything. Once in my teens, I called the police when my *parents* were four hours late getting home.

Scripture repeatedly tells us not to be afraid. Because of God's goodness and power, and because He sent Jesus to die for us and His Holy Spirit to guide us, our fears don't have to rule our lives. We may well face hard things, but God has promised to be with us through it all.

> **TODAY'S READING**
> **Isaiah 51:12–16**
>
> **I, even I, am he who comforts you.**
> Isaiah 51:12

One passage that has helped me profoundly in fearful moments is Isaiah 51:12–16. Here, God reminded His people, who had endured tremendous suffering, that He was still with them, and that His comforting presence is the ultimate reality. No matter how bad things may seem: "I, even I, am he who comforts you," He told them through the prophet Isaiah (V. 12).

I *love* that promise. Those eight words have been an emotion-steadying anchor for my soul. I've clung to this promise repeatedly when life has felt overwhelming, when my own "constant terror" (V. 13) has felt oppressive. Through this passage, God reminds me to lift my eyes from my fears and in faith and dependence to look to the One who "stretches out the heavens" (V. 13)—the One who promises to comfort us.

ADAM HOLZ

Lord, sometimes the struggles we face in life seem so big. But You are bigger. Help us to cling to Your promise of comfort in fearful moments and to experience Your loving provision as we trust You.

God's comforting presence is more powerful than our fears.

He Knows Us

Did God know about me as I drove at night on a 100-mile journey to my village? Given the condition I was in, the answer was not simple. My temperature ran high and my head ached. I prayed, "Lord, I know you are with me, but I'm in pain!"

Tired and weak, I parked by the road near a small village. Ten minutes later, I heard a voice. "Hello! Do you need any help?" It was a man with his companions from the community. Their presence felt good. When they told me the name of their village, *Naa mi n'yala* (meaning, "The King knows about me!"), I was amazed. I had passed this community dozens of times without stopping. This time, the Lord used its name to remind me that, indeed, He, the King, was with me while I was alone on that road in my ailing condition. Encouraged, I pressed on toward the nearest clinic.

> TODAY'S READING
> Psalm 139:1–14
>
> **You have searched me, LORD, and you know me. You know when I sit and when I rise.**
>
> Psalm 139:1–2

God knows us thoroughly as we go about our everyday chores, at different locations and situations, no matter our condition (PSALM 139:1–4, 7–12). He does not abandon us or forget us; nor is He so busy that He neglects us. Even when we are in trouble or in difficult circumstances—"darkness" and "night" (VV. 11–12)—we are not hidden from His presence. This truth gives us such hope and assurance that we can praise the Lord who has carefully created us and leads us through life (V. 14). 🌿

LAWRENCE DARMANI

Thank You, Lord, that You always know where I am and how I am doing. You know me inside and out. I'm thankful I can count on You to care.

No matter where we are, God knows about us.

Hiding Our Hurts

was guest-speaking in a local church and my topic was an honest story about presenting our brokenness before God and receiving the healing He wants to give. Before closing in prayer, the pastor stood in the center aisle, looked deeply into the eyes of his gathered congregants, and said, "As your pastor I have the privilege of seeing you midweek and hearing your heart-breaking stories of brokenness. Then in our weekend worship services, I have the pain of watching you hide your hurt away."

TODAY'S READING
Hebrews 4:12–13

The word of God . . . judges the thoughts and attitudes of the heart. Hebrews 4:12

My heart ached at the hidden hurts God came to heal. The writer of Hebrews describes the Word of God as alive and active. Many have understood this "word" to be the Bible, but it's even more than that. Jesus is the *living* Word of God. He evaluates our thoughts and attitudes—and loves us still.

Jesus died to give us access to God's presence, all the time. And while we all know it's not wise to share *everything* with *everyone*, we also know that God intends His church be a place where we can live unapologetically as broken and forgiven followers of Christ. It's to be a place where we "carry each other's burdens" (GALATIANS 6:2).

What are you hiding from others today? And how are you trying to hide from God as well? God sees us through Jesus. And He still loves us. Will we let Him? 🌱   *ELISA MORGAN*

Who will you prayerfully consider letting help you carry your burdens?

God sees us with the eyes of a Father.

Our Daily Bread

The Best Gift

When I was packing up to go home to London, my mother approached me with a gift—one of her rings I had long admired. Surprised, I asked, "What's this for?" She replied, "I think you should enjoy it now. Why wait until I die? It doesn't fit me anyway." With a smile I received her unexpected gift, an early inheritance that brings me joy.

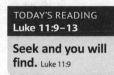

TODAY'S READING
Luke 11:9–13

Seek and you will find. Luke 11:9

My mom gave me a material gift, but Jesus promises that His Father will give the Holy Spirit to those who ask (LUKE 11:13). If parents who are marred with sin can provide necessities (such as fish or eggs) for their children, how much more will our Father in heaven give to His children. Through the gift of the Holy Spirit (JOHN 16:13), we can experience hope, love, joy, and peace even in times of trouble—and we can share these gifts with others.

Growing up, we may have had parents who were unable to love and care for us fully. Or we may have had mothers and fathers who were shining examples of sacrificial love. Or our experience may have been somewhere in between. Whatever we've known with our earthly parents, we can hold onto the promise that our heavenly Father loves us unceasingly. He gave His children the gift of the Holy Spirit. 🌿

AMY BOUCHER PYE

Heavenly Father, I'm amazed at Your love for me.
Help me to dwell in Your presence this day,
sharing Your love with those I meet.

Our Father gives good gifts.

No Co-Signer Required

When a person without a long history of paying his or her bills on time wants to obtain a loan to purchase a home or car, lenders are often reluctant to take the financial risk. Without a track record, that person's promise to repay what he borrows is insufficient for the bank.

The would-be borrower usually resorts to finding someone who does have a history of making good on their debts, asking them to put their name on the loan too. The co-signer's promise assures the lender the loan will be repaid.

TODAY'S READING
Hebrews 6:13–20

People swear by someone greater than themselves, and the oath confirms what is said. Hebrews 6:16

When someone makes a promise to us—whether for financial, marital, or other reasons—we expect them to keep it. We want to know that God will keep His promises too. When He promised Abraham that He would bless him and give him "many descendants" (HEBREWS 6:14; SEE GENESIS 22:17), Abraham took God at His word. As the Creator of all that exists, there is no one greater than He; only God could guarantee His own promise.

Abraham had to wait for the birth of his son (HEBREWS 6:15) (and never saw how innumerable his offspring would grow to be), but God proved faithful to His promise. When He promises to be with us always (13:5), to hold us securely (JOHN 10:29), and to comfort us (2 CORINTHIANS 1:3–4), we too can trust Him to be true to His word. 🕊 *KIRSTEN HOLMBERG*

Lord, thank You for being so trustworthy. I need no other promises but Your word. Help me to trust You more and more each day.

God's promises are sure.

Our Daily Bread

I Just Can't Do It

"**I just can't do it!**" lamented the dejected student. On the page he could see only small print, difficult ideas, and an unforgiving deadline. He needed the help of his teacher.

We might experience similar despair when we read Jesus's Sermon on the Mount. "Love your enemies" (MATTHEW 5:44). Anger is as bad as murder (V. 22). Lust equals adultery (V. 28). And if we dare think we can live up to these standards, we bump into this: "Be perfect, therefore, as your heavenly Father is perfect" (V. 48).

> **TODAY'S READING**
> **1 Corinthians 1:26–31**
>
> **The law was our tutor to bring us to Christ, that we might be justified by faith.**
> Galatians 3:24 NKJV

"The Sermon on the Mount produces despair," says Oswald Chambers. But he saw this as good, because at "the point of despair we are willing to come to [Jesus] as paupers to receive from Him."

In the counterintuitive way God so often works, those who know they can't do it on their own are the ones who receive God's grace. As the apostle Paul put it, "Not many of you were wise by human standards. . . . But God chose the foolish things of the world to shame the wise" (1 CORINTHIANS 1:26–27).

In God's wisdom, the Teacher is also our Savior. When we come to Him in faith, through His Spirit we enjoy His "righteousness, holiness and redemption" (V. 30), and the grace and power to live for Him. That's why He could say, "Blessed are the poor in spirit, for theirs is the kingdom of heaven" (MATTHEW 5:3). 🌿

TIM GUSTAFSON

Thank You, Lord, for blessing those who are poor in spirit, who mourn, and who hunger and thirst for Your righteousness. You are our righteousness!

Through the Son we can enjoy life in God's kingdom.

What's Your Passion?

One of the tellers at my bank has a photograph of a Shelby Cobra roadster on his window. (The Cobra is a high-performance automobile built by the Ford Motor Company.)

One day, while transacting business at the bank, I asked him if that was his car. "No," he replied, "that's my passion, my reason to get up every morning and go to work. I'm going to own one someday."

TODAY'S READING
Psalm 20:6-9

Some trust in chariots and some in horses, but we trust in the name of the LORD our God. Psalm 20:7

I understand this young man's passion. A friend of mine owned a Cobra, and I drove it on one occasion! It's a mean machine! But a Cobra, like everything else in this world, isn't worth living for. Those who trust in things apart from God "are brought to their knees and fall," according to the psalmist (PSALM 20:8).

That's because we were made for God and nothing else will do—a truth we validate in our experience every day: We buy this or that because we think these things will make us happy, but like a child receiving a dozen Christmas presents or more, we ask ourselves, "Is this all?" Something is always missing.

Nothing this world has to offer us—even very good things—fully satisfies us. There is a measure of enjoyment in them, but our happiness soon fades away (1 JOHN 2:17). Indeed, "God cannot give us happiness and peace apart from Himself," C. S. Lewis concluded. "There is no such thing." 🌿 *DAVID H. ROPER*

I have found Him whom my soul so long has craved! Jesus satisfies my longings—through His blood I now am saved. *CLARA WILLIAMS*

There is a longing in every heart that only Jesus can satisfy.

Through the Cross

My coworker Tom keeps an 8" by 12" glass cross on his desk. His friend Phil, who like Tom is a cancer survivor, gave it to him to help him look at everything "through the cross." The glass cross is a constant reminder of God's love and good purposes for him.

That's a challenging idea for all believers in Jesus, especially during difficult times. It's much easier to focus on our problems than on God's love.

The apostle Paul's life was certainly an example of having a cross-shaped perspective. He described himself in times of suffering as being "persecuted, but not abandoned; struck down, but not destroyed" (2 CORINTHIANS 4:9). He believed

> **TODAY'S READING**
> **2 Corinthians 4:8–18**
>
> [Nothing] will be able to separate us from the love of God that is in Christ Jesus our Lord. Romans 8:39

that in the hard times, God is at work, "achieving for us an eternal glory that far outweighs them all. So we fix our eyes not on what is seen, but on what is unseen" (VV. 17–18).

To "fix our eyes . . . on what is unseen" doesn't mean we minimize the problems. Paul Barnett, in his commentary on this passage, explains, "There is to be confidence, based on the certainty of God's purposes for [us] . . . . On the other hand, there is the sober recognition that we groan with hope mingled with pain."

Jesus gave His life for us. His love is deep and sacrificial. As we look at life "through the cross," we see His love and faithfulness. And our trust in Him grows. 🌿   *ANNE CETAS*

Father, teach us who You are. Increase our trust in You.
Fill our minds with Your perspective.

Look at everything through the cross.

Home Sweet Home

"**W**hy do we** have to leave our home and move?" my son asked. It's difficult to explain what a home is, especially to a five-year-old. We were leaving a house, but not our home, in the sense that home is where our loved ones are. It's the place where we long to return after a long trip or after a full day's work.

TODAY'S READING
John 14:1–14

I am going there to prepare a place for you. John 14:2

When Jesus was in the upper room just hours before He died, He told His disciples, "Do not let your hearts be troubled" (JOHN 14:1). The disciples were uncertain of their future because Jesus had predicted His death. But Jesus reassured them of His presence and reminded them they would see Him again. He told them, "My Father's house has many rooms . . . . I am going there to prepare a place for you" (V. 2). He could have used other words to describe heaven. However, He chose words that describe not an uncomfortable or unfamiliar place but a place where Jesus, our loved One, would be.

C. S. Lewis wrote, "Our Father refreshes us on the journey with some pleasant inns, but will not encourage us to mistake them for home." We can thank God for the "pleasant inns" in life, but let's remember that our real home is in heaven where we "will be with the Lord forever" (1 THESSALONIANS 4:17).   *KEILA OCHOA*

Dear Lord, I thank You for heaven, my eternal home.

We look forward to being with the Lord forever.

Our Daily Bread

Shelter from the Storm

When I lived in Oklahoma I had a friend who "chased" tornados. John tracked the storms carefully through radio contact with other chasers and local radar, trying to keep a safe distance while observing their destructive paths so he could report sudden changes to people in harm's way.

One day a funnel cloud changed course so abruptly John found himself in grave danger. Fortunately, he found shelter and was spared.

John's experience that afternoon makes me think of another destructive path: sin in our lives. The Bible tells us, "Each person is tempted when they are dragged away by their own evil desire and

> TODAY'S READING
> **James 1:12–18**
>
> **But as for me, how good it is to be near God! I have made the Sovereign LORD my shelter.** Psalm 73:28 NLT

enticed. Then, after desire has conceived, it gives birth to sin; and sin, when it is full-grown, gives birth to death" (JAMES 1:14–15).

There's a progression here. What may at first seem harmless can soon spin out of control and wreak havoc. But when temptation threatens, God offers us shelter from the gathering storm.

God's Word tells us He would never tempt us, and we can blame our choices only on ourselves. But when we "are tempted, he will also provide a way out so that [we] can endure it" (1 CORINTHIANS 10:13). As we turn to Him and call on Him for help in the moment of temptation, Jesus gives us the strength we need to overcome.

Jesus is our shelter forever. 🌱

JAMES BANKS

Lord Jesus, You conquered sin and death forever through Your cross and empty tomb! Help me to live and thrive in the forgiveness only You can give.

Our Savior calms temptation's storm.

Hope Anyway

Among the hundreds of articles I've written for *Our Daily Bread* since 1988, a few stick in my mind. One such article is from the mid-1990s when I told of a time our three girls were away at camp or on mission trips, so six-year-old Steve and I had some guy time.

As we were enjoying an excursion to the airport, Steve turned to me and said, "It's not as much fun without Melissa," his eight-year-old sister and sidekick. Neither of us knew then how poignant those words would turn out to be. Life indeed has not been "as much fun" for the years since Mell died in a car accident as a teenager. The passage of time may

> **TODAY'S READING**
> **Psalm 34:15–18**
>
> **My comfort in my suffering is this: Your promise preserves my life.**
> Psalm 119:50

dull the ache, but nothing takes the pain away completely. Time cannot heal that wound. But here's something that can help: listening to, meditating on, and savoring the solace promised by the God of all comfort.

Listen: "Because of the LORD's great love we are not consumed, for his compassions never fail" (LAMENTATIONS 3:22).

Meditate: "In the day of trouble he will keep me safe in his dwelling" (PSALM 27:5).

Savor: "My comfort in my suffering is this: Your promise preserves my life" (119:50).

Life can never be the same again when someone we love is gone. But God's promises bring hope and comfort. *DAVE BRANON*

Thank You, God, that You are near. You're always by my side.
I'm grateful for Your comfort in my pain and for Your peace.

God's Word is the true source of comfort.

Watchful Care

Before he raced out the door to school, I asked my son if he had brushed his teeth. Asking again, I reminded him of the importance of telling the truth. Unmoved by my gentle admonishment, he half-jokingly informed me that what I really needed was a security camera in the bathroom. Then I could check for myself if he had brushed his teeth and he wouldn't be tempted to lie.

TODAY'S READING
Jeremiah 23:20–24

"Do not I fill heaven and earth?" declares the LORD.
Jeremiah 23:24

While the presence of a security camera may help remind us to follow the rules, there are still places we can go unnoticed or ways we can avoid being seen. Although we may evade or trick a security camera, we fool ourselves if we think we are ever outside the gaze of God.

God asks, "Who can hide in secret places so that I cannot see them?" (JEREMIAH 23:24). There is both an encouragement and a warning in His question.

The warning is that we cannot hide from God. We can't outrun or fool Him. Everything we do is visible to Him.

The encouragement is that there is no place on earth or in the heavens where we are outside the watchful care of our heavenly Father. Even when we feel alone, God is with us. No matter where we go today, may the awareness of that truth encourage us to choose obedience to His Word and receive comfort—He watches over us. 🌱

LISA SAMRA

Lord Jesus, thank You that there is nowhere I can go that is outside of
Your loving gaze. Knowing You see me, help me to honor You
with my words and actions.

We are never outside the watchful care of our heavenly Father.

Jesus Knows Why

I **have friends** who've received partial healing but still struggle with painful aspects of their diseases. Other friends have been healed of an addiction but still struggle with feelings of inadequacy and self-loathing. And I wonder, *Why doesn't God heal them completely—once and for all?*

In Mark 8:22–26, we read the story of Jesus healing a man born blind. Jesus first took the man away from the village. Then He spit on the man's eyes and "put his hands on him." The man said he now saw people who looked "like trees walking around." Then Jesus touched the man's eyes again, and this time he saw "everything clearly."

> **TODAY'S READING**
> **Mark 8:22–26**
>
> **When Jesus had finished saying these things, the crowds were amazed at his teaching.** Matthew 7:28

In His ministry, Jesus's words and actions often amazed and baffled the crowd and His followers (MATTHEW 7:28; LUKE 8:10; 11:14) and even drove many of them away (JOHN 6:60–66). No doubt this two-part miracle also caused confusion. Why not *immediately* heal this man?

We don't know why. But Jesus knew what the man—and the disciples who viewed his healing—needed in that moment. And He knows what we need today to draw us closer in our relationship with Him. Though we won't always understand, we can trust that God is working in our lives and the lives of our loved ones. And He will give us the strength, courage, and clarity we need to persevere in following Him.

ALYSON KIEDA

Dear Lord, thank You for knowing us so well and for providing what we need most. Give us eyes to see You and a heart to understand Your Word.

Open our eyes, Lord, we want to see Jesus. ROBERT CULL

Perfect Imperfection

A **college professor** of mine, picking up on my perfectionism-induced procrastination, gave me some wise advice. "Don't let perfect be the enemy of good," he said, explaining that striving for perfect performance can prevent the risks necessary for growth. Accepting that my work would always be imperfect would give me the freedom to keep growing.

TODAY'S READING
Ephesians 3:8–19

The apostle Paul explained an even more profound reason to let go of our own efforts to perfect ourselves: it can blind us to our need for Christ.

Paul had learned this the hard way. After years striving to perfectly obey God's law, encountering Jesus changed everything (GALATIANS 1:11–16). Paul realized

> I pray that out of his glorious riches he may strengthen you with power through his Spirit in your inner being. Ephesians 3:16

that if his own efforts were enough to be whole and right with God, "then there was no need for Christ to die" (2:21 NLT). Only by letting go of—*dying* to—self-reliance, could he experience Jesus living in him (V. 20). Only in his imperfection could he experience God's perfect power.

This *doesn't* mean we shouldn't resist sin (V. 17); but it *does* mean we should stop relying on our own strength to grow spiritually (V. 20).

In this lifetime, we will always be works in progress. But as our hearts humbly accept our constant need for the only perfect One, Jesus makes His home there (EPHESIANS 3:17). Rooted in Him, we are free to grow ever deeper in the love "too great" to ever "understand fully" (V. 19 NLT). 🌿   MONICA BRANDS

Lord, so often we exchange the joy and freedom of life with You for the
burden of relying on ourselves. Help us to humbly rely on You instead.

We are free to grow in Jesus's love.

Unselfish Service

A small collection of people stood together, dwarfed by the size of the huge tree lying on the lawn. An elderly woman leaned on her cane and described watching the previous night's windstorm as it blew down "our majestic old elm tree. Worst of all," she continued, voice cracking with emotion, "it destroyed our lovely stone wall too. My husband built that wall when we were first married. He loved that wall. I loved that wall! Now it's gone; just like him."

Next morning, as she peeked out at the tree company workers cleaning up the downed tree, a big smile spread across her face. In between the branches she could just make out two adults and the boy who mowed her lawn carefully measuring and rebuilding her beloved stone wall!

The prophet Isaiah describes the kind of service God favors: acts that lift the hearts of those around us, like the wall repairers did for the elderly woman. This passage teaches that God values unselfish service to others over empty spiritual rituals. In fact, God exercises a two-way blessing on the selfless service of His children. First, God uses our willing acts of service to aid the oppressed and needy (ISAIAH 58:7–10). *Then* God honors those engaged in such service by building or rebuilding our reputations as powerful positive forces in His kingdom (VV. 11–12). What service will you offer this day? ❧   *RANDY KILGORE*

> **TODAY'S READING**
> **Isaiah 58:6–12**
>
> **If you spend yourselves in behalf of the hungry and satisfy the needs of the oppressed, then your light will rise in the darkness.**
>
> Isaiah 58:10

Thank You, Father, for the acts of others You use to lift us up, and for calling us to do the same.

Selfless service to others brings honor to God.

Lavish Expressions of Love

On our wedding anniversary, my husband, Alan, gives me a large bouquet of fresh flowers. When he lost his job during a corporate restructure, I didn't expect this extravagant display of devotion to continue. But on our nineteenth anniversary, the color-splashed blossoms greeted me from their spot on our dining room table. Because he valued continuing this annual tradition, Alan saved some money each month to ensure he'd have enough for this personal show of affection.

TODAY'S READING
2 Corinthians 9:6–15

You will be enriched in every way so that you can be generous on every occasion.

2 Corinthians 9:11

My husband's careful planning exhibited exuberant generosity, similar to what Paul encouraged when he addressed the Corinthian believers. The apostle complimented the church for their intentional and enthusiastic offerings (2 CORINTHIANS 9:2, 5), reminding them that God delights in generous and cheerful givers (VV. 6–7). After all, no one gives more than our loving Provider, who's always ready to supply all we need (VV. 8–10).

We can be generous in all kinds of giving, caring for one another because the Lord meets all of our material, emotional, and spiritual needs (V. 11). As we give, we can express our gratitude for all God has given us. We can even motivate others to praise the Lord and give from all God has given them (VV. 12–13). Openhanded giving, a lavish expression of love and gratitude, can demonstrate our confidence in God's provision for all His people. 🌱

XOCHITL DIXON

Lord, please help us trust Your abundant love and generosity, so we can give to others as You so faithfully give to us.

Generous giving displays courageous confidence in God's loving and faithful provision.

Bees and Snakes

Some problems have Daddy's name written all over them. For instance, my kids recently discovered bees had moved into a crack in our concrete front porch. So, armed with bug spray, I went out to do battle.

I got stung. Five times.

TODAY'S READING
Matthew 7:7–11

I don't like being stung by insects. But better me than my kids or wife. Taking care of my family's well-being is at the top of my job description after all. My children recognized a need, and they asked me to address it. They trusted me to protect them from something they feared.

In Matthew 7, Jesus teaches that we too should bring our needs to God (v. 7), trusting Him with our requests. To illustrate, Jesus gives a case study in character: "Which of you, if your son asks for

> **If you, then, though you are evil, know how to give good gifts to your children, how much more will your Father in heaven give good gifts to those who ask him!** Matthew 7:11

bread, will give him a stone? Or if he asks for a fish, will give him a snake?" (vv. 9–10). For loving parents, the answer is obvious. But Jesus answers anyway, challenging us not to lose faith in our Father's generous goodness: "If you, then, though you are evil, know how to give good gifts to your children, how much more will your Father in heaven give good gifts to those who ask him!" (v. 11).

I can't imagine loving my kids more. But Jesus assures us that even the best earthly father's love is eclipsed by God's love for us. ❧ *ADAM HOLZ*

Father, thank You for loving us so much more than even the best father here ever could. Help us to do as Jesus said with everything that's on our hearts; to ask, seek, and knock in our relationship with You.

We can rely on our Father for everything we need.

Our Daily Bread

Hope in Grief

When I was nineteen, one of my close friends was killed in a car accident. In the following weeks and months, I walked each day in a tunnel of grief. The pain of losing someone so young and wonderful clouded my vision, and at times I even felt unaware of what was going on around me. I felt so blinded by pain and grief that I simply could not see God.

TODAY'S READING
Luke 24:13–32

Then their eyes were opened and they recognized him, and he disappeared from their sight. Luke 24:31

In Luke 24, two disciples, confused and brokenhearted after Jesus's death, didn't realize they were walking with their resurrected Teacher Himself, even as He explained from Scripture why the promised Savior had to die and rise again. Only when He took bread and broke it was it revealed that this was Jesus (VV. 30–31). Although the followers of Jesus had faced death in all its horror when Jesus died, through His resurrection from the dead God showed them how to hope again.

Like those disciples, we might feel weighed down with confusion or grief. But we can find hope and comfort in the reality that Jesus is alive and at work in the world—and in us. Although we still face heartache and pain, we can welcome Christ to walk with us in our tunnel of grief. As the Light of the world (JOHN 8:12), He can bring rays of hope to brighten our fog. 🌱

AMY BOUCHER PYE

Lord God, thank You for being the light in the darkness.
Bring hope when I'm sad and confused,
and help me to see Your glory.

Though we grieve, we have hope in Jesus.

Overcoming Challenges

We gathered monthly to hold one another accountable to our individual goals. My friend Mary wanted to reupholster the seats of her dining room chairs before the year's end. At our November meeting she wittily reported her progress from October: "It took ten months and two hours to recover my chairs." After months of not being able to obtain the materials required, or find the quiet hours away from her demanding job and her toddler's needs, the project took merely two hours of committed work to finish.

The Lord called Nehemiah to a far greater project: to bring restoration to Jerusalem after its walls had lain in ruin

TODAY'S READING
Nehemiah 6:1–9, 15

So the wall was completed on the twenty-fifth of Elul, in fifty-two days.

Nehemiah 6:15

for 150 years (NEHEMIAH 2:3–5, 12). As he led the people in the labor, they experienced mockery, attacks, distraction, and temptation to sin (4:3, 8; 6:10–12). Yet God equipped them to stand firm—resolute in their efforts—completing a daunting task in just fifty-two days.

Overcoming such challenges requires much more than a personal desire or goal; Nehemiah was driven by an understanding that God appointed him to the task. His sense of purpose invigorated the people to follow his leadership despite incredible opposition. When God charges us with a task—whether to repair a relationship or share what He's done in our lives—He gives us whatever skills and strength are necessary to continue in our effort to do what He's asked, no matter what challenges come our way. 🍞 _KIRSTEN HOLMBERG_

Lord, please equip me with Your strength to persevere and finish the tasks You've given me. May my labors bring You glory.

God equips us to overcome obstacles and complete the tasks He's given us to do.

Sinners Like Us

have a friend—her name is Edith—who told me about the day she decided to follow Jesus.

Edith cared nothing for religion. But one Sunday morning she walked into a church near her apartment looking for something to satisfy her discontented soul. The text that day was Luke 15:1–2, which the pastor read from the King James Version: "Then drew near unto him all the publicans and sinners for to hear him. And the Pharisees and scribes murmured, saying, This man receiveth sinners, and eateth with them."

That's what it said, but this is what Edith heard: "This man receives sinners and Edith with them." She sat straight up in her pew! Eventually she realized her mistake, but the thought that Jesus welcomed sinners—*and that included Edith*—stayed with her. That afternoon she decided to "draw near" to Jesus and listen to Him. She began to read the Gospels, and soon she decided to put her faith in Him and follow Him.

> TODAY'S READING
> **Luke 15:1–7**
>
> **This man welcomes sinners and eats with them.** Luke 15:2

The religious folks of Jesus's day were scandalized by the fact that He ate and drank with sinful, awful people. Their rules prohibited them from associating with such folk. Jesus paid no attention to their made-up rules. He welcomed the down-and-out and gathered them to Him, no matter how far gone they were.

It's still true, you know: Jesus receives sinners and (your name). 🕮

DAVID H. ROPER

Heavenly Father, we can't thank You enough for the radical love of Your Son, who drew all of us outcasts and moral failures to Him, and made the way for us to come to You in joy and boldness.

God pursues us in our restlessness, receives us in our sinfulness, holds us in our brokenness. *SCOTTY SMITH*

Love Without Limits

A wise friend advised me to avoid using the words "you always" or "you never" in an argument—especially with my family. How easy it is to criticize others around us and to feel unloving toward those we love. But there is never any variation in God's enduring love for us all.

Psalm 145 overflows with the word *all*. "The LORD is good to all; he has compassion on all he has made" (V. 9). "The LORD is trustworthy in all he promises and faithful in all he does. The LORD upholds all who fall and lifts up all who are bowed down" (VV. 13–14). "The LORD watches over all who love him" (V. 20).

>
> TODAY'S READING
> **Psalm 145:8–21**
>
> **The LORD is good to all; he has compassion on all he has made.**
>
> Psalm 145:9

A dozen times in this psalm we are reminded that God's love is without limit and favoritism. And the New Testament reveals that the greatest expression of it is seen in Jesus Christ: "For God so loved the world that he gave his one and only Son, that whoever believes in him shall not perish but have eternal life" (JOHN 3:16).

Psalm 145 declares that "the LORD is near to all who call on him, to all who call on him in truth. He fulfills the desires of those who fear him; he hears their cry and saves them" (VV. 18–19).

God's love for us always endures, and it never fails! ✿

DAVID C. MCCASLAND

Father in heaven, we are awed by Your love for us that never changes, never fails, and never ends. We praise You for demonstrating Your limitless love for us through Jesus our Savior and Lord.

There is never any variation in God's enduring love for us all.

Healing Flood

've always loved a good thunderstorm. As kids, whenever a storm was truly incredible—with booming thunder and buckets of heavy rain pounding down—my siblings and I would make a mad dash around the outside of our house, slipping and sliding along the way. When it was time to go back inside, we were soaked to the bone.

It was an exhilarating taste—for just a few minutes—of being immersed in something so powerful we couldn't quite tell whether we were having fun or terrified.

This picture comes to mind when, as in Psalm 107, Scripture compares God's restoration to a barren wilderness transformed into "pools of water" (V. 35). Because the kind of storm that transforms a desert into an oasis isn't a gentle shower—it's a downpour, flooding every crack of parched ground with new life.

> TODAY'S READING
> **Psalm 107:1–16, 35–36**
>
> **He turned the desert into pools of water and the parched ground into flowing springs.** Psalm 107:35

And isn't that the kind of restoration we long for? When our stories feel like tales of aimless wandering because we are "hungry and thirsty"—*starving*—for healing that never seems to arrive (VV. 4–5), we need more than a bit of hope. And when deep-rooted patterns of sin leave us trapped "in utter darkness" (VV. 10–11), our hearts need more than a little change.

That's exactly the kind of transformation our God can bring (V. 20). It's never too late to bring our fears and shame to the One who's more than able to break our chains and flood our darkness with His light (VV. 13–14). 🌿

MONICA BRANDS

Father, help us turn to You with our burdens, trusting Your love and power to write a new story of healing and transformation.

God's power transforms.

To My Dear Friend

What the apostle John did for his friend Gaius in the first century is a dying art in the twenty-first century. John wrote him a letter.

One writer for the *New York Times,* Catherine Field, said, "Letter-writing is among our most ancient of arts. Think of letters and the mind falls on Paul of Tarsus," for example. And we can add the apostle John.

In his letter to Gaius, John included hopes for good health of body and soul, an encouraging word about Gaius's faithfulness, and a note about his love for the church. John also spoke of a problem in

TODAY'S READING
3 John

The elder, to my dear friend Gaius, whom I love in the truth. 3 John 1

the church, which he promised to address individually later. And he wrote of the value of doing good things for God's glory. All in all, it was an encouraging and challenging letter to his friend.

Digital communication may mean letter-writing on paper is fading away, but this shouldn't stop us from encouraging others. Paul wrote letters of encouragement on parchment; we can encourage others in a variety of ways. The key is not the *way* we encourage others, but that we take a moment to let others know we care for them in Jesus's name!

Think of the encouragement Gaius experienced when he opened John's letter. Could we similarly shine God's love on our friends with a thoughtful note or an uplifting call?

DAVE BRANON

Lord, help us know how to encourage others who need
a spiritual boost from us.

Encouraging words bring hope to the human spirit.

Radical Love

Just one week before her scheduled wedding date, Sarah's engagement ended. Despite her sadness and disappointment, she decided not to waste the food she had purchased for her wedding reception. She did, however, decide to change the celebration plans. She took down the gift table and revamped the guest list, inviting the residents of local homeless shelters to the feast.

> TODAY'S READING
> **Luke 14:7–14**
>
> **When you give a banquet, invite the poor, the crippled, the lame, the blind.** Luke 14:13

Jesus upheld this sort of no-strings-attached kindness when speaking to the Pharisees, saying, "When you give a banquet, invite the poor, the crippled, the lame, the blind, and you will be blessed" (LUKE 14:13–14). He noted that the blessing would come from God because these guests would not be able to repay the host. Jesus approved of helping people who couldn't supply charity donations, sparkling conversation, or social connections.

When we consider that Jesus spoke these words as He sat at a meal given by a Pharisee, His message seems provocative and radical. But real love is radical. I've heard it said that love is giving to meet the needs of others without expecting anything in return. This is how Jesus has loved each of us. He saw our inner poverty and responded by giving His life for us.

Knowing Christ personally is a journey into His infinite love. All of us are invited to explore "how wide and long and high and deep is the love of Christ" (EPHESIANS 3:18). 🌿

JENNIFER BENSON SCHULDT

Dear God, help me to explore the depths of Your love. I want to give to others what You have given to me.

How deep is the Father's love for us!

Hard Mysteries

s my friend and I went for a walk, we talked about our love for the Bible. She surprised me when she said, "Oh, but I don't like the Old Testament much. All of that hard stuff and vengeance—give me Jesus!"

We might resonate with her words when we read a book like Nahum, perhaps recoiling at a statement such as, "The LORD takes vengeance and is filled with wrath" (NAHUM 1:2). And yet the next verse fills us with hope: "The LORD is slow to anger but great in power" (V. 3).

When we dig more deeply into the subject of God's anger, we understand that when He exercises it, He's most often defending His people or His name. Because of His overflowing love, He seeks justice for wrongs committed and the redemption of those who have turned from Him. We see this not only in the Old Testament, as He calls His people back to Himself, but also in the New, when He sends His Son to be the sacrifice for our sins.

> TODAY'S READING
> **Nahum 1:1–7**
>
> **The LORD is slow to anger but great in power.** Nahum 1:3

We may not understand the mysteries of the character of God, but we can trust that He not only exercises justice but is also the source of all love. We need not fear Him, for He is "good, a refuge in times of trouble. He cares for those who trust in him" (V. 7).

AMY BOUCHER PYE

Father God, You are good. You are loving and You are merciful.
Help me to understand more fully some of the mysteries
of Your redeeming love today.

God's justice and mercy intersect at the cross.

The Joy of Giving

t was a dreary week. I had been feeling lethargic and listless, although I couldn't figure out why.

Near the end of the week, I found out that an aunt had kidney failure. I knew I had to visit her—but to be honest, I felt like postponing the visit. Still, I made my way to her place, where we had dinner, chatted, and prayed together. An hour later, I left her home feeling upbeat for the first time in days. Focusing on someone else rather than myself had somehow improved my mood.

Psychologists have found that the act of giving can produce satisfaction, which comes when the giver sees the recipient's gratitude. Some experts even believe that humans are wired to be generous!

> TODAY'S READING
> **1 Thess. 5:12–24**
>
> **Encourage the disheartened, help the weak, be patient with everyone.**
>
> 1 Thessalonians 5:14

Perhaps that's why Paul, when encouraging the church in Thessalonica to build up their faith community, urged them to "help the weak" (1 THESSALONIANS 5:14). Earlier, he had also cited Jesus's words, "It is more blessed to give than to receive" (ACTS 20:35). While this was said in the context of giving financially, it applies as well to the giving of time and effort.

When we give, we get an insight into how God feels. We understand why He's so delighted to give us His love, and we share in His joy and the satisfaction of blessing others. I think I'll be visiting my aunt again soon.   *LESLIE KOH*

Father, You have made me to give to others just as You have given to me.
Teach me to give so that I can truly reflect Your character
and be more like You today.

The giver is the greatest recipient.

When the Bottom Drops Out

During the 1997 Asian Financial Crisis, more people were looking for work than there were jobs available. I was one of those job seekers. After nine anxious months, I landed employment as a copywriter. But the company soon fell on bad times and I was jobless again.

TODAY'S READING
1 Kings 17:15–24

Ever been there? It seems like the worst is over when suddenly the bottom drops out on you. The widow at Zarephath could relate (1 KINGS 17:12). Due to a famine, she was preparing the last meal for herself and her son when the prophet Elijah requested a bite to eat. She reluctantly agreed and God provided a continuous supply of flour and oil (VV. 10–16).

Let us then approach God's throne of grace with confidence, so that we may receive mercy and find grace to help us in our time of need. Hebrews 4:16

But then her son fell ill. His health declined until he stopped breathing. The widow cried out, "What do you have against me, man of God? Did you come to remind me of my sin and kill my son?" (V. 18).

At times, we may want to respond like the widow—wondering if God is punishing us. We forget that bad things can happen in this fallen world.

Elijah took the concern to God, praying earnestly and honestly for the boy, and God raised him up! (VV. 20–22).

When the bottom drops out on us, may we—like Elijah—realize that the faithful One will not desert us! We can rest in God's purposes as we pray for understanding. ❧ 		*POH FANG CHIA*

God is good in both the good times and the bad.

Dedicated to Love

As a convert to Jesus Christ, Nabeel Qureshi has written books to help his readers understand the people in the religion he left. His tone is respectful, and Qureshi always displays a heart of love for his people.

Qureshi dedicated one of his books to his sister, who has not yet put her faith in Jesus. The dedication is brief, but powerful. "I am begging God for the day that we can worship him together," he wrote.

We get a sense of that kind of love as we read Paul's letter to the church in Rome. "My heart is filled with bitter sorrow and unending grief," he said, "for my people, my Jewish brothers and sisters. I would be willing to be forever cursed—cut off from Christ!—if that would save them" (ROMANS 9:2–3 NLT).

> **TODAY'S READING**
> **Romans 9:1–5**
>
> **My heart's desire and prayer to God for the Israelites is that they may be saved.** Romans 10:1

Paul loved the Jewish people so much that he would have chosen separation from God if only they would accept Christ. He understood that by rejecting Jesus, his people were rejecting the one true God. This motivated him to appeal to his readers to share the good news of Jesus with everyone (10:14–15).

Today, may we prayerfully dedicate ourselves to the love that aches for those close to us! 🌱

TIM GUSTAFSON

Father, we ask You to fill our hearts with Your love for others.
We hold _____ up to You and beg for them
to see the truth about Your Son Jesus.

*We must love those for whom Christ died
as well as those in whom Christ lives.*

A Good Daddy

When our son, Xavier, was younger, business trips often pulled my husband away from home. Though his father called often, there were rough nights when the calls alone didn't comfort Xavier. To help soothe our son when he felt he needed his dad, I'd pull out our photo albums as he prepared for bedtime. I'd point out the images that showed them spending time together and ask, "Do you remember this?"

Memory after memory encouraged our son, who often said, "I have a good daddy."

I understood Xavier's need to be reminded of his father's love when he couldn't see him. Whenever I'm going through tough or lonely times, I too long to know I'm loved, especially by my heavenly Father.

> **TODAY'S READING**
> **Psalm 63**
>
> **On my bed I remember you; I think of you through the watches of the night.** Psalm 63:6

David proclaimed his deep yearning for God as he hid from his enemies in the desert (PSALM 63:1). Remembering his personal encounters with God's limitless power and satisfying love led him to praise (VV. 2–5). Through his most difficult nights, David could still rejoice in his dependable Father's loving care (VV. 6–8).

During our dark times, when we feel as if God's not there for us, we need reminders of who God is and how He's demonstrated His love. Reflecting on our personal experiences with Him, as well as His actions recorded in Scripture, can affirm the countless ways our good Abba Father loves us. 🕊 *XOCHITL DIXON*

Lord, thanks for demonstrating Your endless love to Your people, in our lives and through the words You preserved in Scripture.

Remembering God's works, which reveal His character, reassures us of His love.

Our Daily Bread

A Hopeful Lament

To visit Clifton Heritage National Park in Nassau, Bahamas, is to revisit a tragic era in history. Where the land meets the water, stone steps lead up a cliff. Slaves brought to the Bahamas by ship in the eighteenth century would ascend these steps, often leaving family behind and entering a life of inhumane treatment. At the top, there is a memorial to those slaves. Cedar trees have been carved into the shapes of women looking out to sea toward the homeland and family members they've lost. Each sculpture is scarred with marks of the slave captain's whip.

TODAY'S READING
Lamentations 3:49–58

I called on your name, LORD, from the depths of the pit. Lamentations 3:55

These sculptures of women mourning what they've lost remind me of the importance of recognizing the injustices and broken systems in the world, and lamenting them. Lamenting does not mean that we are without hope; rather, it's a way of being honest with God. It should be a familiar posture for Christians; about forty percent of the Psalms are psalms of lament, and in the book of Lamentations, God's people cry out to Him after their city has been destroyed by invaders (3:55).

Lament is a legitimate response to the reality of suffering, and it engages God in the context of pain and trouble. Ultimately, lament is hopeful: when we lament what is not right, we call ourselves and others to be active in seeking change.

And that's why the sculpture garden in Nassau has been named "Genesis"—the place of lament is recognized as the place of new beginnings. 🌱

AMY PETERSON

We can trust God to bring something new out of our seasons of lament.

That Smiling Man

Going to the grocery store isn't something I particularly enjoy. It's just a mundane part of life—something that has to be done.

But there is one part of this task I've unexpectedly come to look forward to: checking out in Fred's lane. Fred, you see, turns checkout into show time. He's amazingly fast, always has a big smile, and even dances (and sometimes sings!) as he acrobatically flips (unbreakable) purchases into a plastic bag. Fred clearly enjoys a job that could be seen as one of the most tedious around. And for just a moment, his cheerful spirit brightens the lives of people in his checkout lane.

> **TODAY'S READING**
> **Colossians 3:18–23**
>
> **Whatever you do, work at it with all your heart, as working for the Lord, not for human masters.**
> Colossians 3:23

The way Fred does his job has won my respect and admiration. His cheerful attitude, desire to serve, and attention to detail all line up well with the apostle Paul's description of how we are to work in Colossians 3:23: "Whatever you do, work at it with all your heart, as working for the Lord."

When we're in relationship with Jesus, any job we have to do gives us an opportunity to reflect His presence in our lives. No task is too small . . . or too big! Tackling our responsibilities—whatever they may be—with joy, creativity, and excellence gives us an opportunity to influence those around us, no matter our job. 🌿

ADAM HOLZ

Lord, help me to tackle everything on my plate today with grace, enthusiasm, and joy, knowing that my attitude may affect others in ways I'm not even aware of.

The best way to do satisfying work is to do it for the Lord.

Our Daily Bread

Help from Heaven

SOS, the Morse code signal, was created in 1905 because sailors needed a way to indicate extreme distress. The signal gained notoriety in 1910 when used by the sinking ship *Steamship Kentucky,* saving all forty-six people aboard.

While SOS may be a more recent invention, the urgent cry for help is as old as humanity. We hear it often in the Old Testament story of Joshua, who faced opposition from fellow Israelites (JOSHUA 9:18) and challenging terrain (3:15–17) for more than fourteen years as the Israelites

TODAY'S READING
Joshua 10:6–15

Surely the LORD was fighting for Israel!
Joshua 10:14

slowly conquered and settled the land God had promised them. During this struggle "the LORD was with Joshua" (6:27).

In Joshua 10, the Israelites go to the aid of the Gibeonites, allies of Israel who were being attacked by five kings. Joshua knew that he needed the Lord's help to defeat so many powerful enemies (V. 12). God responded with a hailstorm, even stopping the sun in the middle of the sky to give Israel more time to defeat the enemy. Joshua 10:14 recounts, "Surely the LORD was fighting for Israel!"

If you are in the midst of a challenging situation, you can send out an SOS to God. Although help will look different than the assistance Joshua received, perhaps help comes through an unexpected job, an understanding doctor, or peace in the midst of grief. Be encouraged that these are ways He is responding to your call for help and fighting for you. 🌱   *LISA SAMRA*

Thank You, Father, for walking with me on this difficult journey and hearing me when I cry out to You.

As we cry out to God for help, we can trust that He will be with us.

The Gift of Time

I headed into the post office in a big hurry. I had a number of things on my to-do list, but as I entered I was frustrated to find a long line backing up all the way to the door. "Hurry up and wait," I muttered, glancing at my watch.

My hand was still on the door when an elderly stranger approached me. "I can't get this copier to work," he said, pointing to the machine behind us. "It took my money and I don't know what to do." Immediately I knew what God wanted *me* to do. I stepped out of line and was able to fix the problem in ten minutes.

TODAY'S READING
Luke 6:37–38

The man thanked me and then left. As I turned to get back in line, it was *gone*. I walked straight to the service counter.

My experience that day reminds me of Jesus's words: "Give, and it will be

A generous person will prosper; whoever refreshes others will be refreshed.

Proverbs 11:25

given to you. A good measure, pressed down, shaken together and running over, will be poured into your lap. For with the measure you use, it will be measured to you" (LUKE 6:38).

My wait seemed shorter because God interrupted my hurry. By turning my eyes to others' needs and helping me give of my time, He gave me a gift. It's a lesson I hope to remember, next time I look at my watch. 🌿 *JAMES BANKS*

Heavenly Father, all of the time I have is in Your hands, a gift from You. Please show me how to use it to bring glory and honor to You.

Sometimes our to-do list needs to wait.

Riding the Rapids

The rafting guide escorted our group to the river's edge and directed us all to put on life jackets and grab paddles. As we climbed into the boat, he assigned us seats to balance the boat's weight, providing stability when we encountered rapids. After highlighting the thrills the watery voyage ahead would hold for us, he detailed a series of directions we could expect to hear—and would need to follow—to effectively steer the boat through the white water. He assured us that even though there might be tense moments on the way, our journey would be both exciting and safe.

TODAY'S READING
Isaiah 43:1–7

When you pass through the rivers, they will not sweep over you.

Isaiah 43:2

Sometimes life feels like a white-water rafting trip, one that contains more rapids than we might like. God's promise to Israel, through the prophet Isaiah, can guide our feelings when we fear the worst is happening: "When you pass through the rivers, they will not sweep over you" (ISAIAH 43:2). The Israelites faced an overwhelming fear of rejection by God as they went into exile as a consequence of their sin. Yet instead, He affirms them and promises to be with them because He loves them (vv. 2, 4).

God won't abandon us in the rough waters. We can trust Him to guide us through the rapids—our deepest fears and most painful troubles—because He also loves us and promises to be with us. 🌾 *KIRSTEN HOLMBERG*

Thank You, Lord, for being my guide through troubled waters. Help me to trust You even when the journey is wild and scary.

God steers us through difficult times.

The Lord Speaks

We can find nearly every argument in the book of Job about why there is pain in the world, but the arguing never seems to help Job much. His is a crisis of relationship more than a crisis of doubt. *Can he trust God?* Job wants one thing above all else: an appearance by the one Person who can explain his miserable fate. He wants to meet God Himself, face to face.

> TODAY'S READING
> **Job 38:1–11**
>
> **Will the one who contends with the Almighty correct him?** Job 40:2

Eventually Job gets his wish. God shows up in person (SEE JOB 38:1). He times His entrance with perfect irony, just as Job's friend Elihu is expounding on why Job has no right to expect a visit from God.

No one—not Job, nor any of his friends—is prepared for what God has to say. Job has saved up a long list of questions, but it is God, not Job, who asks the questions. "Brace yourself like a man," He begins; "I will question you, and you shall answer me" (V. 3). Brushing aside thirty-five chapters' worth of debates on the problem of pain, God plunges into a majestic poem on the wonders of the natural world.

God's speech defines the vast difference between the God of all creation and one puny man like Job. His presence spectacularly answers Job's biggest question: Is anybody out there? Job can only respond, "Surely I spoke of things I did not understand, things too wonderful for me to know" (42:3). 🌱

PHILIP YANCEY

Lord, we have so many questions about life and its unfairness.
You have shown Yourself good to us. Help us to trust You
for what we cannot understand.

No calamity is beyond God's sovereignty.

Our Daily Bread

Heart Hunger

Riding along with my husband on some errands, I scrolled through emails on my phone and was surprised at an incoming advertisement for a local donut shop, a shop we had just passed on the right side of the street. Suddenly my stomach growled with hunger. I marveled at how technology allows vendors to woo us into their establishments.

As I clicked off my email, I mused over God's constant yearning to draw me closer. He always knows where I am and longs to influence my choices. I wondered, *Does my heart growl in desire for Him the way my stomach did over the idea of a donut?*

In John 6, following the miraculous feeding of the five thousand, the disciples eagerly ask Jesus to *always* give

> TODAY'S READING
> **John 6:32–40**
>
> **I am the bread of life. Whoever comes to me will never go hungry, and whoever believes in me will never be thirsty.**
>
> John 6:35

them "the bread that . . . gives life to the world" (vv. 33–34). Jesus responds in verse 35, "I am the bread of life. Whoever comes to me will never go hungry and whoever believes in me will never be thirsty." How amazing that a relationship with Jesus can provide constant nourishment in our everyday lives!

The donut shop's advertisement targeted my body's craving, but God's continuous knowledge of my heart's condition invites me to recognize my ongoing need for Him and to receive the sustenance only He can provide. ❧   *ELISA MORGAN*

Dear God, remind me of my need for Your daily bread of presence.

Jesus alone offers the only bread that truly satisfies.

Jesus Reached Out

Sometimes life gets busy—classes are hard, work is exhausting, the bathroom needs to be cleaned, and a coffee date is on the day's schedule. It gets to the point where I force myself to read the Bible for a few minutes a day and tell myself I'll spend more time with God next week. But it doesn't take long before I'm distracted, drowning in the day's tasks, and forget to ask God for help of any kind.

> **TODAY'S READING**
> Matthew 14:22–33
>
> **Immediately Jesus reached out his hand and caught him.** Matthew 14:31

When Peter was walking on water toward Jesus, he quickly became distracted by the wind and waves. Like me, he began to sink (MATTHEW 14:29-30). But as soon as Peter cried out, "immediately Jesus reached out his hand and caught him" (VV. 30-31).

I often feel as if I have to make it up to God after being so busy and distracted that I lose sight of Him. But that's not how God works. As soon as we turn to Him for help, Jesus reaches out without hesitation.

When we're unsettled by the chaos of life, it's easy to forget that God is standing in the middle of the storm with us. Jesus asked Peter, "Why did you doubt?" (V. 31). No matter what we're going through, He is there. He is here. Next to us at that moment, in this moment, ready to reach out and rescue us.

JULIE SCHWAB

Lord, help me to turn to You in the midst of my busyness and life's distractions. Thank You for always being here, ready to catch me.

God is waiting for us to turn to Him so He can reach out and help.

Our Daily Bread

Sky Garder

While in London, a friend arranged for my wife Marlene and me to visit the Sky Garden. On the top floor of a thirty-five-story building in London's business district, the Sky Garden is a glass-encased platform filled with plants, trees, and flowers. But the sky part captured our attention. We gazed down from a height of over 500 feet, admiring St. Paul's Cathedral, the Tower of London, and more. Our views of the capital city were breathtaking—providing a helpful lesson on perspective.

TODAY'S READING
Psalm 102:1–2, 18–28

He looked down from His holy height. Psalm 102:19 NASB

Our God has a perfect perspective of everything we experience. The psalmist wrote, "For He looked down from His holy height; from heaven the Lord gazed upon the earth, to hear the groaning of the prisoner, to set free those who were doomed to death" (PSALM 102:19–20 NASB).

Like the hurting people pictured in Psalm 102, we are often locked into the present with its struggles, "groaning" with despair. But God sees our lives from beginning to end. Our Lord is never caught off guard by the things that can blindside us. As the psalmist anticipated, His perfect perspective will lead to an ultimate rescue that sets free even those "doomed to death" (vv. 20, 27–28).

In difficult moments, remember: We may not know what is coming next, but our Lord does. We can trust Him with every moment that stretches before us. 🌱   *BILL CROWDER*

Focusing on Christ puts everything else into perspective.

Marvelous Maker

As an amateur photographer, I enjoy capturing glimpses of God's creativity with my camera. I see His fingerprints on each delicate flower petal, each vibrant sunrise and sunset, and each cloud-painted and star-speckled sky canvas.

My camera's powerful zoom option allows me to take photos of the Lord's creatures too. I've snapped shots of a chattering squirrel in a cherry blossom tree, a colorful butterfly flitting from bloom to bloom, and sea turtles sunning on a rocky, black beach. Each one-of-a-kind image prompted me to worship my marvelous Maker.

> **TODAY'S READING**
> **Psalm 104:24–34**
>
> **How many are your works, LORD! In wisdom you made them all; the earth is full of your creatures.** Psalm 104:24

I'm not the first of God's people to praise Him while admiring His unique creations. The writer of Psalm 104 sings of the Lord's many works of art in nature (V. 24). He regards "the sea, vast and spacious, teeming with creatures beyond number" (V. 25) and rejoices in God for providing constant and complete care for His masterpieces (VV. 27–31). Considering the majesty of the God-given life around him, the psalmist bursts with worshipful gratitude: "I will sing to the LORD all my life; I will sing praise to my God as long as I live" (V. 33).

While reflecting on the Lord's magnificent and immense creation, we can look closely at His intentional creativity and attention to detail. And like the psalmist, we can sing to our Creator with thankful praise for how powerful, majestic, and loving He is and always will be. Hallelujah! 🌿   *XOCHITL DIXON*

God's works are marvelous, and so is He.

In Progress or Completed?

t's satisfying to finish a job. Each month, for instance, one of my job responsibilities gets moved from one category to another, from "In Progress" to "Completed." I *love* clicking that "Completed" button. But last month when I clicked it, I thought, *If only I could overcome rough spots in my faith so easily! It can seem like the Christian life is always in progress, never completed.*

Then I remembered Hebrews 10:14. It describes how Christ's sacrifice redeems us totally. So in one important sense, that "completed button" *has* been pressed for us. Jesus's death did for us what we couldn't do for ourselves: He made us acceptable in God's eyes when we place our faith in Him. It is finished, as Jesus Himself said (JOHN 19:30). Paradoxically, even though His sacrifice is complete and total, we spend the rest of our lives living into that spiritual reality—"being made holy," as Hebrews' author writes.

> **TODAY'S READING**
> **Hebrews 10:5–14**
>
> **For by one sacrifice he has made perfect forever those who are being made holy.**
>
> Hebrews 10:14

The fact that Jesus has finished something that's still being worked out in our lives is hard to understand. When I'm struggling spiritually, it's encouraging to remember that Jesus's sacrifice for me—and for you—is *complete* . . . even if our living it out in this life is still a work in *progress*. Nothing can stop His intended end from being achieved eventually: being transformed into His likeness (SEE 2 CORINTHIANS 3:18). 🌿 *ADAM HOLZ*

Jesus, thank You for giving Your life for us. Help us trust You as we grow into followers whose lives look more and more like Yours, knowing that You are the one who makes us complete.

God is at work to make us who He intends us to be.

A Prayer to Point Us Home

One of the first prayers I learned as a little boy was "Now I lay me down to sleep, I pray the Lord my soul to keep..." It was a prayer I learned from my parents, and I taught it to my son and daughter when they were little. As a child, I found great comfort in placing myself in God's hands with those words before I fell asleep.

TODAY'S READING
Luke 23:44–48

There's a similar prayer neatly tucked away in the "prayer book" of the Bible, the Psalms. Some biblical scholars suggest that the phrase "Into your hands I commit my spirit" (PSALM 31:5) was a "bedtime" prayer taught to children in Jesus's day.

Yet to all who did receive him, to those who believed in his name, he gave the right to become children of God.

John 1:12

You may recognize that prayer as Jesus's final cry from the cross. But Jesus added one more word to it: *Father* (LUKE 23:46). By praying that word in the moments before His death, Jesus demonstrated His intimate relationship with the Father and pointed believers toward their home with Him (JOHN 14:3).

Jesus died on the cross so we could live in the wonder of a relationship with God as our heavenly Father. How comforting it is to know that because of Jesus's sacrificial love for us, we can rest in God's care as His children! We can close our eyes without fear because our Father watches over us and has promised to wake us up to life with Him (1 THESSALONIANS 4:14). 🌾

JAMES BANKS

Lord Jesus, I receive the gift of forgiveness You offer me through the cross. Help me to turn from my sins and follow You, all the way home.

A bright new morning awaits us in Jesus.

God's Care for Us

My young grandsons enjoy dressing themselves. Sometimes they pull their shirts on backwards and often the younger one puts his shoes on the wrong feet. I usually don't have the heart to tell them; besides, I find their innocence endearing.

I love seeing the world through their eyes. To them, everything is an adventure, whether walking the length of a fallen tree, spying a turtle sunning itself on a log, or excitedly watching a fire truck roar by. But I know that even my little grandsons are not truly innocent. They can make up a dozen excuses about why they can't stay in their beds

TODAY'S READING
Genesis 3:1–13

The LORD God made garments of skin for Adam and his wife and clothed them.

Genesis 3:21

at night and are quick to yank a wanted toy from the other. Yet I love them dearly.

I picture Adam and Eve, God's first people, as being in some ways like my grandchildren. Everything they saw in the garden must have been a marvel as they walked with God. But one day they willfully disobeyed. They ate of the one tree they were forbidden to eat (GENESIS 2:15–17; 3:6). And that disobedience immediately led to lies and blame-shifting (3:8–13).

Still, God loved and cared for them. He sacrificed animals in order to clothe them (V. 21)—and later He provided a way of salvation for all sinners through the sacrifice of His Son (JOHN 3:16). He loves us that much! 🌿   *ALYSON KIEDA*

Dear Lord, thank You for loving us, despite our sin, and for making a way
for us to be with You forever!

Jesus loves us so much He sacrificed Himself for our sins.

An Enduring Happiness

Often we hear that happiness comes from doing things our own way. That, however, is not true. That philosophy leads only to emptiness, anxiety, and heartache.

Poet W. H. Auden observed people as they attempted to find an escape in pleasures. He wrote of such people: "Lost in a haunted wood, / Children afraid of the night / Who have never been happy or good."

The psalmist David sings of the remedy for our fears and unhappiness. "I sought the LORD, and he answered me; he delivered me from all my fears" (PSALM 34:4). Happiness is doing things God's way, a fact that can be verified every day. "Those who look to him are radiant," writes David (V. 5). Just try it and you'll see. That's what he means when he says, "Taste and see that the LORD is good" (V. 8).

> **TODAY'S READING**
> **Psalm 34:1–14**
>
> **Whoever of you loves life and desires to see many good days.... Turn from evil and do good.**
>
> Psalm 34:12,14

We say, "Seeing is believing." That's how we know things in this world. Show me proof and I'll believe it. God puts it the other way around. Believing is seeing. "Taste and *then* you will see."

Take the Lord at His word. Do the very next thing He is asking you to do and you will see. He will give you grace to do the right thing and more: He will give you Himself—the only source of goodness—and with it, enduring happiness. 🌱 *DAVID H. ROPER*

Lord, sometimes we must simply pray: "I believe. Help my unbelief."
Help us trust You by doing what You have given us to do today.

Happiness is doing the right thing.

We Would See Jesus

As I looked down at the pulpit where I was sharing prayers at a funeral, I glimpsed a brass plaque bearing words from John 12:21: "Sir, we would see Jesus" (KJV). Yes, I thought, how fitting to consider how we saw Jesus in the woman we were celebrating with tears and smiles. Although she faced challenges and disappointments in her life, she never gave up her faith in Christ. And because God's Spirit lived in her, we could see Jesus.

> **TODAY'S READING**
> John 12:20–26
>
> **They came to Philip…with a request. "Sir," they said, "we would like to see Jesus."**
> John 12:21

John's gospel recounts how after Jesus rode into Jerusalem (SEE JOHN 12:12–16), some Greeks approached Philip, one of the disciples, asking, "Sir,… we would like to see Jesus" (V. 21). They were probably curious about Jesus's healings and miracles, but as they weren't Jewish, they weren't allowed into the inner courts of the temple. When their request was passed along to Jesus, He announced that His hour had come to be glorified (V. 23). And by that, He meant that He would die for the sins of many. He would fulfill His mission to reach not only the Jews but the Gentiles (the "Greeks" in verse 20), and now they would see Jesus.

After Jesus died, He sent the Holy Spirit to dwell in His followers (14:16–17). Thus as we love and serve Jesus, we see Him active in our lives. And, amazingly, those around us too can see Jesus! ❀   *AMY BOUCHER PYE*

Lord Jesus Christ, I am humbled and amazed that You would come and live in me. Help me to share this amazing gift with those I meet today.

We can see Jesus in the lives of His followers.

Generous Givers

After reviewing all God had already done throughout our church's history, leaders presented the congregation with a proposal for a new gym to help us better serve our community. The leadership team announced they'd be the first to sign pledge notes to fund the construction. I initially prayed with a heart soured by self-ishness, not wanting to offer more money than we had already committed to give. Still, my husband and I agreed to pray for the ongoing project. While considering all God continued providing for us, we eventually decided on a monthly offering. The combined gifts of our church family paid for the entire building.

> **TODAY'S READING**
> **1 Chronicles 29:1–14**
>
> **Everything comes from you, and we have given you only what comes from your hand.**
>
> 1 Chronicles 29:14

Grateful for the many ways God's used that gym for community events since we celebrated opening its doors for ministry, I'm reminded of another generous giver—King David. Though the Lord didn't choose him to build His temple, David invested all his resources to the project (1 CHRONICLES 29:1–5). The leaders under him and the people they served gave generously too (VV. 6–9). The king acknowledged all they'd contributed had first been given to them by God—the Creator, Sustainer, and Owner of everything (VV. 10–16).

When we recognize God owns it all, we can commit to grateful, generous, and faithful giving for the benefit of others. And we can trust the Lord will provide—and may even use the generosity of others to help us when we're in need. 🌿

XOCHITL DIXON

Lord, please help us remember You own it all as we commit to giving You our all, willingly and selflessly.
God gives first, and He always outgives His most generous givers.

Unfrozen

At a roundtable discussion about reconciliation, one participant wisely said, "Don't freeze people in time." He observed how we tend to remember mistakes people make and never grant them the opportunity to change.

There are so many moments in Peter's life when God could have "frozen" him in time. But He never did. Peter—the impulsive disciple—"corrected" Jesus, earning a sharp rebuke from the Lord (MATTHEW 16:21–23). He famously denied Christ (JOHN 18:15–27), only to be restored later (21:15–19). And he once contributed to racial divisions within the church.

TODAY'S READING
Galatians 2:11–16

When Cephas came to Antioch, I opposed him to his face. Galatians 2:11

The issue arose when Peter (also called Cephas) had separated himself from the Gentiles (GALATIANS 2:11–12). Only recently he associated freely with them. But some Jews arrived who insisted that circumcision was required for believers in Christ, so Peter began avoiding the uncircumcised Gentiles. This marked a dangerous return to the law of Moses. Paul called Peter's behavior "hypocrisy" (V. 13). Because of Paul's bold confrontation, the issue was resolved. Peter went on to serve God in the beautiful spirit of unity He intends for us.

No one needs to remain frozen in their worst moments. In God's grace we can embrace each other, learn from each other, confront each other when it's necessary, and grow together in His love. ❤   *TIM GUSTAFSON*

Lord, draw us close to You today, so that we may also be closer to each other. Protect Your church's unity. Give us understanding where there is distrust. Heal us where we are divided.

If we confront someone, we should have one goal in mind: restoration, not embarrassment. CHUCK SWINDOLL

Serve Continually

When educational psychologist Benjamin Bloom, researching how to develop talent in young people, examined the childhoods of 120 elite performers—athletes, artists, scholars—he found that all of them had one thing in common: they had practiced intensively for long periods of time.

Bloom's research suggests that growing in any area of our lives requires discipline. In our walk with God, too, cultivating the spiritual discipline of regularly spending time with Him is one way we can grow in our trust in Him.

> TODAY'S READING
> **Daniel 6:10–22**
>
> **Has your God, whom you serve continually, been able to rescue you?** Daniel 6:20

Daniel is a good example of someone who prioritized a disciplined walk with God. As a young person, Daniel started making careful and wise decisions (1:8). He also was committed to praying regularly, "giving thanks to God" (6:10). His frequent seeking of God resulted in a life in which his faith was easily recognized by those around him. In fact, King Darius described Daniel as a "servant of the living God" (v. 20) and twice described him as a person who served God "continually" (vv. 16, 20).

Like Daniel, we desperately need God. How good to know that God works in us so that we long to spend time with Him! (PHILIPPIANS 2:13). So let us come every day before God, trusting that our time with Him will result in a love that will overflow more and more and in a growing knowledge and understanding of our Savior (1:9–11). 🌾

KEILA OCHOA

Father, I thank You for the privilege of serving You. Help me to spend regular time with You in order to grow in my knowledge of You.

Time with God transforms us.

Learning to Trust

When I was a teenager I sometimes challenged my mother when she tried to encourage me to have faith. "Trust God. He will take care of you," she would tell me. "It's not that simple, Mom!" I would bark back. "God helps those who help themselves!"

But those words, "God helps those who help themselves" are nowhere to be found in Scripture. Instead, God's Word teaches us to depend on Him for our daily needs. Jesus tells us, "Look at the birds of the air; they do not sow or reap or store away in barns, and yet your heavenly Father feeds them. Are you not much more valuable than they? Can any one of you by worrying add a single hour to your life?" (MATTHEW 6:26–27).

> TODAY'S READING
> **Matthew 6:25–34**
>
> **Every good and perfect gift is from above, coming down from the Father of the heavenly lights, who does not change like shifting shadows.** James 1:17

Everything we enjoy—even the strength to earn a living and "help ourselves"—are gifts from a heavenly Father who loves us and values us beyond our ability to fathom.

As Mom neared the end of her life, Alzheimer's disease robbed her of her creative mind and memories, but her trust in God remained. She lived in our home for a season, where I was given a "front-row seat" to observe God's provision for her needs in unexpected ways—ways that helped me see she had been right all along. Instead of worrying, she entrusted herself to the One who promised to take care of her. And He showed Himself faithful. 🖉

JAMES BANKS

Loving Lord, please help me to trust You to take care of me today, tomorrow, and forever!

Don't worry about tomorrow—God is already there.

You Love Me?

As a teenager, I went through the typical season of rebellion against my mother's authority. My father died before I entered adolescence, so my mom had to navigate these turbulent parenting waters without his help.

I recall thinking that Mom didn't want me to ever have any fun—and maybe didn't even love me—because she frequently said no. I see now that she said no to activities that weren't good for me precisely *because* she loves me.

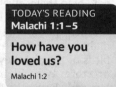

TODAY'S READING
Malachi 1:1–5

How have you loved us?

Malachi 1:2

The Israelites questioned how much God loved them because of their time in captivity in Babylon. But that captivity was God's correction for their continued rebellion against Him. So now, God sent the prophet Malachi to them. His opening words from the Lord were, "I have loved you" (MALACHI 1:2). Israel replied skeptically, inquiring as to how God has loved them, as if to say, "Really?" But God, through Malachi, reminded them of the way He had demonstrated that love: He had chosen them over the Edomites.

We all go through difficult seasons in life. We may be tempted to question God's love for us during those times. Let's recall the many ways He's shown us His unfailing love. When we stop to consider His goodness, we find that He is indeed a loving Father. 🌱

KIRSTEN HOLMBERG

Lord, You have shown tender care for me over the course of my life.
You've been present with me in difficult seasons.
Help me to always remember Your love.

Our heavenly Father corrects us and comforts us.

The House on the Rock

After living in their house for several years, my friends realized that their living room was sinking—cracks appeared on the walls and a window would no longer open. They learned that this room had been added without a foundation. Rectifying the shoddy workmanship would mean months of work as builders laid a new foundation.

They had the work done, and when I visited them afterwards, I couldn't see much difference (although the cracks were gone and now the window opened). But I understood that a solid foundation matters.

This is true in our lives as well.

Jesus shared a parable about wise and foolish builders to illustrate the folly of not listening to Him (LUKE 6:46–49). Those who hear and obey His words are like the person who builds a house on a firm

TODAY'S READING
Luke 6:46–49

When a flood came, the torrent struck that house but could not shake it, because it was well built. Luke 6:48

foundation, unlike those who hear but ignore His words. Jesus assured His listeners that when the storms come, their house would stand. Their faith would not be shaken.

We can find peace knowing that as we listen to and obey Jesus, He forms a strong foundation for our lives. We can strengthen our love for Him through reading the Bible, praying, and learning from other Christians. Then when we face the torrents of rain lashing against us—whether betrayal, pain, or disappointment—we can trust that our foundation is solid. Our Savior will provide the support we need. ✿   *AMY BOUCHER PYE*

Lord God, I want to build my house on a rock. Help me to know that
my solid foundation rests in You, with Your Word giving me
wisdom and strength.

Hearing and obeying Jesus gives our lives a strong foundation.

Call for Help

After five deaths and fifty-one injuries in elevator accidents in 2016, New York City launched an ad campaign to educate people on how to stay calm and be safe. The worst cases were people who tried to save themselves when something went wrong. The best plan of action, authorities say, is simply, "Ring, relax, and wait." New York building authorities made a commitment to respond promptly to protect people from injury and extract them from their predicament.

In the book of Acts, Peter preached a sermon that addressed the error of trying to save ourselves. Luke, who wrote the book, records some remarkable events in which believers in Christ were speaking in languages they did not know (ACTS 2:1–12). Peter got up to explain to his Jewish brothers and sisters that what they were witnessing was the fulfillment of an ancient prophecy (JOEL 2:28–32)—the outpouring of the Spirit and a day of salvation. The blessing of the Holy Spirit was now visibly seen in those who called on Jesus for rescue from sin and its effects. Then Peter told them how this salvation is available for anyone (V. 21). Our access to God comes not through keeping the Law but through trusting Jesus as Lord and Messiah.

If we are trapped in sin, we cannot save ourselves. Our only hope for being rescued is acknowledging and trusting Jesus as Lord and Messiah. 🌢

MARVIN WILLIAMS

> **TODAY'S READING**
> **Acts 2:14–21**
>
> **Everyone who calls on the name of the Lord will be saved.**
>
> Acts 2:21

Have you called on Jesus to rescue you from your sin?

Rescue comes to those who call on Jesus for help.

Officer Miglio's Heart

Back at the police station, Officer Miglio slumped wearily against a wall. A domestic violence call had just consumed half his shift. Its aftermath left a boyfriend in custody, a young daughter in the emergency room, and a shaken mother wondering how it had come to this. This call would wear on the young officer for a long time.

> **TODAY'S READING**
> **Matthew 18:1–10**
>
> **See that you do not despise one of these little ones. For I tell you that their angels in heaven always see the face of my Father in heaven.**
>
> Matthew 18:10

"Nothing you could do, Vic," said his sergeant sympathetically. But the words rang hollow. Some police officers seem able to leave their work at work. Not Vic Miglio. Not the tough cases like this one.

Officer Miglio's heart reflects the compassion of Jesus. Christ's disciples had just come to Him with a question: "Who, then, is the greatest in the kingdom of heaven?" (MATTHEW 18:1). Calling a small child to Him, He told His disciples, "Unless you change and become like little children, you will never enter the kingdom of heaven" (V. 3). Then He gave a stern warning to anyone who would harm a child (V. 6). In fact, children are so special to Him that Jesus told us, "Their angels in heaven always see the face of my Father in heaven" (V. 10).

How comforting, then, that Jesus's love for children is connected to His love for us all! That's why He invites us, through childlike faith, to become His sons and daughters. *TIM GUSTAFSON*

Remind us always, Lord, to love children as You love them, even as we
come to You with the trusting faith of a small child.

Our earthly families may fail us, but our heavenly Father never will.

Strength for Your Journey

Hinds Feet on High Places, a classic allegory of the Christian life, is based on Habakkuk 3:19. The story follows the character Much-Afraid as she goes on a journey with the Shepherd. But Much-Afraid is scared so she asks the Shepherd to carry her.

The Shepherd kindly replies, "I could carry you all the way up to the High Places myself, instead of leaving you to climb there. But if I did, you would never be able to develop hinds' feet, and become my companion and go where I go."

Much-Afraid echoes the questions of the Old Testament prophet Habakkuk (and if I'm honest, my questions too): "Why must I experience suffering?" "Why is my journey difficult?"

> TODAY'S READING
> **Habakkuk 3:16–19**
>
> **The Sovereign LORD is my strength; he makes my feet like the feet of a deer, he enables me to tread on the heights.** Habakkuk 3:19

Habakkuk lived in Judah in the late seventh century BC before the Israelites were taken into exile. The prophet found himself in a society that overlooked social injustice and was immobilized by the fear of imminent invasion by the Babylonians (HABAKKUK 1:2–11). He asked the Lord to intervene and remove suffering (1:13). God replied that He would act justly but in His timing (2:3).

In faith, Habakkuk chose to trust the Lord. Even if the suffering did not end, the prophet believed that God would continue to be his strength.

We too can take comfort that the Lord is our strength to help us endure suffering and will also use the most challenging of life's journeys to deepen our fellowship with Christ. 🕊 *LISA SAMRA*

God, sometimes my suffering seems too much to bear. Help me to trust You and continue to walk with You on this journey.

We can trust the Lord to be our strength in tough times.

Finding the Way Home

Sometimes this journey through life can be so difficult that we're simply overwhelmed, and it seems there's no end to the darkness. During such a time in our own family's life, my wife emerged one morning from her quiet time with a new lesson learned. "I think God wants us *not to forget in the light what we're learning in this darkness.*"

Paul writes this same thought to the Corinthians (2 CORINTHIANS 1), after describing the terrible difficulties he and his team endured in Asia. Paul wants the Corinthians to understand how God can redeem even our darkest moments. We're comforted, he says, so we may learn how to comfort others (V. 4). Paul and his team were learning things from God during their trials that they could use to comfort and advise the Corinthians when they faced similar difficulties. And God does that for us as well, if we're willing to listen. He will redeem our trials by teaching us how to use what we've learned in them to minister to others.

> TODAY'S READING
> **2 Corinthians 1:3–11**
>
> **[God] comforts us in all our troubles, so that we can comfort those in any trouble with the comfort we ourselves receive from God.**
>
> 2 Corinthians 1:4

Are you in the darkness now? Be encouraged by Paul's words and experience. Trust that God is right now directing your steps and that He's also stamping His truths on your heart so you can share them with others who are in similar circumstances. You've been there before, and you know the way home.

RANDY KILGORE

Father, help those who are hurting today so they may see and know Your loving presence in their darkest hours.

Never forget in the light what you learn in the darkness.

Beyond the Stars

n 2011, the National Aeronautics and Space Administration celebrated thirty years of space research. In those three decades, shuttles carried more than 355 people into space and helped construct the International Space Station. After retiring five shuttles, NASA has now shifted its focus to deep-space exploration.

TODAY'S READING
Psalm 8:1–9

You have set your glory in the heavens. Psalm 8:1

The human race has invested massive amounts of time and money, with some astronauts even sacrificing their lives, to study the immensity of the universe. Yet the evidence of God's majesty stretches far beyond what we can measure.

When we consider the Sculptor and Sustainer of the universe who knows each star by name (ISAIAH 40:26), we can understand why the psalmist David praises His greatness (PSALM 8:1). The Lord's fingerprints are on "the moon and the stars, which [He] set in place" (V. 3). The Maker of the heavens and the earth reigns above all, yet He remains near all His beloved children, caring for each intimately and personally (V. 4). In love, God gives us great power, responsibility, and the privilege to care for and explore the world He's entrusted to us (VV. 5–8).

As we study our star-spattered night skies, our Creator invites us to seek Him with passion and persistence. He hears every prayer and song of praise flowing from our lips. 🌱

XOCHITL DIXON

Loving Creator of the universe, thank You for being mindful of us.

***The greatness of God is evident in His awesome vastness
and intimate nearness.***

Building Bridges

I n our neighborhood, high concrete walls surround our homes. Many of these walls are enhanced with electric barbed wires lining the top. The purpose? To ward off robbers.

Frequent power outages are also a problem in our community. These outages render the front gate-bell useless. Because of the wall, a visitor may be kept out in the scorching sun or torrential rain during these outages. Yet even when the gate-bell works, to admit the visitor might depend on who they are. Our fence-walls serve a good purpose, but they can become walls of discrimination—even when the visitor is obviously not an intruder.

> TODAY'S READING
> John 4:7–14, 39–42
>
> **There is neither Jew nor Gentile, neither slave nor free, nor is there male and female, for you are all one in Christ Jesus.**
> Galatians 3:28

The Samaritan woman whom Jesus met at the well had a similar difficulty with discrimination. The Jews had nothing to do with Samaritans. When Jesus asked her for a drink, she said, "You are a Jew and I am a Samaritan woman. How can you ask me for a drink?" (JOHN 4:9). As she began to open up to Jesus, she had a life-changing experience that positively affected her and her neighbors (VV. 39–42). Jesus became the bridge that broke the wall of hostility and favoritism.

The lure to discriminate is real, and we need to identify it in our lives. As Jesus showed us, we can reach out to all people regardless of nationality, social status, or reputation. He came to build bridges.  *LAWRENCE DARMANI*

Lord, thank You for teaching me not to discriminate among people. Help me to see people through Your eyes so that I may honor You.

Jesus breaks down the walls of discrimination.

Muscling Through

Competitive bodybuilders put themselves through a rigorous training cycle. During the initial months, they emphasize gaining size and strength. As the competition nears, the focus shifts to losing any fat that hides the muscle. In the final days before the competition, they consume less water than normal so their muscle tissue is easily visible. Because of the reduced consumption of nourishment, the competitors are actually at their weakest on the day of competition, despite appearing strong.

> **TODAY'S READING**
> 2 Chron. 20:2–3,14–22
>
> **Alarmed, Jehoshaphat resolved to inquire of the LORD, and he proclaimed a fast for all Judah.**
>
> 2 Chronicles 20:3

In 2 Chronicles 20, we read of the opposite reality: acknowledging weakness in order to experience God's strength. "A vast army is coming against you," people told King Jehoshaphat. So "he proclaimed a fast for all Judah" (V. 3), depriving himself and all his people of nourishment. Then they asked God for help. When he finally mustered his military, Jehoshaphat placed singers who praised God at the front of his army (V. 21). As they began to sing, the Lord "set ambushes against the men . . . who were invading Judah, and they were defeated" (V. 22).

Jehoshaphat's decision demonstrated deep faith in God. He purposefully chose not to depend on his own human and military prowess but instead to lean on God. Rather than trying to muscle our way through the trials we face, may we turn to Him and allow Him to be our strength. ❧   *KIRSTEN HOLMBERG*

We must recognize our weakness to experience God's strength.

Unchanging Love

When I was in high school I played on the varsity tennis team. I spent many hours of my teenage years trying to improve my skills on four concrete courts located just two blocks from my home.

The last time I visited that city, one of the first things I did was drive to the tennis courts, hoping to watch others play and reminisce for a moment. But the old courts, so familiar to my memory, were nowhere to be seen. In their place was a vacant field, inhabited only by an occasional weed waving silently in the breeze.

> **TODAY'S READING**
> **Psalm 103:13–22**
>
> **The world and its desires pass away, but whoever does the will of God lives forever.**
> 1 John 2:17

That afternoon remains in my mind as a stark reminder of the brevity of life. One of the places where I expended some of my best youthful strength no longer existed! Reflecting on that experience later brought me to this truth, expressed by an aging King David: "The life of mortals is like grass, they flourish like a flower of the field; the wind blows over it and it is gone, and its place remembers it no more. But from everlasting to everlasting the LORD's love is with those who fear him" (PSALM 103:15–17).

We grow older and the world around us may change, but God's love doesn't. He can always be trusted to take care of those who turn to Him. 🌿 *JAMES BANKS*

Faithful Father, thank You for Your love that never changes!
Help me to love You by serving You faithfully today.

In our changing world, we can always depend on our unchanging God.

Being Real with God

bow my head, close my eyes, lace my fingers together and begin to pray. *"Dear Lord, I'm coming to you today as your child. I recognize your power and goodness. . ."* Suddenly, my eyes snap open. I remember that my son hasn't finished his history project, which is due the next day. I recall that he has an after-school basketball game, and I imagine him awake until midnight finishing his schoolwork. This leads me to worry that his fatigue will put him at risk for the flu!

TODAY'S READING
1 Peter 5:6–10

Cast all your anxiety on him because he cares for you. 1 Peter 5:7

C. S. Lewis wrote about distractions during prayer in his book *The Screwtape Letters.* He noted that when our minds wander, we tend to use willpower to steer ourselves back to our original prayer. Lewis concluded, though, that it was better to accept "the distraction as [our] present problem and [lay] that before [God] and make it the main theme of [our] prayers."

A persistent worry or even a sinful thought that disrupts a prayer may become the centerpiece of our discussion with God. God wants us to be real as we talk with Him and open up about our deepest concerns, fears, and struggles. He is not surprised by anything we mention. His interest in us is like the attention we would receive from a close friend. That's why we're encouraged to give all of our worries and cares to God—because He cares for us (1 PETER 5:7). 🌱   *JENNIFER BENSON SCHULDT*

Dear God, You know what's on my mind today. Help me to experience
the peace that comes from sharing my concerns with You.

Distractions don't have to derail our prayers.

They Smelled Like Christ

Hot and dusty, Bob dismounted from the bus he had ridden to a city far from home. He was tired from a long day of travel and grateful that he would be able to have dinner with friends of friends who lived in the area. They welcomed him in, and he immediately felt a sense of peace. He felt at home, comfortable, safe, and valued.

Later, wondering why he had felt such peace in an unfamiliar place, Bob found an answer in 2 Corinthians. The apostle Paul describes people who follow God as having the "pleasing aroma of Christ." "That's exactly it!" Bob said to himself. His hosts had "smelled like" Christ.

TODAY'S READING
2 Corinthians 2:14–17

For we are to God the pleasing aroma of Christ among those who are being saved.

2 Corinthians 2:15

When Paul says that God leads His people in Christ's "triumphal procession" spreading the fragrance of His truth, he's referring to a practice in the ancient world. Victorious armies would burn incense as they marched through the streets. For their supporters, the smell brought joy. In the same way, Paul says the people of God carry a pleasing fragrance to those who believe. It isn't something we create on our own but something God gives as He leads us in spreading the knowledge of Him.

Bob is my dad, and that trip to a faraway town took place more than forty years ago, but he's never forgotten it. He's still telling the story of the people who smelled like Christ. 🌱

AMY PETERSON

Heavenly Father, thank You for leading Your people in triumph and spreading the fragrance of Your truth through us.

Who smells like Christ to you?

How to Stand Firm

I t was a cold, icy winter's day, and my mind was on getting from my warm vehicle to a warm building. The next thing I knew I was on the ground, my knees turned inward and my lower legs turned outward. Nothing was broken, but I was in pain. The pain would get worse as time went by and it would be weeks before I was whole again.

Who among us hasn't taken a spill of some sort? Wouldn't it be nice to have something or someone to keep us on our feet all the time? While there are no guarantees of surefootedness in the physical sense, there is One who stands

TODAY'S READING
Jude 1:24–25

To him who is able to keep you from stumbling. Jude 1:24

ready to assist us in our quest to honor Christ in this life and prepare us to stand joyfully before Him in the next.

Every day we face temptations (and even false teachings) that seek to divert us, confuse us, and entangle us. Yet, it's not ultimately through our own efforts that we remain on our feet as we walk in this world. How assuring to know that when we hold our peace when tempted to speak angrily, to opt for honesty over deceit, to choose love over hate, or to select truth over error—we experience God's power to keep us standing (JUDE 1:24). And when we appear approved before God when Christ returns, the praise that we offer now for His sustaining grace will echo throughout eternity (V. 25). 🌱   *ARTHUR JACKSON*

Father, thank You for Your constant care for our souls.

Dressed in His righteousness alone, faultless to stand before the throne.
EDWARD MOTE

He Knows Our Names

During a visit to the National September 11 Memorial in New York City, I quickly photographed one of the twin reflecting pools. Around these two pools, the names of the nearly 3,000 people who died in the World Trade Center attacks are etched into bronze panels. Later, while looking more closely at the photo, my eyes were drawn to the hand of a woman resting on a name. Many people come to this place to touch a name and remember someone they loved.

TODAY'S READING
Psalm 23:1–6

Do not fear, for I have redeemed you; I have summoned you by name; you are mine. Isaiah 43:1

The prophet Isaiah reminded God's people of His unfailing love and concern for them, even though they had often turned away from Him. The Lord said, "Do not fear, for I have redeemed you; I have summoned you by name; you are mine" (ISAIAH 43:1).

In the 23rd Psalm, David wrote, "Even though I walk through the darkest valley [the valley of the shadow of death], I will fear no evil, for you are with me . . . . Surely your goodness and love will follow me all the days of my life, and I will dwell in the house of the LORD forever" (vv. 4, 6).

God never forgets us. No matter where we are or whatever our situation, He knows our names and holds us fast in His unfailing love. 🌱 *DAVID C. MCCASLAND*

Father in heaven, thank You for calling us by name and surrounding us with Your love, today and forever.

God knows our names and He holds us fast in His love.

Is There Wi-Fi?

As I was preparing to go on a mission trip with some young people, the most frequently asked question was, "Is there Wi-Fi?" And I assured them there would be. So just imagine the wails and groans one night when the Wi-Fi was down!

Many of us become anxious when we're separated from our smartphones. And when we do have our iPhones or Androids in our hands, we can be fixated on our screens.

> TODAY'S READING
> **Proverbs 15:9–21**
>
> **A wise person is hungry for knowledge, while the fool feeds on trash.** Proverbs 15:14 NLT

Like many things, the internet and all that it allows us to access can become either a distraction or a blessing. It depends on what we do with it. In Proverbs we read, "A wise person is hungry for knowledge, while the fool feeds on trash" (15:14 NLT).

Applying the wisdom of God's Word to life, we can ask ourselves: Do we check our social networks compulsively throughout the day? What does that say about the things we hunger for? And do the things we read or view online encourage sensible living (VV. 16–21), or are we feeding on trash—gossip, slander, materialism, or sexual impurity?

As we yield to the work of the Holy Spirit, we can fill our minds with things that are "true, and honorable, and right, and pure, and lovely, and admirable" (PHILIPPIANS 4:8 NLT). By God's wisdom we can make good choices that honor Him. ❧ *POH FANG CHIA*

God, help me to use my time well and to fill my mind with what is pure.

What we let into our minds shapes the state of our souls.

What's in a Name?

"**G**ip" **Hardin,** a Methodist preacher, named his son after the famous preacher John Wesley, reflecting Gip's hopes and aspirations for his baby boy. John Wesley Hardin, however, tragically chose a different path than his ministry-minded namesake. Claiming to have killed forty-two men, Hardin became one of the most notorious gunfighters and outlaws of the American West of the late 1800s.

In the Bible, as in many cultures today, names hold special significance. Announcing the birth of God's Son, an angel instructed Joseph to name Mary's child "Jesus, because he will save his people from their sins" (MATTHEW 1:21). The meaning of Jesus's name—"Jehovah saves"—confirmed His mission to save from sin.

Unlike Hardin, Jesus completely and thoroughly lived up to His name. Through His death and resurrection, He accomplished His mission of rescue.

TODAY'S READING
Matthew 1:18–25

She will give birth to a son, and you are to give him the name Jesus.

Matthew 1:21

John affirmed the life-giving power of Jesus's name, saying, "But these are written that you may believe that Jesus is the Messiah, the Son of God, and that by believing you may have life in his name" (JOHN 20:31). The book of Acts invites everyone to trust Him, for, "Salvation is found in no one else, for there is no other name under heaven given to mankind by which we must be saved" (ACTS 4:12).

All who call on Jesus's matchless name in faith can experience for themselves the forgiveness and hope He provides. Have you called on His name? 🌿

BILL CROWDER

Thank You, Father, for providing salvation through Your Son, Jesus.
I love You.

Jesus's name is also His mission—to seek and to save that which was lost.

The Ultimate Satisfaction

As we distributed snacks for children at a Bible School program, we noticed a little boy who devoured his snack. Then he also ate the leftovers of the children at his table. Even after I gave him a bag of popcorn, he still wasn't satisfied. As leaders, we were concerned as to why this little boy was so hungry.

It occurred to me that we can be like that boy when it comes to our emotions. We look for ways to satisfy our deepest longings, but we never find what fully satisfies us.

The prophet Isaiah invites those who are hungry and thirsty to "come, buy and eat" (ISAIAH 55:1). But then he asks, "Why spend money on what is not bread,

> **TODAY'S READING**
> **Isaiah 55:1–7**
>
> **Come, all you who are thirsty, come to the waters; and you who have no money, come, buy and eat!** Isaiah 55:1

and your labor on what does not satisfy?" (V. 2). Isaiah is talking about more than just physical hunger here. God can satisfy our spiritual and emotional hunger through the promise of His presence. The "everlasting covenant" in verse 3 is a reminder of a promise God made to David in 2 Samuel 7:8–16. Through David's family line, a Savior would come to reconnect people to God. Later, in John 6:35 and 7:37, Jesus extended the same invitation Isaiah gave, thus identifying Himself as the Savior foretold by Isaiah and other prophets.

Hungry? God invites you to come and be filled in His presence.

LINDA WASHINGTON

Father, I long to know You more.
Only You can satisfy my deepest desires.

Only God will satisfy our spiritual hunger.

Good for You?

Because I like dark chocolate, I once Googled "Is dark chocolate good for you?" I got a variety of results—some good, some bad. You can do the same for almost any food product. Is milk good for you? Is coffee good for you? Is rice good for you? There is a dizzying array of answers to these questions, so you have to be aware that the search itself may not be good for you. It may give you a headache!

TODAY'S READING
Psalm 119:65–72

You are good, and what you do is good; teach me your decrees.

Psalm 119:68

But if you're looking for something that's one-hundred percent good for you all the time, can I recommend the Word of God? Listen to what it can do for the follower of Jesus who is seeking to build a relationship with God.

It can keep you pure (PSALM 119:9, 11).

It blesses you (LUKE 11:28).

It makes you wise (MATTHEW 7:24).

It gives light and understanding (PSALM 119:130).

It helps you grow spiritually (1 PETER 2:2).

Our God is good: "The LORD is good to all," says Psalm 145:9. And in His goodness, He's provided those who love Him with a guide that helps us see how to enhance our relationship with Him. As we try to decide how to live in a world full of choices, praise God that He's told us in Scripture what's good for us. Let's say with the psalm-writer: "How sweet are your words to my taste, sweeter than honey to my mouth" (PSALM 119:103).

DAVE BRANON

God, thank You for leaving us Your inspired Word. Help us to read it
carefully, interpret it correctly, and apply it enthusiastically in our lives.
God's Word is the only sure foundation for life.

The Right Way to Pray

I admire people who record prayer requests in journals tattered from daily handling, those who keep track of every prayer and praise and then faithfully update their lists. I'm inspired by those who gather with others to pray and whose kneeling wears out the carpet at their bedsides. For years, I tried to copy their styles, to emulate a perfect prayer life, and to imitate the eloquence of the so-much-more-articulate-than-me folks. I strived to unravel what I thought was a mystery, as I longed to learn the right way to pray.

> TODAY'S READING
> **Matthew 6:5–15**
>
> **When you pray, go into your room, close the door and pray to your Father, who is unseen.** Matthew 6:6

Eventually, I learned that our Lord simply desires prayer that begins and ends with humility (MATTHEW 6:5). He invites us into an intimate exchange through which He promises to listen (V. 6). He never requires fancy or memorized words or phrases (V. 7). He assures us that prayer is a gift, an opportunity to honor His majesty (VV. 9–10), to display our confidence in His provision (V. 11), and to affirm our security in His forgiveness and guidance (VV. 12–13).

God assures us He hears and cares about every single spoken and unspoken prayer, as well as the prayers that slip down our cheeks as silent tears. As we place our trust in God and His perfect love for us, we can be sure praying with a humble heart that's surrendered to and dependent on Him is always the *right* way to pray. 🖋   XOCHITL DIXON

Lord, thank You for reminding us You hear every prayer.

Calling on Jesus as our loving Savior and Lord is the right way to pray.

Legacies of Love

was paging through my great-grandmother's Bible when a treasure fell into my lap. On a small scrap of paper, in a young child's handwriting, were the words, "Blessed are the poor in spirit: for theirs is the kingdom of heaven. Blessed are they that mourn: for they shall be comforted" (MATTHEW 5:3–4 KJV). Scribbled beside those verses in wobbly cursive was my mother's signature.

My great-grandmother had a habit of teaching her grandchildren to write out Scripture verses so they would learn them and take them to heart. But the story behind this verse brought tears to my eyes. My grandfather died when my mother was very young, and her little brother (my uncle) died just weeks later.

> **TODAY'S READING**
> **2 Timothy 1:1–5**
>
> **Let your light shine before others, that they may see your good deeds and glorify your Father in heaven.** Matthew 5:16

It was in that tragic season that my great-grandmother pointed my mother to Jesus and the comfort only He can give.

Paul wrote Timothy, "I am reminded of your sincere faith, which first lived in your grandmother Lois and in your mother Eunice and, I am persuaded, now lives in you also" (2 TIMOTHY 1:5). Faith isn't inherited, but it is *shared*. Timothy's mother and grandmother s*hared their faith with him,* and he believed.

When we encourage those close to us to have hope in Jesus, we offer them a legacy of love. Through a simple note, my mother left evidence of my great-grandmother's love for her Savior and her family. Oh, to share Him with those who come after us!

JAMES BANKS

Thank You for those who shared Your love with me, Father.
Please help me to point others to Your salvation today.

When we share our faith, we share the greatest treasure of all.

Engraved on His Hands

n Charles Spurgeon's many years at his London church during the 1800s, he loved to preach on the riches of Isaiah 49:16, which says that God engraves us on the palms of His hands. He said, "Such a text as this is to be preached hundreds of times!" This thought is so precious that we can run over it in our minds again and again.

Spurgeon makes the wonderful connection between this promise of the Lord to His people, the Israelites, and God's Son, Jesus, on the cross as He died for us. Spurgeon asked, "What are these wounds in Your hands? . . . The engraver's tool was the nail, backed by the hammer. He must be fastened to the Cross, that His people might be truly engraved on the palms of His hands." As the Lord promised to engrave His people on His palms, so Jesus stretched out His arms on the cross, receiving the nails in His hands so we could be free of our sins.

> TODAY'S READING
> **Isaiah 49:14–18**
>
> **See, I have engraved you on the palms of my hands.** Isaiah 49:16

If and when we're tempted to think that God has forgotten us, we only need to look at our palms and remember God's promise. He has put indelible marks on His hands for us; He loves us that much.

AMY BOUCHER PYE

Lord God, how vast is Your love for me! You keep me ever before You.
I know You'll never leave me, and I'm grateful.

The Lord engraves us on the palms of His hands.

A Fitting Time

Yesterday I purchased an airline ticket to send my first-born child to college. I'm surprised the keyboard on my computer still functions, given the waterworks my eyes unleashed on it during the flight selection process. I have so enjoyed my eighteen years of daily life with her that I am saddened by the prospect of her departure. Yet I wouldn't rob her of the opportunity that lies ahead simply because I'll miss her. At this juncture in her life, it is fitting for her to embark on a new journey to discover adulthood and explore another part of the country.

TODAY'S READING
Ecclesiastes 3:1–14

He has made everything beautiful in its time. Ecclesiastes 3:11

As this season of my parenting draws to a close, another one begins. It will undoubtedly bring both new challenges and new delights. Solomon, Israel's third king, wrote that God appoints "a time for everything, and a season for every activity under the heavens" (ECCLESIASTES 3:1). We humans have little control over the events of our lives—whether we view those events as favorable or not. But God, in His mighty power, makes "everything beautiful in its time" (V. 11).

In seasons of heartache, we can trust God to bring something good from them in time. Our comforts and joys may come and go, but God's works "will endure forever" (V. 14). We may not relish every season—some are quite painful—yet He can bring beauty to them all. 🕊

KIRSTEN HOLMBERG

Father, You have permitted this season in my life.
Help me to be content in the midst of it, and to recognize
Your power and might are at work.

God brings beauty from all seasons.

Where to Find Hope

Elizabeth struggled for a long time with drug addiction, and when she recovered wanted to help others in return. So she started writing notes and anonymously placing them throughout her city. Elizabeth tucks these notes under car windshield wipers and tacks them on poles in parks. She used to look for signs of hope; now she leaves them for others to find. One of her notes concluded with these words: "Much love. Hope sent."

Hope with love—that's what Jesus gives. He brings us His love with each new day and strengthens us with that hope. His love is not rationed out to us drop by drop but flows out of His heart freely and is poured lavishly into ours: "We know how dearly God loves us, because he has given us the Holy Spirit to fill our hearts with his love" (ROMANS 5:5 NLT).

> **TODAY'S READING**
> **Romans 5:1–11**
>
> **And hope does not put us to shame, because God's love has been poured out into our hearts through the Holy Spirit, who has been given to us.**
>
> Romans 5:5

He desires to use the hard times to develop perseverance and character and bring us a satisfying, hope-filled life (VV. 3–4). And even when we're far from Him, He still loves us (VV. 6–8).

Are you looking for signs of hope? The Lord gives hope with love through inviting us to grow in a relationship with Him. Our hope for a fulfilling life is anchored in His unfailing love.

ANNE CETAS

I'm grateful, God, for the love You lavishly pour on me. Please bring me contentment in You and confidence in what You are doing in me.

Hope is the anchor of the soul.

Unexpected Ways

n 1986, five-year-old Levan Merritt fell twenty feet into the gorilla enclosure of England's Jersey zoo. As parents and onlookers cried out for help, a full-grown male silverback, named Jambo, placed himself between the motionless boy and several other gorillas. Then he began to gently stroke the child's back. When Levan began to cry, Jambo led the other gorillas into their own enclosure as zoo-keepers and an ambulance driver came to the rescue. More than thirty years later Levan still talks about Jambo the gentle giant—his guardian angel who had acted in a shockingly unexpected way, changing his perception of gorillas forever.

> **TODAY'S READING**
> **1 Kings 19:1–12**
>
> **Anyone who has seen me has seen the Father.** John 14:9

Elijah may have expected God to act in certain ways, but the God of gods used a rock-shattering wind, a powerful earthquake, and raging fire to show His prophet how *not* to think of Him. Then He used a gentle whisper to show His heart and to express His presence (1 KINGS 19:11–12).

Elijah had seen God's power before (18:38–39). But he didn't fully understand the One who wants to be known as more than the greatest and most fearsome of gods (19:10, 14).

Eventually, that quiet whisper found fullness of meaning in the powerful gentleness of Jesus, who said, "Anyone who has seen me has seen the Father" (JOHN 14:9). Then He quietly allowed Himself to be nailed to a tree—an unexpected, compassionate act by the great God who loves us. 🌱

MART DEHAAN

Father in heaven, please help us to find courage in Your whisper—and in the ways of Your Son. Have mercy on us for not seeing beyond Your power to a love we've barely begun to know.

God won't shout if we only need a whisper.

The Blessing of Encouragers

The 2010 movie *The King's Speech* tells the story of England's King George VI, who unexpectedly became monarch when his brother abandoned the throne. With the country on the brink of World War II, government officials wanted a well-spoken leader because of the increasingly influential role of radio. King George VI, however, struggled with a stuttering problem.

TODAY'S READING
Acts 9:26–31

But Barnabas took [Saul] and brought him to the apostles. Acts 9:27

I was especially drawn to the film's portrayal of George's wife, Elizabeth. Throughout his struggle to overcome his speech difficulty, she was his constant source of encouragement. Her steadfast devotion provided the support he needed to overcome his challenge and rule well during the war.

The Bible highlights the stories of encouragers who gave powerful assistance during challenging circumstances. Moses had Aaron and Hur's support during Israel's battles (EXODUS 17:8–16). Elizabeth encouraged her pregnant relative Mary (LUKE 1:42–45).

After his conversion, Paul needed the support of Barnabas, whose name literally means "son of encouragement." When the disciples were fearful of Paul, Barnabas, at the risk of his own reputation, vouched for him (ACTS 9:27). His endorsement was essential to Paul being welcomed by the Christian community. Barnabas later served as Paul's traveling and preaching companion (ACTS 14). Despite the dangers, they worked together to proclaim the gospel.

Believers in Jesus are still called to "encourage one another and build each other up" (1 THESSALONIANS 5:11). May we be eager to offer encouragement to help support others, especially as they face difficult circumstances.   *LISA SAMRA*

The encouragement of a friend can make all the difference.

Listening to Your Brother

"**Y**ou need to listen** to me, I'm your brother!" The plea came from a concerned older brother in my neighborhood and was directed to a younger sibling who was moving farther away from him than the older child was comfortable with. Clearly the older child was better able to judge what was best in the situation.

How many of us have resisted the wise counsel of a brother or sister? If you've had to face the consequences of resisting the good advice of someone more mature, you're not alone.

One of the greatest resources we can have as believers in Jesus is a family—those who are spiritually related because of a common faith in Him. This family includes mature men and women who love God and each other. Like the little brother in my neighborhood, we sometimes need a word of caution or correction to get us back on track. This is particularly true when we offend someone or someone offends us. Doing what's right can be difficult. Yet Jesus's words in Matthew 18:15–20 show us what to do when offenses happen within our spiritual family.

> TODAY'S READING
> **Matthew 18:15–20**
>
> **Whoever turns a sinner from the error of their way will save them from death and cover over a multitude of sins.**
> James 5:20

Thankfully, our gracious heavenly Father places in our lives people who are prepared to help us honor Him and others. And when we listen, things go better in the family (V. 15).

ARTHUR JACKSON

Father, we praise You for placing us in Your spiritual family.
Help us to learn and grow through the wise words and godly behavior
of mature believers.

Wisdom grows when we listen to the words of mature believers.

Walking God's Way

"**W**e're going *this* way," I said as I touched my son's shoulder and redirected him through the crowd to follow his mom and sisters in front of us. I'd done this more often as the day wore on at the amusement park our family was visiting. He was getting tired and more easily distracted. *Why can't he just follow them?* I wondered.

TODAY'S READING
Isaiah 30:15–21

Whether you turn to the right or to the left, your ears will hear a voice behind you, saying, "This is the way; walk in it." Isaiah 30:21

Then it hit me: *How often do I do exactly the same thing? How often do I veer from obediently walking with God, enchanted by the temptations to pursue what I want instead of seeking His ways?*

Think of Isaiah's words from God for Israel: "Whether you turn to the right or to the left, your ears will hear a voice behind you, saying, 'This is the way; walk in it' " (ISAIAH 30:21). Earlier in that chapter, God had rebuked His people for their rebelliousness. But if they would trust His strength instead of their own ways (V. 15), He promised to show His graciousness and compassion (V. 18).

One expression of God's graciousness is His promise to guide us by His Spirit. That happens as we talk to Him about our desires and ask in prayer what He has for us. I'm thankful God patiently directs us, day-by-day, step-by-step, as we trust Him and listen for His voice. 🌱

ADAM HOLZ

Father, You've promised to guide us through the ups and downs and decisions we face in life. Help us to trust and follow You, and to actively listen for Your guiding voice.

God patiently directs us as we trust Him and listen for His voice.

Our Daily Bread

Many Beautiful Things

Just before her death, artist and missionary Lilias Trotter looked out a window and saw a vision of a heavenly chariot. According to her biographer, a friend asked, "Are you seeing many beautiful things?" She answered, "Yes, many, many beautiful things."

TODAY'S READING
Mark 14:1–9

She has done a beautiful thing to me. Mark 14:6

Trotter's final words reflect God's work in her life. Not only in death, but throughout her life, He revealed much beauty to her and through her. Although a talented artist, she chose to serve Jesus as a missionary in Algeria. John Ruskin, a famous painter who tutored her, is said to have commented, "What a waste," when she chose the mission field over a career in art.

Similarly, in the New Testament, when a woman came to Simon the Leper's house with an alabaster jar and poured perfume on Jesus's head, those present saw it as a waste. This expensive perfume was worth a year's common wages, so some of the people present thought it could have been used to help the poor. However, commending this woman's deep devotion to Him, Jesus said, "She has done a beautiful thing to me" (MARK 14:6).

Every day we can choose to let Christ's life shine in our lives and display His beauty to the world. To some, it may seem a waste, but let us have willing hearts to serve Him. May Jesus say we have done many beautiful things for Him. 🌢 *KEILA OCHOA*

Dear Father, help me express my love to You in beautiful ways.

May our lives display the beauty of God.

It's Not About the Fish

Sighted numerous times off the coast of Australia's South Queensland, Migaloo is the first albino humpback whale ever documented. The splendid creature, estimated at more than forty feet long, is so rare that Australia passed a law specifically to protect him.

The Bible tells us about a "huge fish" so rare that God had provided it especially to swallow a runaway prophet (JONAH 1:17). Most know the story. God told Jonah to take a message of judgment to Nineveh. But Jonah wanted nothing to do with the Ninevites, who had a reputation for cruelty to just about everyone—

TODAY'S READING
Jonah 3:10–4:4

When God saw what they did and how they turned from their evil ways, he relented. Jonah 3:10

including the Hebrews. So he fled. Things went badly. From inside the fish, Jonah repented. Eventually he preached to the Ninevites, and they repented too (3:5–10).

Great story, right? Except it doesn't end there. While Nineveh repented, Jonah pouted. "Isn't this what I said, LORD?" he prayed. "I knew that you are a gracious and compassionate God, slow to anger and abounding in love" (4:2). Having been rescued from certain death, Jonah's sinful anger grew until even his prayer became suicidal (V. 3).

The story of Jonah isn't about the fish. It's about our human nature and the nature of the God who pursues us. "The Lord is patient with you," wrote the apostle Peter, "not wanting anyone to perish, but everyone to come to repentance" (2 PETER 3:9). God offers His love to brutal Ninevites, pouting prophets, and you and me. 🌼

TIM GUSTAFSON

Father, we tend to look at what others "deserve" and forget we need Your love just as much. Help us live in Your love and tell others about it.

Our love has limits; God's love is limitless.

When We're Weary

Sometimes trying to do the right thing can be exhausting. We may wonder, *Do my well-intentioned words and actions make any difference at all?* I wondered this recently when I sent a prayerfully thought-out email meant to encourage a friend, only to have it met with an angry response. My immediate reaction was a mixture of hurt and anger. *How could I be so misunderstood?*

Before I responded out of anger, I remembered that we won't always see the results (or the results we desire) when we tell someone about how Jesus loves them. When we do good things for others

TODAY'S READING
Galatians 6:1–10

Let us not become weary in doing good. Galatians 6:9

hoping to draw them to Him, they may spurn us. Our gentle efforts to prompt someone to right action may be ignored.

Galatians 6 is a good place to turn when we're discouraged by someone's response to our sincere efforts. Here the apostle Paul encourages us to consider our motives—to "test our actions"—for what we say and do (VV. 1-4). When we have done so, he encourages us to persevere: "Let us not become weary in doing good, for at the proper time we will reap a harvest if we do not give up. Therefore, as we have opportunity, let us do good to all people" (VV. 9-10).

God wants us to continue living for Him, which includes praying for and telling others about Him—"doing good." He will see to the results.

ALYSON KIEDA

Dear God, thank You for the encouragement we receive from Your Word. Help us to persevere in doing good.

We can leave the results of our lives in God's hands.

Asking God First

Early in our marriage, I struggled to figure out my wife's preferences. *Did she want a quiet dinner at home or a meal at a fancy restaurant? Was it okay for me to hang out with the guys, or did she expect me to keep the weekend free for her?* Once, instead of guessing and deciding first, I asked her, "What do you want?"

"I'm fine with either," she replied with a warm smile. "I'm just happy you thought of me."

> TODAY'S READING
> **Psalm 37:3–7, 23–24**
>
> **Take delight in the LORD, and he will give you the desires of your heart.** Psalm 37:4

At times I've wanted desperately to know *exactly* what God wanted me to do—such as which job to take. Praying for guidance and reading the Bible didn't reveal any specific answers. But one answer was clear: I was to trust in the Lord, take delight in Him, and commit my way to Him (PSALM 37:3–5).

That's when I realized that God usually gives us the freedom of choice—if we first seek to put His ways before our own. That means dropping choices that are plainly wrong or would not please Him. It might be something immoral, ungodly, or unhelpful toward our relationship with Him. If the remaining options please God, then we're free to choose from them. Our loving Father wants to give us the desires of our hearts—hearts that take delight in Him (V. 4). 🌱

LESLIE KOH

Teach me, O God, to put You first in everything I do.
Show me how to take delight in You, that my heart will be
transformed to be like Yours.

Do your decisions please God?

Gleaning the Fields

A **Tanzanian friend** has a vision for redeeming a piece of desolate land in the capital city of Dodoma. Recognizing the needs of some local widows, Ruth wants to transform these dusty acres into a place to keep chickens and grow crops. Her vision to provide for those in need is rooted in her love for God, and was inspired by her biblical namesake, Ruth.

God's laws allowed the poor or the foreigner to glean (harvest) from the edges of the fields (LEVITICUS 19:9–10). Ruth (in the Bible) was a foreigner, and was therefore allowed to work in the fields, gathering food for her and her mother-in-law. Gleaning in Boaz's field, a close relative, led to Ruth and Naomi ultimately finding a home and protection. Ruth used her ingenuity and effort in the work of the day—gathering food from the edges of the field— and God blessed her.

> TODAY'S READING
> **Ruth 2:1–12**
>
> **Ruth the Moabite said to Naomi, "Let me go to the fields and pick up the leftover grain behind anyone in whose eyes I find favor."** Ruth 2:2

The passion of my friend Ruth and the dedication of the biblical Ruth stir me to give thanks to God for how He cares for the poor and downtrodden. They inspire me to seek ways to help others in my community and more broadly as a means of expressing my thanks to our giving God. How might you worship God through extending His mercy to others? 🌾

AMY BOUCHER PYE

Jesus, You desire that no one would go hungry.
Open our eyes to the ways we can help those in need.
May we share Your love, for Your glory.

God cares for the vulnerable.

Unlocking a Mystery

When I came home from work one day and saw a pair of lady's high-heel shoes next to the driveway, I was sure I knew whose they were. So I put them in the garage to give to my daughter Lisa when she returned to the house to pick up her children. But when I checked with Lisa, I found they didn't belong to her. In fact, no one in our family claimed them, so I put them back where I'd found them. The next day, they were gone. Mysterious.

> **TODAY'S READING**
> **Ephesians 3:1–12**
>
> **This mystery is that through the gospel the Gentiles are heirs together with Israel.** Ephesians 3:6

Did you know that the apostle Paul wrote of a mystery in his letters? But the mystery he described was so much more than some kind of "whodunit." In Ephesians 3, for example, Paul spoke of a mystery that "was not made known to people in other generations" (V. 5). This mystery is that, while in the past God revealed Himself through Israel, now, through Jesus, Gentiles—those outside of Israel—could be "heirs together with Israel" (V. 6).

Think about what this means: all who trust Jesus as Savior can love and serve God together. We can all equally "approach [Him] with freedom and confidence" (V. 12). And through the church's unity the world will see God's wisdom and goodness (V. 10).

Praise God for our salvation. It unlocks for us the mystery of unity as people of any and all backgrounds become one in Jesus. 🌿

DAVE BRANON

Thank You, Jesus, for the unity all believers can enjoy in You.
Help us to serve together as equal members of Your body.

Unity in Christ breaks down barriers and builds the church.

For Our Friends

I n Emily Bronte's novel *Wuthering Heights,* a cantankerous man who often quotes the Bible to criticize others is memorably described as "the wearisomest self-righteous Pharisee that ever ransacked a Bible to rake [apply] the promises to himself and fling the curses to his neighbours."

It's a funny line; and it may even bring particular people to mind. But aren't we *all* a bit like this—prone to condemn others' failures while excusing our own?

In Scripture some people amazingly did the exact opposite; they were willing to give up God's promises for them and

TODAY'S READING
John 15:5–17

My command is this: Love each other as I have loved you. John 15:12

even be cursed if it would save others. Consider Moses, who said he'd rather be blotted out of God's book than see the Israelites unforgiven (EXODUS 32:32). Or Paul, who said he'd choose to be "cut off from Christ" if it meant his people would find Him (ROMANS 9:3).

As self-righteous as we naturally are, Scripture highlights those who love others more than themselves.

Because ultimately such love points to Jesus. "Greater love has no one than this," Jesus taught, than "to lay down one's life for one's friends" (JOHN 15:13). Even before we knew Him, Jesus loved us "to the end" (13:1)—choosing death to give us life.

Now we are invited into the family of God, to love and be loved like this (15:9–12). And as we pour into others Christ's unimaginable love, the world will catch a glimpse of Him. 🌾

MONICA BRANDS

Lord, thank You for showing us what it means to love.
Help us to love like You.

When we love Christ, we love others.

God's Brand

Scooping up the smallest children, a frantic maid raced out of the flaming house. As she ran, she called loudly to five-year-old Jacky.

But Jacky didn't follow. Outside, a bystander reacted quickly, standing on the shoulders of a friend. Reaching into the upstairs window, he pulled Jacky to safety—just before the roof caved in. Little Jacky, said his mother Susanna, was "a brand [stick] plucked from the burning." You might know that "brand" as the great traveling minister John Wesley (1703–1791).

TODAY'S READING
Zechariah 3:1–7

I have taken away your sin, and I will put fine garments on you. Zechariah 3:4

Susanna Wesley was quoting Zechariah, a prophet who provides valuable insight into God's character. Relating a vision he had, the prophet takes us into a courtroom scene where Satan is standing next to Joshua the high priest (3:1). Satan accuses Joshua, but the Lord rebukes the devil and says, "Is this not a brand [burning stick] plucked from the fire?" (V. 2 NKJV). The Lord tells Joshua, "I have taken away your sin, and I will put fine garments on you" (V. 4).

Then the Lord gave Joshua this challenge—and an opportunity: "If you will walk in obedience to me and keep my requirements, then you will govern my house" (V. 7).

What a picture of the gift we receive from God through our faith in Jesus! He snatches us from the fire, cleans us up, and works in us as we follow His Spirit's leading. You might call us God's brands plucked from the fire. 🌱

TIM GUSTAFSON

Father, we give You our thanks for rescuing us and making us right with You. We humbly ask for Your Spirit's guidance as we serve You today.

*God rescues us because He loves us;
then He equips us to share His love with others.*

Asking for Help

Her email arrived late in a long day. In truth, I didn't open it. I was working overtime to help a family member manage his serious illness. I didn't have time, therefore, for social distractions.

The next morning, however, when I clicked on my friend's message, I saw this question: "Can I help you in any way?" Feeling embarrassed, I started to answer no. Then I took a deep breath to pause. I noticed then that her question sounded familiar—if not divine.

That's because Jesus asked it. Hearing a blind beggar call out to Him on the Jericho Road, Jesus stopped to ask this man, named Bartimaeus, a similar question. *Can I help?* Or as Jesus said: "What do you want me to do for you?" (MARK 10:51).

> TODAY'S READING
> Mark 10:46–52
>
> **"What do you want me to do for you?" Jesus asked him.** Mark 10:51

The question is stunning. It shows the Healer, Jesus, longs to help us. But first, we're invited to admit needing Him—a humbling step. The "professional" beggar Bartimaeus was needy, indeed—poor, alone, and possibly hungry and downcast. But wanting a new life, he simply told Jesus his most basic need. "Rabbi," he said, "I want to see."

For a blind man, it was an honest plea. Jesus healed him immediately. My friend sought such honesty from me too. So I promised her I'd pray to understand my basic need and, more important, I'd humbly tell her. Do you know your basic need today? When a friend asks, tell it. Then take your plea even higher. Tell God. 🌾

PATRICIA RAYBON

Lord, I am needy. I want to share my heart with You now.
Help me to humbly receive the help of others also.

God opposes the proud but shows favor to the humble. *1 PETER 5:5*

Courageous Stand

Teresa Prekerowa was just a teenager when the Nazis invaded her native Poland at the dawn of World War II. This was in the beginnings of the Holocaust when her Jewish neighbors began to disappear—arrested by the Nazis. So Teresa and other Polish countrymen risked their lives to rescue those neighbors from the Warsaw ghetto and the Nazi purge. Teresa would become one of the premier historians of the war and the Holocaust, but it was her courage to stand against the tide of evil that would list her with the Righteous Among the Nations at the Yad Vashem Holocaust Memorial in Jerusalem.

> **TODAY'S READING**
> **Ephesians 6:10–18**
>
> **Our struggle is not against flesh and blood, but against the rulers, against the authorities, against the powers of this dark world.**
> Ephesians 6:12

Courage is needed to stand against evil. Paul told the church at Ephesus, "For our struggle is not against flesh and blood, but against the rulers, against the authorities, against the powers of this dark world and against the spiritual forces of evil" (EPHESIANS 6:12). Clearly this unseen opposition is more than any of us can face alone, so God has given us the necessary spiritual resources (the "full armor of God") to enable us to "stand against the devil's schemes" (V. 11).

What might that courageous stand involve? It may be working against injustice or intervening on behalf of someone you know who is vulnerable or victimized. Whatever form the conflict may take, we can have courage—our God has already provided what we need to stand for Him and against evil. ✒

BILL CROWDER

God enables us to stand for Him.

Our Daily Bread

Better Than Ever

The story is told of a group of salmon fishermen who gathered in a Scottish inn after a long day of fishing. As one was describing a catch to his friends, his arm swept across the table and knocked a glass against the wall, shattering it and leaving a stain on the white plaster surface. The man apologized to the innkeeper and offered to pay for the damage, but there was nothing he could do; the wall was ruined. A man seated nearby said, "Don't worry." Rising, he took a painting implement from his pocket and began to sketch around the ugly stain. Slowly there emerged the head of a magnificent stag. The man was Sir E. H. Landseer, Scotland's foremost animal artist.

> **TODAY'S READING**
> **Psalm 51:9-13**
>
> **Restore to me the joy of your salvation and grant me a willing spirit, to sustain me.**
> Psalm 51:12

David, Israel's illustrious king who penned Psalm 51, brought shame on himself and his nation by his sins. He committed adultery with the wife of one of his friends and engineered the death of that friend—both deeds worthy of death. It would seem his life was ruined. But he pled with God: "Restore to me the joy of your salvation and grant me a willing spirit, to sustain me" (V. 12).

Like David we have shameful acts in our past and the memories that accompany them, recollections that taunt us in the middle of the night. There's so much we wish we could undo or redo.

There is a grace that not only forgives sin but also uses it to make us better than before. God wastes nothing. DAVID H. ROPER

Lord, I've failed You again. Please forgive me again. Change me.
Turn me around. Teach me to follow Your ways.

God has both an all-seeing eye and all-forgiving heart.

Twinkle

"**T**winkle, Twinkle, Little Star**"** is an English lullaby. Its lyrics, originally a poem by Jane Taylor, capture the wonder of God's universe where stars hang "up above the world so high." In the rarely published later stanzas, the star acts as a guide: "As your bright and tiny spark lights the traveler in the dark."

In Philippians, Paul challenges believers in Philippi to be blameless and pure as they "shine . . . like stars in the sky" while offering the good news of the gospel to all around them (2:15–16). We wonder how we can shine like stars. We often feel inadequate and struggle to think our "light" is bright enough to make a difference. But

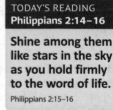

TODAY'S READING
Philippians 2:14–16

Shine among them like stars in the sky as you hold firmly to the word of life.

Philippians 2:15–16

stars don't *try* to be stars. They just are. Light changes our world. And it changes us. God brought physical light into our world (GENESIS 1:3); and through Jesus, God brings spiritual light into our lives (JOHN 1:1–4).

We who have God's light in us are to shine in such a way that those around us see light and are drawn to its source. As effortlessly as a star hanging in the night sky, our light makes a difference because of what it is: Light! When we simply shine, we follow Paul's directive to "hold firmly to the word of life" in a world in deep darkness, and we draw others to the source of our hope: Jesus. 🌿

ELISA MORGAN

Dear God, may Your light shine out of the very cracks of our beings as we hold out the Word of life to others.

Jesus brings light into our life.

A Warm Welcome for All

During a recent vacation, my wife and I visited a famous athletic complex. The gates were wide open, and it appeared that we were welcome to visit. We enjoyed touring the grounds and admiring the well-manicured sports fields. As we were about to leave, someone stopped us and coldly told us we were not supposed to be there. Suddenly, we were reminded that we were outsiders—and it felt uncomfortable.

TODAY'S READING
Hebrews 13:1–3

Let us do good to all people, especially to those who belong to the family of believers.

Galatians 6:10

On that vacation we also visited a church. Again, the doors were open, so we walked in. What a difference! Many people greeted us warmly and made us feel right at home. We walked out of that church service knowing we were welcomed and accepted.

Sadly, it isn't uncommon for outsiders to receive the unspoken message "you're not supposed to be here" when they visit a church. But Scripture calls us to be hospitable to all. Jesus said we are to love our neighbors as ourselves, which surely means welcoming them into our lives and our churches (MATTHEW 22:39). In Hebrews, we're reminded to "show hospitality to strangers" (13:2). Both Luke and Paul instruct us to show active love to people with social and physical needs (LUKE 14:13–14; ROMANS 12:13). And among the body of believers, we have a special responsibility to show love (GALATIANS 6:10).

When we welcome all people openly and with Christlike love, we reflect our Savior's love and compassion. 🌿 *DAVE BRANON*

Lord, open our hearts to all people who enter our lives—showing them
Christlike love and godly hospitality. Help us to make everyone
we meet feel the warm welcome of Jesus's love.

When we practice hospitality, we share God's goodness.

Our Singing Father

No one told me before my wife and I had children how important singing would be. My children are now six, eight, and ten. But all three had problems sleeping early on. Each night, my wife and I took turns rocking our little ones, praying they'd nod off quickly. I spent hundreds of hours rocking them, desperately crooning lullabies to (hopefully!) speed up the process. But as I sang over our children night after night, something amazing happened: It deepened my bond of love and delight for them in ways I had never dreamed.

> **TODAY'S READING**
> **Zephaniah 3:14–20**
>
> **The LORD your God is with you, the Mighty Warrior who saves. He will take great delight in you; in his love he will…rejoice over you with singing.** Zephaniah 3:17

Did you know Scripture describes our heavenly Father singing over His children too? Just as I sought to soothe my children with song, so Zephaniah concludes with a portrait of our heavenly Father singing over His people: "He will take great delight in you; in his love he will … rejoice over you with singing" (3:17).

Much of Zephaniah's prophetic book warns of a coming time of judgment for those who'd rejected God. Yet that's not where it ends. Zephaniah concludes not with judgment but with a description of God not only rescuing His people from all their suffering (VV. 19–20) but also tenderly loving and rejoicing over them with song (V. 17).

Our God is not only a "Mighty Warrior who saves" and restores (V. 17) but a loving Father who tenderly sings songs of love over us. 🌱 *ADAM HOLZ*

Father, help us to embrace Your tender love and "hear" the songs You sing.

Our heavenly Father delights in His children like a parent singing to a newborn baby.

Much More Than Words

At a dedication ceremony during which a Bible translated into a local African language was presented, the area chief was presented with his own copy. In appreciation, he lifted the Bible to the skies and exclaimed, "Now we know God understands our language! We can read the Bible in our own native mother-tongue."

No matter our language, our heavenly Father understands it. But often we feel unable to express our deepest longings to Him. The apostle Paul encourages us to pray regardless of how we feel. Paul speaks of our suffering world and our own pain: "The whole creation has been groaning as in the pains of childbirth" (ROMANS 8:22), and he compares that to the Holy Spirit's work on our behalf. "The Spirit helps us in our weakness," he writes. "We do not know what we ought to pray for, but the Spirit himself intercedes for us through wordless groans" (V. 26).

>
> TODAY'S READING
> **Romans 8:22–30**
>
> **In the same way, the Spirit helps us in our weakness.**
> Romans 8:26

God's Holy Spirit knows us intimately. He knows our longings, our heart-language, and our unspoken words, and He helps us in our communication with God. His Spirit draws us to be transformed into the image of God the Son (V. 29).

Our heavenly Father understands our language and speaks to us through His Word. When we think our prayers are weak or too short, His Holy Spirit helps us by speaking through us to the Father. He yearns for us to talk with Him in prayer. 🌱

LAWRENCE DARMANI

Thank You, Lord, for understanding my language and innermost longings. When my prayers are weak and dry, bear me up through Your Spirit.

When we feel weak in our prayers,
God's Spirit helps us in ways we can't imagine.

Singing to the Firing Squad

Two men convicted of drug trafficking had been on death row for a decade. While in prison, they learned of God's love for them in Jesus, and their lives were transformed. When it came time for them to face the firing squad, they faced their executioners reciting the Lord's Prayer and singing "Amazing Grace." Because of their faith in God, through the power of the Spirit they were able to face death with incredible courage.

TODAY'S READING
Mark 14:16–26

I trusted in the LORD when I said, "I am greatly afflicted." Psalm 116:10

They followed the example of faith set by their Savior, Jesus. When Jesus knew that His death was imminent, He spent part of the evening singing with friends. It's remarkable that He could sing under such circumstances, but what's even more remarkable is what He sang. On that night, Jesus and his friends had a Passover meal, which always ends with a series of Psalms known as the Hallel, Psalms 113–118. Facing death, that night Jesus sang about the "cords of death" entangling Him (PSALM 116:3). Yet He praised God's faithful love (117:2) and thanked Him for salvation (118:14). Surely these Psalms comforted Jesus on the night before His crucifixion.

Jesus's trust in God was so great that even as He approached His own death—a death He had done nothing to deserve!—He chose to sing of God's love. Because of Jesus, we too can have confidence that whatever we face, God is with us. AMY PETERSON

God, strengthen our faith in You so that when we face trials, or even approach death, we can sing with confidence about Your love.

How sweet is the sound of God's amazing grace!

Stories of Jesus

As a girl I loved to visit my small local library. One day, looking at the bookshelves holding the young adult section, I reasoned I could probably read every book. In my enthusiasm I forgot one important fact—new books were regularly added to the shelves. Although I gave it a valiant effort, there were simply too many books.

New books continue to fill more and more bookshelves. The apostle John likely would be amazed with the availability of books today since his five New Testament books, the Gospel of John; 1, 2, and 3 John; and Revelation, were handwritten on parchment scrolls.

TODAY'S READING
1 Jn. 1:1–4; Jn. 21:24–25

Jesus did many other things as well. John 21:25

John wrote those books because he felt compelled by the Holy Spirit to give Christians an eyewitness account of Jesus's life and ministry (1 JOHN 1:1-4). But John's writings contained only a small fraction of all that Jesus did and taught during His ministry. In fact, John said if everything Jesus did were written down "the whole world could not contain the books that would be written" (JOHN 21:25 NLT).

John's claim remains true today. Despite all the books that have been written about Jesus, the libraries of the world still cannot contain every story of His love and grace. We can also celebrate that we have our own personal stories to share and rejoice that we will be proclaiming them forever! (PSALM 89:1). 🌳

LISA SAMRA

To write the love of God above would drain the ocean dry.
Nor could the scroll contain the whole, though stretched from sky to sky.
F.M. LEHMAN

Let your life tell the story of Christ's love and grace.

Safe in His Arms

The weather outside was threatening, and the alert on my cell phone warned about the possibility of flash floods. An unusual number of cars were parked in my neighborhood as parents and others gathered to pick up children at the school bus drop-off point. By the time the bus arrived, it had started to rain. That's when I observed a woman exit her car and retrieve an umbrella from the trunk. She walked towards a little girl and made sure the child was shielded from the rain until they returned to the vehicle. What a beautiful "real time" picture of parental, protective care that reminded me of the care of our heavenly Father.

> **TODAY'S READING**
> **Isaiah 40:9–11**
>
> **He tends his flock like a shepherd: He gathers the lambs in his arms and carries them close to his heart.** Isaiah 40:11

The prophet Isaiah forecast punishment for disobedience followed by brighter days for God's people (ISAIAH 40:1–8). The heavenly dispatch from the mountain (V. 9) assured the Israelites of God's mighty presence and tender care. The good news, then and now, is that because of God's power and ruling authority, anxious hearts need not fear (VV. 9–10). Included in the announcement was news about the Lord's protection, the kind of protection shepherds provide (V. 11): vulnerable young sheep would find safety in the Shepherd's arms; nursing ewes would be led gently.

In a world where circumstances aren't always easy, such images of safety and care compel us to look confidently to the Lord. Those who trust wholeheartedly in the Lord find security and renewed strength in Him (V. 31). 🌱   *ARTHUR JACKSON*

Father, in a world where we are sometimes threatened, we are comforted because of Your gracious care for us—in and through the Lord Jesus Christ.

The good news is that God cares for us!

He Carried Our Burden

t's not unusual for utility bills to be surprisingly high. But Kieran Healy of North Carolina received a water bill that would make your heart stop. The notification said that he owed 100 million dollars! Confident he hadn't used *that* much water the previous month, Healy jokingly asked if he could pay the bill in installments.

Owing a 100-million-dollar debt would be an overwhelming burden, but that pales in comparison to the real—and immeasurable—burden sin causes us to carry. Attempting to carry the burden and consequences of our own sins ultimately leaves us feeling tired and riddled with guilt and shame. The truth is we are incapable of carrying this load.

And we were never meant to. As Peter reminded believers, only Jesus, the sinless Son of God, could carry the heavy

> **TODAY'S READING**
> **1 Peter 1:18–25**
>
> "He himself bore our sins" in his body on the cross, so that we might die to sins and live for righteousness; "by his wounds you have been healed." 1 Peter 2:24

burden of our sin and its weighty consequences (1 PETER 2:24). In His death on the cross, Jesus took all our wrongdoing on Himself and offered us His forgiveness. Because He carried our burden, we don't have to suffer the punishment we deserve.

Instead of living in fear or guilt, the "empty way of life handed down to" us (1:18), we can enjoy a new life of love and freedom (VV. 22–23). 🌻

MARVIN WILLIAMS

Lord, sometimes our guilt and shame can feel so heavy.
Help us to release our past and its pain to You
and experience Your peace, knowing You have carried it all
and have set us free.

Jesus carried the burden of our sin so He could give us the blessing of life.

Ask the Animals

Our grandkids, enraptured, got a close-up look at a rescued bald eagle. They were even allowed to touch him. As the zoo volunteer told about the powerful bird perched on her arm, I was surprised to learn this male had a wingspan of about six and one-half feet, yet because of its hollow bones it weighed only about eight pounds.

This reminded me of the majestic eagle I had seen soaring above a lake, ready to swoop down and snatch its prey in its talons. And I pictured in my mind another big bird—the spindly legged blue heron I had spied standing motionless on the edge of a pond. It was poised to dart its long beak into the water. They're just two among the nearly 10,000 species of birds that can direct our thoughts to our Creator.

TODAY'S READING
Job 12:7–10

Ask the animals, and they will teach you, or the birds in the sky, and they will tell you. Job 12:7

In the book of Job, Job's friends are debating the reasons for his suffering and ask, "Can you fathom the mysteries of God?" (SEE 11:5–9). In response Job declares, "Ask the animals, and they will teach you, or the birds in the sky, and they will tell you" (JOB 12:7). Animals testify to the truth that God designed, cares for, and controls His creation: "In his hand is the life of every creature and the breath of all mankind" (V. 10).

Since God cares for birds (MATTHEW 6:26; 10:29), we can be assured He loves and cares for you and me, even when we don't understand our circumstances. Look around and learn of Him. 🍞

ALYSON KIEDA

God's world teaches us about Him.

Trust Him First

"**D**on't let go, Dad!"

"I won't. I've got you. I promise."

I was a little boy terrified of the water, but my dad wanted me to learn to swim. He would purposefully take me away from the side of the pool into a depth that was over my head, where he was my only support. Then he would teach me to relax and float.

> **TODAY'S READING**
> Isaiah 46:3–13
>
> **Praise the LORD; praise God our savior! For each day he carries us in his arms.** Psalm 68:19 NLT

It wasn't just a swimming lesson; it was a lesson in trust. I knew my father loved me and would never let me be harmed intentionally, but I was also afraid. I would cling tightly to his neck until he reassured me all would be well. Eventually his patience and kindness won out, and I began to swim. But I had to trust him first.

When I feel "over my head" in a difficulty, I sometimes think back on those moments. They help me call to mind the Lord's reassurance to His people: "Even to your old age . . . I am he who will sustain you. I have made you and I will carry you" (ISAIAH 46:4).

We may not always be able to feel God's arms beneath us, but the Lord has promised that He will never leave us (HEBREWS 13:5). As we rest in His care and promises, He helps us learn to trust in His faithfulness. He lifts us above our worries to discover new peace in Him.   *JAMES BANKS*

Abba, Father, I praise You for carrying me through life.
Please give me faith to trust that You are always with me.

God carries us to new places of grace as we trust in Him.

Terrible and Beautiful Things

ear can leave us frozen. We know all the reasons to be afraid—everything that's hurt us in the past, everything that could easily do so again. So sometimes we're stuck—unable to go back; too afraid to move forward. *I just can't do it. I'm not smart enough, strong enough, or brave enough to handle being hurt like that again.*

I'm captivated by how author Frederick Buechner describes God's grace: like a gentle voice that says, "Here is the world. Terrible and beautiful things will happen. Don't be afraid. I am with you."

Terrible things will happen. In our world, hurting people hurt other people, often terribly. Like the psalmist David, we carry our own stories of when evil surrounded us, when, like "ravenous beasts," others wounded us (PSALM 57:4). And so we grieve; we cry out (VV. 1–2).

TODAY'S READING
Psalm 57

Awake, my soul! Awake, harp and lyre! I will awaken the dawn. Psalm 57:8

But because God is with us, *beautiful things can happen too.* As we run to Him with our hurts and fears, we find ourselves carried by a love far greater than anyone's power to harm us (VV. 1–3), a love so deep it fills the skies (V. 10). Even when disaster rages around us, His love is a solid refuge where our hearts find healing (VV. 1, 7). Until one day we'll find ourselves awakening to renewed courage, ready to greet the day with a song of His faithfulness (VV. 8–10).

MONICA BRANDS

Healer and Redeemer, thank You for holding us and healing us with Your endless love. Help us find in Your love the courage to follow You and share Your love with those around us.

God's love and beauty make us brave.

The Prayer and the Chain Saw

respect my Aunt Gladys's intrepid spirit, even if that very spirit concerns me sometimes. The source of my concern came in the form of news she shared in an email: "I cut down a walnut tree yesterday."

You must understand that my chainsaw-wielding aunt is seventy-six years old! The tree had grown up behind her garage. When the roots threatened to burst through the concrete, she knew it had to go. But she did tell us, "I always pray before I tackle a job like that."

While serving as butler to the king of Persia during the time of Israel's exile, Nehemiah heard news concerning the people who had returned to Jerusalem. Some work needed to be done. "The wall of Jerusalem is broken down, and its gates

TODAY'S READING
Nehemiah 1

LORD, let your ear be attentive to the prayer of this your servant. Nehemiah 1:11

have been burned with fire" (NEHEMIAH 1:3). The broken walls left them vulnerable to attack by enemies. Nehemiah had compassion for his people and wanted to get involved. But prayer came first, especially since a new king had written a letter to stop the building efforts in Jerusalem (see Ezra 4). Nehemiah prayed for his people (NEHEMIAH 1:5–10), and then asked God for help before requesting permission from the king to leave (V. 11).

Is prayer your response? It's always the best way to face any task or trial in life. 🌿

LINDA WASHINGTON

Father, Your Holy Spirit reminds us to pray first.
Today, we commit to doing so as Your Spirit prompts us.

Make prayer a first priority, instead of a last resort.

A Piercing Thorn

The thorn pricked my index finger, drawing blood. I hollered and then groaned, drawing back my hand instinctively. But I *shouldn't* have been surprised: trying to prune a thorny bush without gardening gloves was a recipe for exactly what just happened.

The pain throbbing in my finger—and the blood flowing from it—demanded attention. And as I searched for a bandage, I found myself unexpectedly thinking about my Savior. After all, soldiers forced Jesus to don an entire crown of thorns (JOHN 19:1–3). If one thorn hurt this much, I thought, how much

> TODAY'S READING
> **Isaiah 53:1–6**
>
> **But he was pierced for our transgressions . . . and by his wounds we are healed.** Isaiah 53:5

agony would an entire crown of them inflict? And that's just a small portion of the physical pain He suffered. A whip flogged His back. Nails penetrated His wrists and ankles.

But Jesus endured spiritual pain too. Verse 5 of Isaiah 53 tells us, "But he was pierced for our transgressions, he was crushed for our iniquities; the punishment that brought us peace was on him." The "peace" Isaiah talks about here is another way of talking about forgiveness. Jesus allowed Himself to be pierced by nails and a crown of thorns to bring us spiritual peace with God. His sacrifice, His willingness to die on our behalf, paved the way to make a relationship with the Father possible. And He did it, Scripture tells us, for me, for you.

ADAM HOLZ

Father, I can't imagine the pain Your Son endured to wash away my sin. Thank You for sending Him for me, to be pierced for my sins that I might have a relationship with You.

Jesus allowed Himself to be pierced to bring us spiritual peace with God.

Bring Your Boats

Hurricane Harvey brought catastrophic flooding to eastern Texas in 2017. The onslaught of rain stranded thousands of people in their homes, unable to escape the floodwaters. In what was dubbed the "Texas Navy," many private citizens brought boats from other parts of the state and nation to help evacuate stranded people.

The actions of these valiant, generous men and women call to mind the encouragement of Proverbs 3:27, which instructs us to help others whenever we are able. They had the power to act on behalf of those in need by bringing their boats. And so they *did*. Their actions demonstrate a willingness to use whatever resources they had at their disposal for the benefit of others.

> **TODAY'S READING**
> **Proverbs 3:21–31**
>
> **Do not withhold good from those to whom it is due, when it is in your power to act.**
>
> Proverbs 3:27

We may not always feel adequate for the task at hand; often we become paralyzed by thinking we don't have the skills, experience, resources, or time to help others. In such instances, we're quick to sideline ourselves, discounting what we *do* have that might be of assistance to someone else. The Texas Navy couldn't stop the floodwaters from rising, nor could they legislate government aid. But they used what they had within their power—their boats—to come alongside the deep needs of their fellow man. May we all bring our "boats"—whatever they may be—to take the people in our paths to higher ground. 🌼 *KIRSTEN HOLMBERG*

Lord, all that I have is from You. Help me to always use what You've given me to help others.

God provides for His people through His people.

Always Accepted

After several years of struggling to keep up in her studies, Angie was finally taken out of her elite primary school and transferred to a "normal" one. In Singapore's intensely competitive education landscape, where being in a "good" school can improve one's future prospects, many would see this as a failure.

Angie's parents were disappointed, and Angie herself felt as if she had been demoted. But soon after joining her new school, the nine year old realized what it meant to be in a class of average students. "Mummy, I belong here," she said. "I'm finally accepted!"

TODAY'S READING
Luke 19:1–10

The Son of Man came to seek and to save the lost.
Luke 19:10

It reminded me of how excited Zacchaeus must have felt when Jesus invited Himself to the tax collector's home (LUKE 19:5). Christ was interested in dining with those who knew they were flawed and didn't deserve God's grace (V. 10). Having found us— and loved us—as we were, Jesus gives us the promise of perfection through His death and resurrection. We are made perfect through His grace alone.

I've often found my spiritual journey to be one of constant struggle, knowing that my life falls far short of God's ideal. How comforting it is to know that we are always accepted, for the Holy Spirit is in the business of molding us to be like Jesus. 🌱

LESLIE KOH

Father, thank You for loving me as I am, and for making me perfect through Your Son's sacrifice. Teach me to submit to Your daily renewal.

We're not perfect, but we're loved.

My Real Face

For years, feelings of unworthiness and shame over my less-than-godly past had an adverse impact on every aspect of my life. What if others discovered the extent of my blemished reputation? Though God helped me muster up courage to invite a ministry leader to lunch, I strived to *seem* perfect.

I scrubbed my house spotless, whipped up a three-course meal, and donned my best jeans and blouse.

I rushed to turn off the front-yard sprinklers. Twisting the leaking nozzle, I screamed when a gush of water drenched me. With towel-dried hair and smeared makeup, I changed into dry sweat pants and a T-shirt . . . just in time to hear the doorbell. Frustrated, I confessed my morning's antics and motives. My new friend shared her own battles with fear and insecurity stemming from guilt over past failings. After we prayed, she welcomed me to her team of God's imperfect servants.

> **TODAY'S READING**
> **1 Timothy 1:12–17**
>
> **I thank Christ Jesus our Lord, who has given me strength, that he considered me trustworthy, appointing me to his service.** 1 Timothy 1:12

The apostle Paul accepted his new life in Christ, refusing to deny his past or let it stop him from serving the Lord (1 TIMOTHY 1:12–14). Because Paul knew Jesus's work on the cross saved and changed him—the worst of sinners—he praised God and encouraged others to honor and obey Him (VV. 15–17).

When we accept God's grace and forgiveness, we're freed from our past. Flawed but fiercely loved, we have no reason to be ashamed of our real faces as we serve others with our God-given gifts. 🕊

XOCHITL DIXON

Lord, thanks for eliminating our shame and insecurities as You use us to serve You, no matter what our life looked like before You saved us.

God accepts us as we are, and changes us as we serve Him in love.

Treasure in a Pumpkin

As a young mother, I was determined to document my daughter's first year of life. Each month, I took photos of her to illustrate how she had changed and grown. In one of my favorite pictures, she is gleefully sitting in the belly of a hollowed-out pumpkin I purchased from a local farmer. There she sat, the delight of my heart, contained in an overgrown squash. The pumpkin withered in the ensuing weeks, but my daughter continued to grow and thrive.

> **TODAY'S READING**
> **2 Corinthians 4:7–18**
>
> **We have this treasure in jars of clay to show that this all-surpassing power is from God and not from us.**
>
> 2 Corinthians 4:7

The way Paul describes knowing the truth of who Jesus is reminds me of that photo. He likens the knowledge of Jesus in our heart to a treasure stored in a clay pot. Remembering what Jesus did for us gives us the courage and strength to persevere through struggles in spite of being "hard pressed on every side" (2 CORINTHIANS 4:8). Because of God's power in our lives, when we are "struck down, but not destroyed," we reveal the life of Jesus (V. 9).

Like the pumpkin that withered, we may feel the wear and tear of our trials. But the joy of Jesus in us can continue to grow in spite of those challenges. Our knowledge of Him—His power at work in our lives—is the treasure stored in our frail clay bodies. We can flourish in the face of hardship because of His power at work within us. ❧

KIRSTEN HOLMBERG

Dear Father, thank You for putting Your truth into my heart and life.
Help me to bear up under the challenges I face with Your power.
May others see Your work in my life and come to know You too.

God's power is at work within us.

Choosing the Trail

have a beautiful autumn photograph of a young man on horseback in the Colorado mountains as he contemplates which trail ahead to follow. It reminds me of Robert Frost's poem "The Road Not Taken." In it, Frost ponders two pathways that lie before him. Both are equally inviting, but he doubts he will return to this place again, and he must choose one. Frost wrote, "Two roads diverged in a wood, and I—I took the one less traveled by, and that has made all the difference."

In Jesus's Sermon on the Mount (MATTHEW 5-7), the Lord told His listeners, "Enter through the narrow gate. For wide is the gate and broad is the road that

> TODAY'S READING
> **Matthew 7:13-14**
>
> **Small is the gate and narrow the road that leads to life, and only a few find it.** Matthew 7:14

leads to destruction, and many enter through it. But small is the gate and narrow the road that leads to life, and only a few find it" (7:13-14).

On our journey through life, we face many choices about which road to travel. Many pathways seem promising and attractive but only one is the pathway of life. Jesus calls us to travel the road of discipleship and obedience to God's Word—to follow Him instead of the crowd.

As we ponder the road ahead, may God give us wisdom and courage to follow His way—the road of life. It will make all the difference for us and those we love! 🌍 *DAVID C. MCCASLAND*

Lord, as we go through this day, give us eyes to see the narrow road
that leads to life and the courage to follow it.

Choose to walk the road of life with Jesus.

Impossible to Hold

Swimming with friends in the Gulf of Mexico, Caitlyn encountered a shark, which grabbed her legs and pulled at her body. To counter the attack, Caitlyn punched the shark in the nose. The predator unclenched its jaws and swam away in defeat. Although its bite caused multiple wounds, which required over 100 stitches, the shark was unable to keep Caitlyn in its grasp.

This story reminds me of the fact that Jesus delivered a blow to death, ending its power to intimidate and defeat His followers. According to Peter, "It was impossible for death to keep its hold on [Jesus]" (ACTS 2:24).

TODAY'S READING
Acts 2:22–36

It was impossible for death to keep its hold on [Jesus].
Acts 2:24

Peter said these words to a crowd in Jerusalem. Perhaps many of them had been the ones yelling out, "Crucify him!" to condemn Jesus (MATTHEW 27:22). As a result, Roman soldiers fastened Him to a cross where He hung until they confirmed He was dead. Jesus's body was carried to a tomb where it stayed for three days until God resurrected Him. After His resurrection, Peter and others spoke and ate with Him, and after forty days they watched Him ascend into heaven (ACTS 1:9).

Jesus's life on Earth ended amidst physical suffering and mental anguish, yet God's power defeated the grave. Because of this, death—or any other struggle—lacks the ability to keep us in its grip forever. One day all believers will experience everlasting life and wholeness in God's presence. Focusing on this future can help us find freedom today. 🌾 *JENNIFER BENSON SCHULDT*

Dear Jesus, Your victory over death gives me hope! I praise You as the resurrected One who died so that I could have eternal life.

The grip of the grave is no match for the power of God.

Where Is Peace?

"Do you still hope for peace?" a journalist asked Bob Dylan in 1984.

"There is not going to be any peace," Dylan replied. His response drew criticism, yet there's no denying that peace remains ever elusive.

About 600 years before Christ, most prophets were predicting peace. God's prophet wasn't one of them. Jeremiah reminded the people that God had said, "Obey me, and I will be your God and you will be my people" (JEREMIAH 7:23). Yet they repeatedly ignored the Lord and His

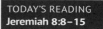

TODAY'S READING
Jeremiah 8:8–15

We have peace with God through our Lord Jesus Christ. Romans 5:1

commands. Their false prophets said, "Peace, peace" (8:11), but Jeremiah predicted disaster. Jerusalem fell in 586 BC.

Peace is rare. But amid Jeremiah's book of dire prophecies we discover a God who loves relentlessly. "I have loved you with an everlasting love," the Lord told His rebellious people. "I will build you up again" (31:3–4).

God is a God of love and peace. Conflict comes because of our rebellion against Him. Sin destroys the world's peace and robs each of us of inner peace. Jesus came to this planet to reconcile us to God and give us that inner peace. "Since we have been justified through faith, we have peace with God through our Lord Jesus Christ," wrote the apostle Paul (ROMANS 5:1). His words are among the most hope-filled ever written.

Whether we live in a combat zone or dwell in a serene neighborhood with nary a whisper of war, Christ invites us into His peace. 🌿

TIM GUSTAFSON

God cannot give us a happiness and peace apart from Himself, because it is not there. *C. S. LEWIS*

The Great Crescendo

My parents taught me to love all sorts of music—from country to classical. So my heart beat rapidly as I walked into the Moscow Conservatory, one of Russia's great music halls, to hear the Moscow National Symphony. As the conductor drove the musicians through a masterful Tchaikovsky piece, themes developed that gradually built to a powerful crescendo—a profound and dramatic musical climax. It was a magical moment, and the audience stood to roar its approval.

The Scriptures move toward the most powerful crescendo of history: the cross and resurrection of Jesus Christ. In the moments following Adam and Eve's fall into sin in the garden of Eden, God promised that a Redeemer would come (GENESIS 3:15), and throughout the Old Testament that theme moved forward. The promise rang out in the Passover lamb (EXODUS 12:21), the hopes of the prophets (1 PETER 1:10), and the longings of the people of God.

> TODAY'S READING
> **1 John 4:14-21**
>
> **The Father has sent his Son to be the Savior of the world.** 1 John 4:14

First John 4:14 confirms where that story had been going: "We have seen and testify that the Father has sent his Son to be the Savior of the world." How? God accomplished His promised rescue of His broken world when Jesus died and rose again to forgive us and restore us to our Creator. And one day He will come again and restore His whole creation.

As we remember what God's Son has done for us, we celebrate the great crescendo of God's grace and rescue for us and His world—Jesus! ❦

BILL CROWDER

Father, Your Son has impacted Your world like nothing else. I'm grateful
He has come for my rescue and will come again to restore Your world.

Celebrate the gift of Jesus!

Unexpected Kindness

My friend was waiting to pay for her groceries when the man in front of her turned around and handed her a voucher for £10 ($14) off her bill. Short on sleep, she burst into tears because of his kind act; then she started laughing at herself for crying. This unexpected kindness touched her heart and gave her hope during a period of exhaustion. She gave thanks to the Lord for His goodness extended to her through another person.

> **TODAY'S READING**
> **Ephesians 2:1–10**
>
> **For we are God's handiwork, created in Christ Jesus to do good works.** Ephesians 2:10

The theme of giving was one the apostle Paul wrote about in his letter to gentile Christians in Ephesus. He called them to leave their old lives behind and embrace the new, saying that they were saved by grace. Out of this saving grace, he explained, flows our desire to "do good works," for we have been created in God's image and are His "handiwork" (2:10). We, like the man at the supermarket, can spread God's love through our everyday actions.

Of course, we don't have to give material things to share God's grace; we can show His love through many other actions. We can take the time to listen to someone when they speak to us. We can ask someone who is serving us how they are. We can stop to help someone in need. As we give to others, we'll receive joy in return (ACTS 20:35). ❧

AMY BOUCHER PYE

Dear Father, You created us in Your image,
and we rejoice that we can share Your love and life.
Help us to see the opportunities to give to others today.

We've been created to share God's love through giving His gifts.

Your Way, Not Mine

Kamil and Joelle were devastated when their eight-year-old daughter Rima was diagnosed with a rare form of leukemia. The disease led to meningitis and a stroke, and Rima lapsed into a coma. The hospital medical team counseled her parents to make arrangements for Rima's funeral, giving her less than a one percent chance of survival.

TODAY'S READING
Luke 22:39–46

Trust in the LORD with all your heart and lean not on your own understanding.
Proverbs 3:5

Kamil and Joelle fasted and prayed for a miracle. "As we pray," Kamil said, "we need to trust God no matter what. And pray like Jesus—not my way, Father, but Yours." "But I want so much for God to heal her!" Joelle answered honestly. "Yes! And we should ask!" Kamil responded. "But it honors God when we give ourselves to Him even when it's hard, because that's what Jesus did."

Before Jesus went to the cross, He prayed: "Father, if you are willing, take this cup from me; yet not my will, but yours be done" (LUKE 22:42). By praying "take this cup," Jesus asked not to go to the cross; but He submitted to the Father out of love.

Surrendering our desires to God isn't easy, and His wisdom can be difficult to understand in challenging moments. Kamil and Joelle's prayers were answered in a remarkable way—Rima is a healthy fifteen year old today.

Jesus understands every struggle. Even when, for our sake, His request was not answered, He showed us how to trust our God in every need. 🐟   *JAMES BANKS*

I want to be "all in" for You, Father. I trust in Your unfailing love and give myself to You as Your servant today.

God always deserves our commitment and praise.

Getting a Grip on Gratitude

The years of weariness caused by chronic pain and frustrations with my limited mobility had finally caught up with me. In my discontent, I became demanding and ungrateful. I began complaining about my husband's caregiving skills. I griped about the way he cleaned the house. Even though he's the best cook I know, I fussed about the lack of variety in our meals. When he finally shared that my grumbling hurt his feelings, I was resentful. He had no idea what I was going through. Eventually, God helped me see my wrongs, and I asked my husband and the Lord for forgiveness.

> TODAY'S READING
> **Numbers 11:1-11**
>
> **Would they have enough if all the fish in the sea were caught for them?** Numbers 11:22

Longing for different circumstances can lead to complaining, and even a form of relationship damaging self-centeredness. The Israelites were familiar with this dilemma. It seems they were never satisfied and always griping about God's provision (EXODUS 17:1-3). Even though the Lord cared for His people in the wilderness by sending them "bread from heaven" (16:4), they began craving other food (NUMBERS 11:4). Instead of rejoicing over the daily miracles of God's faithful and loving care, the Israelites wanted something more, something better, something different, or even something they used to have (VV. 4-6). They took out their frustrations on Moses (VV. 10-14).

Trusting God's goodness and faithfulness can help us get a good grip on gratitude. Today we can thank Him for the countless ways He cares for us. 🌿 *XOCHITL DIXON*

Grateful praise satisfies us and pleases God.

Agreeing to Disagree

I remember hearing my dad talk about how difficult it was to walk away from unending arguments over differing interpretations of the Bible. By contrast he recalled how good it was when both sides agreed to disagree.

But is it really possible to set aside irreconcilable differences when so much seems to be at stake? That's one of the questions the apostle Paul answers in his New Testament letter to the Romans. Writing to readers caught in social, political, and religious conflict, he suggests ways of finding common ground even under the most polarized conditions (14:5–6).

TODAY'S READING
Romans 14:1–13

Let us therefore make every effort to do what leads to peace. Romans 14:19

According to Paul, the way to agree to disagree is to recall that each of us will answer to the Lord not only for our opinions but also for how we treat one another in our differences (V. 10).

Conditions of conflict can actually become occasions to remember that there are some things more important than our own ideas—even more than our interpretations of the Bible. All of us will answer for whether we have loved one another, and even our enemies, as Christ loved us.

Now that I think of it, I remember that my dad used to talk about how good it is not just to agree to disagree but to do so with mutual love and respect. ❦ *MART DEHAAN*

Father, please enable us to be patient and kind with those who don't agree with us about anything or everything.

We can agree to disagree—in love.

Hope in the Darkness

According to legend, Qu Yuan was a wise and patriotic Chinese government official who lived during the time known as the Warring States period (475–246 BC). It has been said that he tried repeatedly to warn his king about an impending threat that would destroy the country, but the king rejected his advice. Eventually, Qu Yuan was exiled. When he learned about the fall of his beloved country to the foe he had warned about, he ended his life.

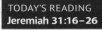

TODAY'S READING
Jeremiah 31:16–26

I will refresh the weary and satisfy the faint. Jeremiah 31:25

Qu Yuan's life resembles some aspects of the life of the prophet Jeremiah. He too served kings who scorned his warnings, and his country was ravaged. However, while Qu Yuan gave in to his despair, Jeremiah found genuine hope. Why the difference?

Jeremiah knew the Lord who offers the only true hope. "There is hope for your descendants," God had assured His prophet. "Your children will return to their own land" (JEREMIAH 31:17). Although Jerusalem was destroyed in 586 BC, it was later rebuilt (SEE NEHEMIAH 6:15).

At some point, we all find ourselves in situations that can cause us to despair. It could be a bad medical report, a sudden job loss, a shattered family. But when life knocks us down, we can still look up—for God is on the throne! He holds our days in His hands, and He holds us close to His heart. 🌸 *POH FANG CHIA*

Lord, fill me up with hope and give me a tangible reminder today that things will turn out right in Your way, in Your time.

The world hopes for the best, but the Lord offers the best hope. JOHN WESLEY

Compassion Fatigue

Anne Frank is well known for her diary describing her family's years of hiding during World War II. When she was later imprisoned in a Nazi death camp, those with her said "her tears [for them] never ran dry," making her "a blessed presence for all who knew her." Because of this, scholar Kenneth Bailey concluded that Anne never displayed "compassion fatigue."

Compassion fatigue can be one of the results of living in a badly broken world. The sheer volume of human suffering can numb even the best intentioned among us. Compassion fatigue, however, was not in Jesus's makeup. Matthew 9:35–36 says, "Jesus went through all the towns and villages, teaching in their synagogues, proclaiming the good news of the kingdom and healing every disease and sickness. When he saw the crowds, he had

> **TODAY'S READING**
> Matthew 9:35–38
>
> **When he saw the crowds, he had compassion on them, because they were harassed and helpless, like sheep without a shepherd.** Matthew 9:36

compassion on them, because they were harassed and helpless, like sheep without a shepherd."

Our world suffers not only from physical needs but also from spiritual brokenness. Jesus came to meet that need and challenged His followers to join Him in this work (vv. 37–38). He prayed that the Father would raise up workers to respond to the needs all around us—people who struggle with loneliness, sin, and illness. May the Father give us a heart for others that mirrors His heart. In the strength of His Spirit, we can express His compassionate concern to those who are suffering. 🌱 *BILL CROWDER*

In a world filled with heartache, we can model the compassion of Jesus.

Our Daily Bread

Catching Foxes

While talking on the phone with a friend who lives by the seaside, I expressed delight at hearing seagulls squawking. "Vile creatures," she responded, for to her they're a daily menace. As a Londoner, I feel the same way about foxes. I find them not cute animals but roaming creatures that leave smelly messes in their wake.

TODAY'S READING
Song 2:14–17

Catch for us the foxes, the little foxes that ruin the vineyards.
Song of Solomon 2:15

Foxes appear in the love poetry of the Song of Solomon, an Old Testament book that reveals the love between a husband and wife and, some commentators believe, between God and His people. The bride warns about little foxes, asking her bridegroom to catch them (2:15). For foxes, hungry for the vineyard's grapes, could tear the tender plants apart. As the bride looks forward to their married life together, she doesn't want vermin disturbing their covenant of love.

How can "foxes" disturb our relationship with God? For me, when I say "yes" to too many requests, I can become overwhelmed and unpleasant. Or when I witness relational conflict, I can be tempted to despair or anger. As I ask the Lord to limit the effect of these "foxes"—those I've let in through an open gate or those that have snuck in—I gain in trust of and love for God as I sense His loving presence and direction.

How about you? How can you seek God's help from anything keeping you from Him? 🌿

AMY BOUCHER PYE

Lord God, You are powerful and You are good.
Please protect my relationship with You, keeping out anything that would
take my eyes off You.

God can guard our relationship with Him.

See Your City

"**S**ee our city the way we do." A Detroit, Michigan, urban development group used that slogan to launch its vision for the city's future. But the project came to a sudden stop when members of the community noticed something missing in the campaign. African Americans make up a large majority of the city's population and workforce. Yet people of color were absent from the crowd of white faces that showed up on signs, banners, and billboards urging all to see the city as they did.

> TODAY'S READING
> **Genesis 12:1–3**
>
> **All peoples on earth will be blessed through you.** Genesis 12:3

The countrymen of Jesus also had a blind spot in their vision for the future. As children of Abraham, they were primarily concerned about the future of Jewish people. They couldn't understand Jesus's concern for Samaritans, Roman soldiers, or anyone else who didn't share their family roots, rabbis, or temple worship.

I relate to the blind spots of Detroit and Jerusalem. I too tend to see only people whose life experience I understand. Yet God has a way of bringing about His unity amid our diversity. We're more alike than we realize.

Our God chose a desert nomad by the name of Abram to bring blessing to all the people of the world (GENESIS 12:1–3). Jesus knows and loves everyone we don't yet know or love. Together we live by the grace and mercy of One who can help us see one another, our cities, and His kingdom—as He does. 🌱 MART DEHAAN

Father in heaven, please open our eyes to people and hearts who are more like us than we are inclined to believe. Help us see our own need of You.

Everyone everywhere is more like us than less like us.

Our Daily Bread

Still the King

One news report called it "the single deadliest day for Christians in decades." The pair of attacks on Sunday worshipers in April 2017 defies our understanding. We simply don't have a category to describe bloodshed in a house of worship. But we can find some help from others who know this kind of pain well.

Most of the people of Jerusalem were in exile or had been slain when Asaph wrote Psalm 74. Pouring out his heart's anguish, he described the destruction of the temple at the hands of ruthless invaders. "Your foes roared in the place where you met with us," Asaph said (v. 4). "They burned your sanctuary to the ground; they defiled the dwelling place of your Name" (v. 7).

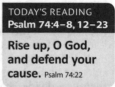

TODAY'S READING
Psalm 74:4–8, 12–23

Rise up, O God, and defend your cause. Psalm 74:22

Yet the psalmist found a place to stand despite the awful reality—providing encouragement that we can do so too. "But God is my King from long ago," Asaph resolved. "He brings salvation on the earth" (v. 12). This truth enabled Asaph to praise God's mighty power even though His salvation seemed absent in the moment. "Have regard for your covenant," Asaph prayed. "Do not let the oppressed retreat in disgrace; may the poor and needy praise your name" (vv. 20–21).

When justice and mercy seem absent, God's love and power are in no way diminished. With Asaph, we can confidently say, "But God is my King." 🌱

TIM GUSTAFSON

Lord, with the psalmist we pray for the honor of Your Name.
Show Yourself strong and compassionate.
Rise up and defend Your cause.

God will defend His Name.

Wisdom's Source

A man filed a lawsuit against a woman, claiming she had his dog. In court, the woman said her dog couldn't be his and told the judge where she had purchased it. The real owner's identity was revealed when the judge released the animal in the courtroom. Tail wagging, it immediately ran to the man!

Solomon, a judge in ancient Israel needed to settle a somewhat similar issue. Two women each claimed to be the mother of the same baby boy. After considering both arguments, he requested a sword to divide the infant in half. The

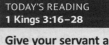

TODAY'S READING
1 Kings 3:16–28

Give your servant a discerning heart.
1 Kings 3:9

real mother begged Solomon to give the baby to the other woman, choosing to save her son's life even if she could not have him (1 KINGS 3:26). Solomon gave the baby to *her*.

Wisdom is necessary as we decide what's fair and moral, right and wrong. If we truly value wisdom, we can ask God for a discerning heart, like Solomon did (V. 9). God may answer our request by helping us balance our needs and desires with the interests of others. He may also help us weigh short-term benefits against long-term (sometimes eternal) gains so we can honor Him in how we live.

Our God is not only a perfectly wise judge, but He is also a personal counselor who is willing to give us godly wisdom in great amounts (JAMES 1:5). 🌿

JENNIFER BENSON SCHULDT

I worship You God, as the true source of wisdom.
Please show me how to make choices that bring honor to Your name.

Need wisdom? Seek it from the Source who alone can provide it—God.

Our Daily Bread

Dad at the Dentist

didn't expect a profound lesson about the Father's heart at the dentist's office—but I got one. I was there with my ten-year-old son. He had an adult tooth coming in under a baby tooth that hadn't fallen out yet. It had to come out. There was no other way.

> **TODAY'S READING**
> Matthew 26:36–39
>
> **My Father, if it is possible, may this cup be taken from me. Yet not as I will, but as you will.** Matthew 26:39

My son, in tears, pleaded with me: "Dad, isn't there another way? Can't we just wait and see? Please, Dad, I don't *want* to have this tooth pulled!" It just about broke my heart, but I told him, "Son, it's got to come out. I'm sorry. There's no other way." And I held his hand as he wriggled and writhed while the dentist removed that stubborn molar, tears in my eyes too. I couldn't take his pain away; the best I could offer was to be present with him in it.

In that moment, I remembered Jesus in the garden of Gethsemane, asking His Father for a different way. How it must have broken the Father's heart to see His beloved Son in such agony! Yet there was no other way to save His people.

In our lives, we sometimes face unavoidable yet painful moments—just like my son did. But because of Jesus's work for us through His Spirit, even in our darkest moments our loving heavenly Father is always present with us (MATTHEW 28:20). *ADAM HOLZ*

Father, thank You for loving us so much that You sent Your beloved Son to save us, even though it must have broken Your heart to do so. In our times of joy or pain, thank You for Your Spirit holding and carrying us.

Our loving heavenly Father promises He is always present with us, even in our darkest moments.

I'm Sorry

In 2005, Collins falsified a report that resulted in McGee being thrown in prison for four years, and McGee vowed to find Collins when he got out and "hurt him." McGee was eventually exonerated, but not before he lost everything. Meanwhile, Collins's many falsified reports were uncovered, he lost his job, and he too spent time behind bars. But both men came to faith in Christ while in prison.

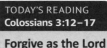

TODAY'S READING
Colossians 3:12–17

Forgive as the Lord forgave you.
Colossians 3:13

In 2015, the two discovered they were working together in the same faith-based company. Collins recalls, "I [told McGee], 'Honestly, I have no explanation, all I can do is say I'm sorry.'" It was "pretty much what I needed to hear," said McGee, who graciously forgave him. The men were able to reconcile because both had experienced the incomparable love and forgiveness of God, who empowers us to "forgive as the Lord forgave [us]" (COLOSSIANS 3:13).

Now the two are great friends. "We have this joint mission . . . of letting the world know that if you owe an apology to somebody, put your pride down and go apologize," said Collins. "And if you're holding something against somebody, let go of the bitterness because it's like drinking poison and hoping it's hurting them."

God calls believers to live in peace and unity. If we have "a grievance against someone," we can bring it to Him. He will help us to reconcile (VV. 13–15; PHILIPPIANS 4:6–7). 🌿   ALYSON KIEDA

Dear Father, thank You for forgiving us when we come to You
in sorrow over our sins. Help us to receive Your forgiveness
and to extend it to others.

Christ sets us free to forgive.

Fathers and Sons

My father was a good father, and, in most respects, I was a dutiful son. But I allowed my father to starve for the one thing I could have given him: myself.

He was a quiet man; I was equally silent. We often worked for hours side-by-side with scarcely a word passing between us. He never asked; I never told him my deepest desires and dreams, my hopes and fears.

In time I woke up to my reticence. Perhaps the perception came when my first son was born, or when, one by one, my sons went out into the world. Now I wish I had been more of a son to my father.

> TODAY'S READING
> **Ephesians 4:31–32**
>
> **He will turn the hearts of fathers to their children and the hearts of children to their fathers.** Malachi 4:6 ESV

I think of all the things I could have told him. And all the things he could have told me. At his funeral I stood beside his casket, struggling to understand my emotions. "It's too late, isn't it?" my wife said quietly. "Exactly."

My comfort lies in the fact that we'll be able to set things right in heaven, for is that not where every tear will be wiped away? (REVELATION 21:4).

For believers in Jesus, death is not the end of affection but the beginning of timeless existence in which there will be no more misunderstandings; relationships will be healed and love will grow forever. There, the hearts of sons will turn to their fathers and the hearts of fathers to their sons (MALACHI 4:6). 🌾

DAVID H. ROPER

Father, thank You for forgiving me and allowing me to experience a restored relationship with You. Help me to seek reconciliation in my broken relationships and deeper connections with others close to me even as I await the healing that will come in Your presence.

In God's power and love, draw closer to others while there's time.

What We Can Do

Even though confined to his bed, 92-year-old Morrie Boogaart knit hats for the homeless in Michigan. He had reportedly made more than 8,000 hats in fifteen years. Instead of focusing on his health or limitations, Mr. Boogaart looked beyond himself and did what he could to place the needs of others above his own. He declared that his work made him feel good and gave him a purpose. He said, "I'm going to do this until I go home to the Lord"—which happened in February 2018. Though most recipients of his hats won't know his story or how much he sacrificed to create each cap, Morrie's simple act of persevering love is now inspiring people across the world.

> TODAY'S READING
> **Philippians 2:1–11**
>
> **In your relationships with one another, have the same mindset as Christ Jesus.** Philippians 2:5

We too can look past our struggles, place others before ourselves, and imitate our loving and compassionate Savior, Jesus Christ (PHILIPPIANS 2:1–5). God in the flesh—the King of Kings—took on the "very nature of a servant" in genuine humility (VV. 6–7). Giving His life—the ultimate sacrifice—He took our place on the cross (V. 8). Jesus gave everything for us . . . all for the glory of God the Father (VV. 9–11).

As believers in Jesus, it's our privilege to show love and demonstrate concern for others through acts of kindness. Even if we don't think we have much to offer, we can adopt the attitude of servanthood. We can actively seek opportunities to make a difference in people's lives by simply doing what we can. 🌱

XOCHITL DIXON

We can model Christ's love by doing what we can to serve others.

His Presence

The anxious father and his teenage son sat before the psychic. "How far is your son traveling?" the psychic asked. "To the big city," the man replied, "and he will be gone for a long time." Handing the father a talisman (a kind of good-luck charm), he said, "This will protect him wherever he goes."

TODAY'S READING
Exodus 3:7–12

I was that boy. However, that psychic and that talisman could do nothing for me. While in that city, I put my faith in Jesus. I threw away the talisman and clung to Christ. Having Jesus in my life guaranteed God's presence.

My presence will go with you, and I will give you rest.

Exodus 33:14

Thirty years later, my father, now a believer, said to me as we rushed my brother to the hospital, "Let us first pray; the Spirit of God goes with you and will be with you all the way!" We had learned that God's presence and power is our only security.

Moses learned a similar lesson. He had a challenging task from God—to lead the people out of bondage in Egypt and into the Promised Land (EXODUS 3:10). But God assured him, "I will be with you" (V. 12).

Our journey too is not without challenges, but we're assured of God's presence. As Jesus told His disciples, "I am with you always, to the very end of the age" (MATTHEW 28:20). 🌿

LAWRENCE DARMANI

When the journey seems long and dreary, dear Lord,
help me to remember that You are traveling with me.

There's no need to fear where you're going when Jesus is going with you.

Confident Hope

Dr. William Wallace was serving as a missionary surgeon in Wuzhou, China, in the 1940s when Japan attacked China. Wallace, who was in charge of Stout Memorial Hospital at the time, ordered the hospital to load his equipment on barges and continue to function as a hospital while floating up and down rivers to avoid infantry attacks.

> **TODAY'S READING**
> **Philippians 1:19–26**
>
> **For to me, to live is Christ and to die is gain.** Philippians 1:21

During dangerous times, Philippians 1:21—one of Wallace's favorite verses—reminded him that if he lived, he had work to do for the Savior; but if he died, he had the promise of eternity with Christ. The verse took on special meaning when he died while falsely imprisoned in 1951.

Paul's writing reflects a deep devotion we can aspire to as followers of Jesus; enabling us to face trials and even danger for His sake. It is devotion enabled by the Holy Spirit and the prayers of those closest to us (V. 19). It's also a promise. Even when we surrender ourselves to continued service under difficult circumstances, it is with this reminder: when our life and work end here, we still have the joy of eternity with Jesus ahead of us.

In our hardest moments, with hearts committed to walking with Christ now, and with our eyes firmly fixed on the promise of eternity with Him, may our days and our acts bless others with the love of God.

RANDY KILGORE

Make of me, Father, a willing servant in times of weakness
and times of strength.

Sacrifices offered to God are opportunities to showcase His love.

Who's Driving?

My neighbor Tim has a figurine on his dashboard of a "wild thing" based on Maurice Sendak's beloved children's book *Where the Wild Things Are*.

Not long ago Tim was following me through traffic and made some abrupt moves to keep up. When we arrived, I asked, "Was that the 'wild thing' driving?"

The following Sunday I forgot my sermon notes at home. I "flew" out of the church to retrieve them, passing Tim along the way. When we met later, he joked, "Was that the wild thing driving?"

TODAY'S READING
Romans 6:1–14

Since we live by the Spirit, let us keep in step with the Spirit. Galatians 5:25

We laughed, but his point hit home—I should have paid attention to the speed limit.

When the Bible describes what it means to live in a relationship with God, it encourages us to "offer every part of [ourselves]" to Him (ROMANS 6:13). I took Tim's response to me that day as a gentle reminder from God to yield my "lead foot," because I am to give all of myself to Him out of love.

The question of "who's driving?" applies to all of life. Do we let the "wild things" of our old sin nature drive us—like worry, fear, or self-will—or do we yield to God's loving Spirit and the grace that helps us grow?

Giving in to God is good for us. Scripture says that God's wisdom takes us down "pleasant ways, and all her paths are peace" (PROVERBS 3:17). Better to follow where He leads. 🌱

JAMES BANKS

Loving Lord, thank You for the grace You give us to obey You,
and the peace You give us as we stay near.

What God requires He also inspires.

Dumb Sheep, Good Shepherd

My friend Chad spent a year as a shepherd in Wyoming. "Sheep are so dumb that they'll only eat what is right in front of them," he told me. "Even if they've eaten all the grass in front of them, they won't turn to look for a fresh patch—they'll just start eating dirt!"

We laughed, and I couldn't help but think about how often the Bible compares humans to sheep. No wonder we need a shepherd! But since sheep are so dumb, not just any shepherd will do. Sheep need a shepherd who cares about them. When the prophet Ezekiel wrote to God's people in exile, captives in Babylon, he compared them to sheep led by bad shepherds. Instead of caring for the flock, Israel's

> **TODAY'S READING**
> **Ezekiel 34:7–16**
>
> As a shepherd looks after his scattered flock when he is with them, so will I look after my sheep. Ezekiel 34:12

leaders had exploited them, profiting from them (V. 3) and then leaving them for the wild animals to devour (V. 5).

But they were not without hope. God, the Good Shepherd, promised to rescue them from the leaders who exploited them. He promised to bring them home, put them in lush pastures, and give them rest. He would heal the injured and go after the lost (VV. 11–16). He would banish wild animals, so that His flock would be safe (V. 28).

Members of God's flock are in need of tender care and direction. How blessed we are to have a Shepherd who is always leading us to green pastures! (V.14). 🌾

AMY PETERSON

Am I listening for the voice of my Shepherd?

Bound to Encourage

The **Steven Thompson Memorial Centipede** is a cross-country meet unlike any other. Each seven-member team runs as a unit, holding a rope for the first two miles of a three-mile course. At the two-mile mark, the team drops the rope and finishes the race individually. Each person's time is, therefore, a combination of the pace the team kept and his or her own speed.

This year, my daughter's team opted for a strategy I had not previously seen: They put the fastest runner at the front and the slowest right behind her. She explained that their goal was for the strongest runner to be near enough to speak words of encouragement to the slowest runner.

> TODAY'S READING
> **Hebrews 10:19–25**
>
> **Let us consider how we may spur one another on toward love and good deeds.** Hebrews 10:24

Their plans depicted for me a passage from the book of Hebrews. The writer urges us to "hold unswervingly to the hope we profess" (HEBREWS 10:23) as we "spur one another on toward love and good deeds" (V. 24). There are certainly many ways of accomplishing this, but the author highlighted one: "not giving up meeting together, as some are in the habit of doing, but encouraging one another" (V. 25). Gathering together with other believers as we're able is a vital aspect of the life of faith.

The race of life can feel like more than we can handle at times, and we may be tempted to drop the rope in hopelessness. As we run together, let's offer one another the encouragement to run strong! ◈

KIRSTEN HOLMBERG

Jesus, thank You for the hope You offer. Thank You for never discouraging us. Help us imitate You by encouraging each other today.

Encouragement is water to the soul.

Dangerous Distractions

Artist **Sigismund Goetze** shocked Victorian-era England with a painting entitled "Despised and Rejected of Men." In it, he portrayed the suffering, condemned Jesus surrounded by people of Goetze's own generation. They were so consumed by their own interests—business, romance, politics—that they were shockingly oblivious to the Savior's sacrifice. Indifferent to Christ, the surrounding crowd, like the mob at the foot of Jesus's cross, had no idea what—or who—they had missed.

> TODAY'S READING
> **John 13:31–35**
>
> **Your love for one another will prove to the world that you are my disciples.** John 13:35 NLT

In our day as well, believers and unbelievers alike can easily become distracted from the eternal. How can followers of Jesus cut through this fog of distraction with the truth of God's great love? We can begin by loving one another as fellow children of God. Jesus said, "Your love for one another will prove to the world that you are my disciples" (JOHN 13:35 NLT).

But real love doesn't stop there. We extend that love by sharing the gospel in hopes of drawing people to the Savior. As Paul wrote, "We are . . . Christ's ambassadors" (2 CORINTHIANS 5:20).

In this way, the body of Christ can both reflect and project God's love, the love we so desperately need, to both each other and to our world. May both efforts, empowered by His Spirit, be a part of cutting through the distractions that hinder us from seeing the wonder of God's love in Jesus.   *BILL CROWDER*

To a world living in the fog of distraction, we bring the light of the good news of Jesus.

Thanks for Who God Is

Among the thousands of sentiments printed on greeting cards, perhaps one of the most touching is this simple statement: "Thanks for being you." If you receive that card, you know that someone cares for you not because you did something spectacular for that person but because you're appreciated for your essence.

I wonder if this kind of sentiment might indicate for us one of the best ways to say "thank you" to God. Sure, there are times when God intervenes in our lives in a tangible way, and we say something like, "Thank You, Lord, for allowing me to get that job." But most often, we can simply say, "Thank You, God, for being who You are."

TODAY'S READING
Psalm 95:1–7

Let us come before him with thanksgiving . . . for the LORD is the great God.

Psalm 95:2–3

That's what's behind verses like 1 Chronicles 16:34: "Give thanks to the LORD, for he is good; his love endures forever." Thank You, God, for who You are—good and loving. And Psalm 7:17: "I will give thanks to the LORD because of his righteousness." Thank You, God, for who You are—the holy One. And "Let us come before him with thanksgiving . . . for the Lord is the great God" (PSALM 95:2–3). Thank You, God, for who You are—the Almighty God of the universe.

Who God is. That's reason enough for us to stop what we're doing and praise and thank Him. Thank You, God, for just being You! 🌐
DAVE BRANON

Thank You, dear God, for being who You are—the Almighty God
who loves us and welcomes our love in return.
Thank You for everything that makes You magnificent.
We stand in awe of You as we praise You with word and song.

There are countless reasons to thank God, including for who He is!

Power of Touch

Dr. Paul Brand, twentieth-century pioneer medical missionary to India, saw firsthand the stigma associated with leprosy. During an appointment, he touched a patient to reassure him treatment was possible. Tears began to stream down the man's face. An attendant explained the tears to Dr. Brand, saying, "You touched him and no one has done that for years. They are tears of joy."

Early in His ministry, Jesus was approached by a man with leprosy, an ancient label for all types of infectious skin diseases. Because of his disease the man was required by the Old Testament law to live outside his community. If the sick man accidentally found himself in close proximity to healthy people, he had to call out, "Unclean! Unclean!" so they could avoid him (LEVITICUS 13:45–46). As a result, the man may have gone months or years without human contact.

> **TODAY'S READING**
> **Mark 1:40–45**
>
> **Moved with compassion, Jesus reached out and touched him.**
>
> Mark 1:41 NLT

Filled with compassion, Jesus reached out His hand and touched the man. Jesus had the power and authority to heal people with just a word (MARK 2:11–12). But as Jesus encountered a man whose physical illness left him feeling isolated and rejected, His touch assured the man that he was not alone but accepted.

As God gives us opportunities, we can extend grace and show compassion with a gentle touch that conveys dignity and value. The simple, healing power of human touch goes a long way to remind hurting people of our care and concern. LISA SAMRA

Lord Jesus, thank You for the personal way You reached out to care
for hurting people. Help me to follow Your example and extend
compassion in my actions.

Caring for others may include a compassionate touch.

Don't Stop Building!

When an opportunity came to take on a new role at work, Simon believed it was a godsend. After praying over the decision and seeking counsel, he felt that God was giving him this opportunity to take on bigger responsibilities. Everything fell into place, and his boss supported his move. Then things began to go wrong. Some colleagues resented his promotion and refused to cooperate. He began to wonder if he should give up.

> **TODAY'S READING**
> **Ezra 5:1–5**
>
> **The eye of their God was watching over [them] … and they were not stopped.** Ezra 5:5

When the Israelites returned to Jerusalem to build the house of God, enemies sought to frighten and discourage them (EZRA 4:4). The Israelites stopped at first, but continued after God encouraged them through the prophets Haggai and Zechariah (4:24–5:2).

Once again, enemies came to hassle them. But this time they persevered, knowing "the eye of their God was watching over [them]" (5:5). They held on firmly to God's instructions and trusted Him to carry them through whatever opposition they'd face. Sure enough, God moved the Persian king to support the temple's completion (VV. 13–14).

Similarly, Simon sought God's wisdom to discern whether he should stay or find a new position. Sensing God calling him to remain, he relied on God's strength to persevere. Over time, he slowly gained his colleagues' acceptance.

As we seek to follow God, wherever He places us, we may face opposition along the way. That's when we need to keep following Him. He will guide us and carry us through. ❧

LESLIE KOH

Remain strong, for God's eye is on you.

Hard Conversations

once drove fifty miles to have a hard conversation with a remote staff person. I had received a report from another employee that suggested he was misrepresenting our company, and I was concerned for our reputation. I felt nudged to offer an opinion that might change his choices.

In 1 Samuel 25, an unlikely person took great personal risk to confront a future king of Israel who was about to make a disastrous choice. Abigail was married to Nabal, whose character matched the meaning of his name ("fool") (VV. 3, 25). Nabal had refused to pay David and his troops the customary wage for protecting his livestock (VV. 10–11). Hearing that David planned a murderous revenge on her household, and knowing her foolish husband wouldn't listen to reason, Abigail prepared a peace offering, rode to meet David, and persuaded him to reconsider (VV. 18–31).

TODAY'S READING
1 Samuel 25:21–35

If it is possible, as far as it depends on you, live at peace with everyone. Romans 12:18

How did Abigail accomplish this? After sending ahead donkeys loaded with food to satisfy David and his men and settle the debt, she spoke truth to David. She wisely reminded David of God's call on his life. If he resisted his desire for revenge, when God made him king, he wouldn't "have on his conscience the staggering burden of needless bloodshed" (V. 31).

You might also know someone dangerously close to a mistake that could harm others and compromise their own future effectiveness for God. Like Abigail, might God be calling you to a hard conversation? 🌾   *ELISA MORGAN*

Dear God, please help me know when to lovingly confront others.

Sometimes following God means difficult conversations.

On the Wrong Side?

When the bridge to Techiman, Ghana, washed out, residents of New Krobo on the other side of the Tano River were stranded. Attendance at Pastor Samuel Appiah's church in Techiman suffered too because many of the members lived in New Krobo—on the "wrong" side of the river.

TODAY'S READING
Philippians 1:12–18

What has happened to me has actually served to advance the gospel. Philippians 1:12

Amid the crisis, Pastor Sam was trying to expand the church's children's home to care for more orphans. So he prayed. Then his church sponsored outdoor meetings across the river in New Krobo. Soon they were baptizing new believers in Jesus. A new church took root. Not only that, New Krobo had space to care for the orphans awaiting housing. God was weaving His restorative work into the crisis.

When the apostle Paul found himself on the "wrong" side of freedom, he didn't lament his situation. In a powerful letter to the church in Philippi, he wrote, "I want you to know, brothers and sisters, that what has happened to me has actually served to advance the gospel" (PHILIPPIANS 1:12). Paul noted how his chains had led to "the whole palace guard" learning about Christ (V. 13). And others had gained confidence to share the good news of Jesus (V. 14).

Despite obstacles, Pastor Sam and the apostle Paul found God showing them new ways to work in their crises. What might God be doing in our challenging circumstances today? 🌿

TIM GUSTAFSON

Lord, sometimes we feel as though we're on the wrong side of a particular situation. We know You are everywhere. Help us see You.

God is at work in the mess. That's the message of the Bible. MATT CHANDLER

A Hidden Ministry

A big academic project was weighing on me, and I was fretting over whether I could complete it by the deadline. In the midst of my anxious thoughts, I received three notes of encouragement from friends who were cheering me on. Each one said, "God brought you to mind today when I was praying." I felt humbled and encouraged that these friends would contact me without knowing what I was going through, and I believed God had used them as His messengers of love.

TODAY'S READING
2 Corinthians 1:8–11

On him we have set our hope that he will continue to deliver us, as you help us by your prayers.

2 Corinthians 1:10–11

The apostle Paul knew the power of prayer when he wrote to the people in the church of Corinth. He said he trusted that God would continue to deliver them from peril "as you help us by your prayers" (2 CORINTHIANS 1:10–11). And when God answered their prayers, He would be glorified as the people gave Him thanks for the "answer to the prayers of many" (V. 11).

My friends and Paul's supporters were engaging in the ministry of intercession, which Oswald Chambers calls "a hidden ministry that brings forth fruit through which the Father is glorified." As we focus our minds and hearts on Jesus, we find Him shaping us, including how we pray. He enables us to give the gift of true intercession to friends, family members, and even strangers.

Has God put someone on your heart and mind for whom you can pray? 🌸

AMY BOUCHER PYE

God hears the prayers of His people.

What We Have

My friend was eager to gather her family and friends for a festive holiday celebration at her home. Each of the guests looked forward to gathering around the table together and wanted to help defray the expense of feeding so many by contributing to the meal. Some would bring bread, others salad or a side dish. For one guest, however, money was exceptionally tight. Although she looked forward to spending the evening with those whom she loved, she couldn't afford to purchase any food. So, instead, she offered to clean the host's home as her gift.

TODAY'S READING
2 Corinthians 8:1–12

For if the willingness is there, the gift is acceptable according to what one has, not according to what one does not have.

2 Corinthians 8:12

She would have been welcome at the table had she come empty-handed. Yet she looked at what she did have to offer—her time and skills—and brought them to the gathering with her whole heart. I think that's precisely the spirit of Paul's words in 2 Corinthians 8. They had been eager to give to help some fellow Christians, and he urged them to follow through on that effort. He commended them for their desire and their willingness, saying their motivation to give is what makes a gift of any size or amount acceptable (V. 12).

We're often quick to compare our giving to that of others, especially when our resources don't afford us the luxury of giving as much as we'd like to. But God views our giving differently: it's our willingness to give what we have that He loves. 🌼

KIRSTEN HOLMBERG

Lord, help me see what You've given me, even if it doesn't seem like much by the world's standards. Help me to give generously.

God loves wholehearted giving of any measure.

A Mother's Love

When Sue's parents divorced when she was young, the legal tussle over her custody and other matters resulted in her being sent to a children's home for a while. Bullied by bigger kids, she felt lonely and abandoned. Her mother visited only once a month, and she hardly saw her father. It was only years later, however, that her mother told her that while the home's rules prevented her from visiting more often, she had stood at the fence every single day, hoping to catch a glimpse of her daughter. "Sometimes," she said, "I would just watch you playing in the garden, just to check if you were okay."

> **TODAY'S READING**
> **Psalm 91:1–6**
>
> **He will call on me, and I will answer him; I will be with him in trouble, I will deliver him and honor him.**
>
> Psalm 91:15

When Sue shared this story, it gave me a glimpse of God's love. Sometimes we may feel abandoned and alone in our struggles. How comforting it is to know that God is in fact watching over us all the time! (PSALM 33:18). Even though we can't see Him, He is there. Like a loving parent, His eyes and His heart are constantly on us wherever we go. Yet, unlike Sue's mom, He can act on our behalf at any time.

Psalm 91 describes God delivering, protecting, and lifting up His children. He is more than a refuge and a shelter. As we navigate the dark valleys of life, we can take comfort in the knowledge that the all-powerful Lord is watching over us and is active in our lives. "I will answer [you]," He declares. "I will be with [you] in trouble, I will deliver [you]" (V. 15). 🌿 *LESLIE KOH*

Lord, thank You for the assurance that we're always under Your watchful care.

Our heavenly Father is ever near.

A Constant Helper

After a spinal injury left Marty paralyzed, he decided to go back to school to earn his MBA. Marty's mother, Judy, helped make his goal a reality. She sat with him through every lecture and study group, jotting notes and handling technology issues. She even assisted him onto the platform when he received his diploma. What might have been unattainable became possible with the consistent, practical help Marty received.

Jesus knew His followers would need a similar kind of support after He left the earth. When He told them about His upcoming absence, He said they would gain a new kind of connection with God through the Holy Spirit. This Spirit would

TODAY'S READING
John 14:15–26

[The Holy Spirit] will remind you of everything I have said to you. John 14:26

be a moment-by-moment helper—a teacher and guide who would not only live *with* them but also be *in* them (JOHN 14:17, 26).

The Spirit would provide Jesus's disciples with internal help from God, which would enable them to endure what they couldn't handle on their own as they fanned out to share the good news. In moments of struggle, the Spirit would remind them of everything Jesus said to them (V. 26): Do not let your hearts be troubled ... Love one another ... I am the resurrection and the life.

Are you facing something that exceeds your own strength and ability? You can depend on the Spirit's constant help. God's Spirit working in you will bring Him the glory He deserves. 🌱

JENNIFER BENSON SCHULDT

Dear God, thank You for the ongoing support available through the Holy Spirit. Help me to rely on Your Spirit when I need help.

When it is a question of God's almighty Spirit, never say, "I can't."
OSWALD CHAMBERS

Quiet Witness

Amy lives in a closed country where it's forbidden to preach the gospel. She's a trained nurse who works in a big hospital, caring for newborn babies. She's such a committed professional that her work stands out, and many women are curious about her. They are moved to ask her questions in private. It's then that Amy shares about her Savior openly.

Because of her good work, some co-workers were envious and accused her of stealing some medicine. Her superiors didn't believe them, and authorities eventually found the culprit. This episode led some of her fellow nurses to ask about her faith. Her example reminds me of what Peter says: "Dear friends . . . . Be careful to live properly among your unbelieving neighbors. Then even if they accuse you of doing wrong, they will see your honorable behavior, and they will give honor to God" (1 PETER 2:11–12 NLT).

> TODAY'S READING
> **1 Peter 2:11–21**
>
> **Be careful to live properly among your unbelieving neighbors.**
>
> 1 Peter 2:12 NLT

Our everyday lives at home, in our work environment, or at school make an impact on others when we let God work in us. We're surrounded by people who are watching the way we speak and behave. Let's depend on God and have Him rule our actions and thoughts. Then we'll influence those who don't believe and this may lead some of them to turn in faith to Jesus. ❧

KEILA OCHOA

Father, help me to live in such a way that Your name
will be honored wherever I go.

Our lives speak louder than our words.

God Is Here

A plaque in our home states "Bidden or not bidden, God is present." A modern version might read, "Acknowledged or unacknowledged, God is here."

Hosea, an Old Testament prophet who lived in the late eighth century BC (755–715), wrote similar words to the Hebrew nation. He encouraged the Israelites to "press on" (HOSEA 6:3) to acknowledge God because they had forgotten Him (4:1). As the people forgot God's presence, they began to turn away from Him (V. 12) and before long there was no room for God in their thoughts (SEE PSALM 10:4).

> **TODAY'S READING**
> **Hosea 6:1–6**
>
> **Let us acknowledge the LORD; let us press on to acknowledge him.**
>
> Hosea 6:3

Hosea's simple but profound insight to acknowledge God reminds us He's near and at work in our lives, in both the joys and struggles.

To acknowledge God might mean that when we get a promotion at work, we recognize God gave us insight to finish our work on time and within budget. If our housing application is rejected, acknowledging God helps to sustain us as we trust Him to work in the situation for our good.

If we don't make it into the college of our choice, we can acknowledge God is with us and take comfort in His presence even in our disappointment. As we enjoy dinner, to acknowledge God may be to remind ourselves of God's provision of the ingredients and a kitchen to prepare the meal.

When we acknowledge God, we remember His presence in both the successes and sorrows, whether big or small, of our lives. ❧

LISA SAMRA

Lord Jesus, please forgive me for the times I am prone to forget You. Help me to acknowledge Your presence in my life.

God is always present and at work.

Putting Up Hay

When I was in college, I worked a summer on a ranch in Colorado. One evening, tired and hungry after a long day of mowing hay, I drove the tractor into the yard. Acting like the hot shot I thought I was, I cranked the steering wheel hard left, stamped on the left brake, and spun the tractor around.

The sickle was down and swept the legs out from under a 500-gallon gasoline tank standing nearby. The tank hit the ground with a resounding boom, the seams split, and all the gasoline spewed out.

The rancher stood nearby surveying the scene.

I got off the tractor, stammered an apology, and—because it was the first thing that popped into my mind— offered to work the rest of the summer without pay.

> **TODAY'S READING**
> **Luke 15:11–24**
>
> **Blessed are those whose transgressions are forgiven.** Romans 4:7

The old rancher stared at the wreckage for a moment and turned toward the house. "Let's go have dinner," he drawled.

A scrap of a story Jesus told passed through my mind—a story about a young man who had done a terrible thing: "Father, I have sinned against heaven and against you," he cried. He intended to add, "Make me like one of your hired servants," but before he could get all the words out of his mouth his father interrupted him. In essence, he said, "Let's go have dinner" (LUKE 15:17–24).

Such is God's amazing grace. 🌾

DAVID H. ROPER

Father, we celebrate Your gracious and lavish forgiveness.
Thank You for the peace and freedom it brings us
as we enjoy a family relationship with You.

What a privilege to be sons and daughters of the King!

A Solid Foundation

Last summer my husband and I toured Fallingwater, a house in rural Pennsylvania designed by architect Frank Lloyd Wright in 1935. I've never seen anything quite like it. Wright wanted to create a home that rose organically out of the landscape, as if it could have grown there—and he accomplished his goal. He built the house around an existing waterfall, and its style mirrors the neighboring rock ledges. Our tour guide explained what made the construction safe: "The whole vertical core of the house," she said, "rests on boulders."

> TODAY'S READING
> **Matthew 7:24–27**
>
> **Everyone who hears these words of mine and puts them into practice is like a wise man who built his house on the rock.**
>
> Matthew 7:24

Hearing her words, I couldn't help but think of Jesus's words to His disciples. During the Sermon on the Mount, Jesus told them that what He was teaching would be the sure foundation for their lives. If they heard His words and put them into practice, they would be able to withstand any storms. Those who heard but didn't obey, in contrast, would be like a house built on sand (MATTHEW 7:24–27). Later, Paul echoed this thought, writing that Christ is the foundation, and we must build upon it with work that will endure (1 CORINTHIANS 3:11).

When we listen to the words of Jesus and obey them, we're building our lives on a steady, rock-solid foundation. Maybe our lives can look a little like Fallingwater, beautiful and built to last on the Rock.

AMY PETERSON

God, help us to hear and obey the words of Jesus!

What are you building your life around?

Lord of the Moment

Not long ago I was working on a construction project at my son's home three hours away. The job took days longer than expected, and each morning I prayed we would finish by sunset. But every evening there was more to be done.

I wondered why. Could there be a reason for the delay? An answer came the next morning. I was picking up a tool when my phone rang and a stranger's voice spoke urgently: "Your daughter was injured in an accident. You need to come immediately."

> TODAY'S READING
> **2 Kings 8:1-6**
>
> **In their hearts humans plan their course, but the LORD establishes their steps.** Proverbs 16:9

She lived near my son, so it took just fourteen minutes to reach her. If I had been home, I would have been three hours away. I followed the ambulance to the hospital and comforted her before surgery. As I sat holding her hand I realized if my project hadn't been delayed, I wouldn't have been there.

Our moments belong to God. This was the experience of a woman whose son God had resurrected through the prophet Elisha (2 KINGS 4:18-37). She left the country because of famine and returned years later to beg the king for her land. At precisely that moment the king was conversing with the prophet's servant Gehazi. "Just as Gehazi was telling the king how Elisha had restored" her son, the woman walked in (8:5). Her request was granted.

We don't know what even the next second brings, but God is graciously able to use any situation for good. May God give us grace to walk with Him expectantly into His appointments for us today. 🖋️   *JAMES BANKS*

Thank You, Lord, for the gift of my life. Help me to be Your faithful servant.

Our lives are better off in God's hands than in our own.

Honoring God with Thanks

The doctor wasn't frowning, despite talking to my husband about his recent cancer diagnosis. Smiling, she offered a suggestion: start each day by giving thanks. "For at least three things," the doctor said. Dan agreed, knowing that gratitude opens our hearts to find encouragement in God's goodness. Thus, Dan starts each day with words of praise. *Thank You, God, for a good night's sleep. For my clean bed. For sunshine. For breakfast on the table. For a smile on my lips.*

> **TODAY'S READING**
> **Psalm 50:8–15**
>
> **Call on me in the day of trouble; I will deliver you, and you will honor me.** Psalm 50:15

Each word is heartfelt. But could it sound trivial? Does our praise in life's small details matter to Almighty God? In Psalm 50, David's chief musician, Asaph, offers a clear answer. God has "no need of a bull from your stall or of goats from your pens" (V. 9). Instead of these once-formal Israelite sacrifices of gratitude, God wants His people to give Him our hearts and lives in gratitude (VV. 14, 23).

As my husband experienced, whole-hearted gratitude helps our spirits flourish. Then when we call on the Lord "in the day of trouble," He will "deliver" us (V. 15). Does this mean Dan will be healed, spiritually and physically, during his two-year treatment? Or not until after this lifetime? We don't know. But for now, Dan delights in showing God he's grateful for His love, and for who God is: Redeemer. Healer. Friend. And friends delight to hear these beautiful words: Thank you. 🌱

PATRICIA RAYBON

My gratitude to God is great to Him.

God Hears

Diane listened as the others in the group asked for prayers for their family members and friends facing challenges or illness. She had a family member who had been struggling with an addiction for years. But Diane kept her request silent. She couldn't bear to see the looks on people's faces or hear the questions or advice that often followed whenever she spoke the words aloud. She felt that this request was usually better left unspoken. Others simply didn't understand how her loved one could be a believer in Jesus and still struggle daily.

TODAY'S READING
Romans 12:9–21

Be joyful in hope, patient in affliction, faithful in prayer. Romans 12:12

Although Diane didn't share her request with that group, she did have a few trusted friends she asked to pray with her. Together they asked God to set her loved one free from the very real bondage of addiction that he might experience freedom in Christ—and that God would give Diane the peace and patience she needed. As she prayed, she found comfort and strength from her relationship with Him.

Many of us have earnest, persistent prayers that seem to go unanswered. But we can be assured that God *does* care and He *does* hear all our requests. He urges us to continue to walk closely with Him, being "joyful in hope, patient in affliction, faithful in prayer" (ROMANS 12:12). We can lean on Him. 🌱

ALYSON KIEDA

Lord, Your Word urges us to pray continually. Help us to be persistent in prayer, and enable us to be faithful partners in prayer with others.

Let us draw near to God with a sincere heart and with the full assurance that faith brings. *HEBREWS 10:22*

A Safe Place

My brothers and I grew up on a wooded hillside in West Virginia that provided a fertile landscape for our imaginations. Whether swinging from vines like Tarzan or building tree houses like the Swiss Family Robinson, we played out the scenarios we found in the stories we read and movies we watched. One of our favorites was building forts and then pretending we were safe from attack. Years later, my kids built forts out of blankets, sheets, and pillows—constructing their own "safe place" against imaginary enemies. It seems almost instinctive to want a hiding place where you can feel safe and secure.

> TODAY'S READING
> **Psalm 17:1–9**
>
> **I call on you, my God, for you will answer me; turn your ear to me and hear my prayer.**
> Psalm 17:6

When David, the singer-poet of Israel, sought a safe place, he looked no further than God. Psalm 17:8 asserts, "[God,] keep me as the apple of your eye; hide me in the shadow of your wings." When you consider the Old Testament record of David's life and the almost constant threats he faced, these words reveal an amazing level of confidence in God (V. 6). In spite of those threats, he was convinced his true safety was found in Him.

We can know that same confidence. The God who promises to never leave or forsake us (HEBREWS 13:5) is the One we trust with our lives every day. Although we live in a dangerous world, our God gives us peace and assurance—both now and forever. He is our safe place. 🌱

BILL CROWDER

Father, the world around me can feel threatening, overwhelming, and dangerous. But You give me peace, strength, and help.

Give God thanks for being your hiding place today.

Thanks for Being You!

When I served as my mom's live-in caregiver at a cancer center, I got to know Lori, another caregiver who lived down the hallway from us with her husband, Frank. I would chat, laugh, vent, cry, and pray with Lori in the shared living areas. We enjoyed supporting each other as we cared for our loved ones.

TODAY'S READING
Psalm 100

Enter his gates with thanksgiving.
Psalm 100:4

One day, I missed the free shuttle that took residents to buy groceries. Lori offered to drive me to the store later that evening. With grateful tears, I accepted her offer. "Thanks for being you," I said. I truly appreciated her for who she was as a person, not just for what she did for me as a friend.

Psalm 100 demonstrates an appreciation of God for who He is, not simply for all He does. The psalmist invites "all the earth" (v. 1) to "worship the Lord with gladness" (v. 2), being confident in knowing "the Lord is God" (v. 3). Our Maker invites us into His presence to "give thanks to him and praise his name" (v. 4). Yes, the Lord remains worthy of our ongoing thankfulness because He "is good," His "love endures forever," and His "faithfulness continues through all generations" (v. 5).

God will always be the Creator and Sustainer of the universe and our intimately loving Father. He deserves our genuine joy-filled gratitude. 🌱

XOCHITL DIXON

Lord, thanks for being You!

Who can you share God's love with today?

Questions at Christmas

Well before the calendar flips to December, Christmas cheer begins to bubble up in our northern town. A medical office drapes its trees and shrubs in close-fitting strings of lights, each a different color, illuminating a breathtaking nighttime landscape. Another business decorates its building to look like an enormous, extravagantly wrapped Christmas present. It's difficult to turn anywhere without seeing evidence of Christmas spirit—or at least seasonal marketing.

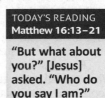

TODAY'S READING
Matthew 16:13–21

"But what about you?" [Jesus] asked. "Who do you say I am?"
Matthew 16:15

Some people love these lavish displays. Others take a more cynical view. But the crucial question isn't how others observe Christmas. Rather, we each need to consider what the celebration means to *us*.

A little more than thirty years after His birth, Jesus asked His disciples, "Who do people say the Son of Man is?" (MATTHEW 16:13). They gave responses others had given: John the Baptist, Elijah, maybe another prophet. Then Jesus made it personal: "Who do *you* say I am?" (V. 15). Peter replied, "You are the Messiah, the Son of the living God" (V. 16).

Many will celebrate Christmas without a thought about who the Baby really is. As we interact with them, we can help them consider these crucial questions: Is Christmas just a heartwarming story about a baby born in a stable? Or did our Creator visit His creation and become one of us? 🌱

TIM GUSTAFSON

Father in heaven, may our Christmas celebrations this year, whether lavish or small, honor the Messiah who came to redeem His creation.

Who do you say Jesus is?

A Hand Up

My children have enjoyed the thrill of a backyard ice-skating rink during our cold Idaho winters. When they were young, learning to skate was challenging: persuading them to deliberately set foot on the hard, icy surface proved difficult because they knew the pain of falling. Each time their feet slid out from under them, my husband or I would reach out to pull them again to their feet, setting them upright and steadying their frames.

TODAY'S READING
Ecclesiastes 4:8–12

If either of them falls down, one can help the other up.

Ecclesiastes 4:10

Having someone there to help us up when we fall is the gift of a helping hand depicted in Ecclesiastes. Working with another makes our work sweeter and more effective (4:9), and a friend brings warmth to our lives. When we encounter challenges, it helps to have someone come alongside with practical and emotional support. These relationships can give us strength, purpose, and comfort.

When we find ourselves flattened on the cold ice of life's hardships, is there a helping hand nearby? If so, it might be from God. Or when someone else needs a friend, could we be God's answer to lift them up? In being a companion, we often find one. If it appears that no one is nearby to lift us to our feet again, we can find comfort in knowing that God is our ever-present help (PSALM 46:1). As we reach out to Him, He's ready to steady us with His firm grip. 🌱   KIRSTEN HOLMBERG

Thank You, Father, for helping me up when life knocks me down. Thank You for the people You've used to encourage and strengthen me. Yours is the most faithful friendship I have.

How can you open yourself more fully to God's presence in your life?

Lonely Christmas

The loneliest Christmas I ever spent was in my grand-father's cottage near Sakogu, northern Ghana. I was just fifteen, and my parents and siblings were a thousand kilometers away. In previous years, when I'd been with them and my village friends, Christmas was always big and memorable. But this Christmas was quiet and lonely. As I lay on my floor mat early Christmas morning, I remembered a local song: *The year has ended; Christmas has come; the Son of God is born; peace and joy to everybody.* Mournfully, I sang it over and over.

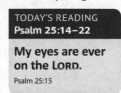

TODAY'S READING
Psalm 25:14-22

My eyes are ever on the LORD.

Psalm 25:15

My grandmother came and asked, "What song is that?" My grandparents didn't know about Christmas—or about Christ. So I shared what I knew about Christmas with them. Those moments brightened my loneliness.

Alone in the fields with only sheep and occasional preda-tors, the shepherd boy David experienced loneliness. It would not be the only time. Later in his life he wrote, "I am lonely and afflicted" (PSALM 25:16). But David didn't allow loneliness to cause him to be despondent. Instead, he sang: "My hope, LORD, is in you" (V. 21).

From time to time we all face loneliness. Wherever Christ-mas may find you this year, in loneliness or in companionship, you can enjoy the season with Christ. 🌿   *LAWRENCE DARMANI*

Lord, thank You that with You I'm not alone even
in my times of loneliness. This Christmas, help me to enjoy my
fellowship with You and to reach out to others.

With Jesus at Christmas, we're never alone.

God's Hidden Hand

My friend was adopted by a missionary couple from the United States and grew up in Ghana. After his family moved back to the US, he began college but had to drop out. Later, he signed on with the military, which eventually helped him pay for college and took him all over the world. Through it all, God was at work, preparing him for a special role. Today, he writes and edits Christian literature that ministers to an international audience.

TODAY'S READING
Psalm 139:13–18

All the days ordained for me were written in your book before one of them came to be. Psalm 139:16

His wife also has an interesting story. She failed her chemistry exams during her first year of college due to the strong medication she had to take for epilepsy. After some careful deliberation, she switched from studying science to studying American Sign Language, which had a more manageable workload. Reflecting on that experience, she says, "God was redirecting my life for a greater purpose." Today, she is making His life-changing Word accessible to the hearing-impaired.

Do you sometimes wonder where God is leading you? Psalm 139:16 acknowledges God's sovereign hand in our lives: "Your eyes saw my unformed body; all the days ordained for me were written in your book before one of them came to be." We don't know how God will use the circumstances of our life, but we can rest in the knowledge that God knows everything about us and is directing our footsteps. Though His sovereign hand may seem hidden, He's never absent. 🕊

POH FANG CHIA

Dear Lord, help me to trust You even when I don't understand.

What steps can you take to discern God's leading
or to act on His call for your life?

Home

Recently a friend who sold homes for a living died of cancer. As my wife and I reminisced about Patsy, Sue recalled that many years ago Patsy had led a man to faith in Jesus and he became a good friend of ours.

How encouraging to recall that Patsy not only helped families find homes to live in here in our community, but she also helped others make sure they had an eternal home.

As Jesus prepared to go to the cross for us, He showed a keen interest in our eternal accommodations. He told His disciples, "I go to prepare a place for you" and reminded them that there would be plenty of room in His Father's house for all who trusted Him (JOHN 14:2 NKJV).

TODAY'S READING
John 14:1-6

In My Father's house are many mansions; if it were not so, I would have told you. I go to prepare a place for you. John 14:2 NKJV

We love to have a nice home in this life—a special place for our family to eat, sleep, and enjoy each other's company. But think of how amazing it will be when we step into the next life and discover that God has taken care of our eternal accommodations. Praise God for giving us life "to the full" (JOHN 10:10), including His presence with us now and our presence with Him later in the place He is preparing for us (14:3).

Thinking of what God has in store for those who trust Jesus can challenge us to do as Patsy did and introduce others to Him. 🌱   *DAVE BRANON*

Lord, while we anticipate the home You're preparing for us,
may we tell others they too can enjoy forever the home You're preparing
for all who believe in Jesus.

*Who can you talk to today about their need for an eternal home
and the assurance that would bring them?*

Steadfast Love

"**I love you!**" my dad called out as I slammed the car door and headed into school. I was in sixth grade, and for months we had played out basically the same scenario every morning. We arrived at school, Dad said, "Have a great day! I love you!" and all I said was "Bye." I wasn't angry with him or ignoring him. I was simply so wrapped up in my own thoughts that I didn't notice his words. Nevertheless, my dad's love remained steadfast.

> **TODAY'S READING**
> **Psalm 136:1–9**
>
> **Give thanks to the LORD, for he is good. His love endures forever.**
> Psalm 136:1

God's love is like that—and more. It endures forever. The Hebrew word that expresses this steadfast kind of love is *hesed*. It's used over and over again in the Old Testament, and twenty-six times in Psalm 136 alone! No modern word can fully capture the meaning; we translate it "kindness," "loving-kindness," "mercy," or "loyalty." *Hesed* is a love that is based on covenant commitment; love that is loyal and faithful. Even when God's people sinned, He was faithful in loving them. Steadfast love is an integral part of the character of God (EXODUS 34:6).

When I was a child, I sometimes took my dad's love for granted. Sometimes now I do the same thing with my heavenly Father's love. I forget to listen to God and respond. I forget to be grateful. Yet I know that God's love for me remains steadfast—a reality that provides a sure foundation for all of my life. 🌿

AMY PETERSON

God, we praise You for Your steadfast love to us!
Even when we're faithless, You're faithful.

Take time to show the love of God to someone today.

"The Lord's"

I t doesn't take much to notice that getting "inked" is very popular these days. Some tattoos are so small that one barely notices them. Others—from athletes to actors to everyday people—have opted to cover much of their bodies with multicolored inks, words, and designs. The trend seems like it's here to stay, a trend that netted $3 billion in revenue in 2014—and an additional $66 million for tattoo removal.

> **TODAY'S READING**
> Isaiah 44:1–5
>
> **The Spirit himself testifies with our spirit that we are God's children.**
>
> Romans 8:16

Regardless of how you may feel about tattoos, Isaiah 44 speaks metaphorically about people writing something on their hands: "The Lord's" (v. 5). This "self-tattoo" is the climax of an entire paragraph that speaks of the Lord's care for those He had chosen (v. 1). They could count on His help (v. 2); and their land and descendants were marked for blessing (v. 3). Two simple, powerful words, "The Lord's," affirmed that God's people knew they were His possession and that He would take care of them.

Those who come to God through faith in Jesus Christ can confidently say of themselves, "The Lord's!" We are His people, His sheep, His offspring, His inheritance, His dwelling. These are the things we cling to in the varied seasons of life. While we may have no external mark or tattoo, we can take heart that we have the witness of God's Spirit in our hearts that we belong to Him (SEE ROMANS 8:16–17). 🍃   *ARTHUR JACKSON*

Father, the expressions of Your love and care are all around me
and Your Spirit lives within me. Thank You!

How can the truth that you belong to God impact how you live?

Expect the Messiah

The repairman looked young—too young to fix our problem, a car that wouldn't start. "He's just a kid," my husband, Dan, whispered to me, showing his doubt. His disbelief in the young man sounded like the grumbling in Nazareth where citizens doubted who Jesus was.

"Isn't this the carpenter's son?" they asked (MATTHEW 13:55) when Jesus taught in the synagogue. Scoffing, they were surprised to hear that someone they knew was healing and teaching, and asked, "Where did this man get this wisdom and these miraculous powers?" (V. 54). Instead of trusting in Jesus, they were offended by the authority He displayed (VV. 15, 58).

TODAY'S READING
Matthew 13:53–58

"Isn't this the carpenter's son? Isn't his mother's name Mary?"
Matthew 13:55

In this same way, we may struggle to trust in our Savior's wisdom and power, especially in the familiar and ordinary details of our daily lives. Failing to expect His help, we may miss out on the wonder of His life transforming our own (V. 58).

As Dan found, the help he needed stood right in front of him. Finally agreeing to accept the young man's aid, my husband allowed him to look at our old car's battery. By switching just one bolt, the mechanic had the car running in seconds—engine humming and lights ablaze. "It lit up like Christmas," Dan said.

So too may we expect and experience the Messiah bringing fresh light, life, and help into our daily journey with Him. ❧

PATRICIA RAYBON

When I doubt You, Lord, help my unbelief.
What are some practical ways you can remind yourself or others that God is in control and He is able?

The "No-Secret" Secret

A coworker confessed to me that he didn't think he was "Jesus material." I listened as he described what he called his "comfortable, narcissistic" life, and how it didn't satisfy him. "But here's my problem, I've been trying to be good, even caring, but it isn't working. It seems that the very things I want to do, I can't do, and the things I want to stop doing, I just keep doing."

"What's your secret?" he asked me in complete sincerity. "My secret," I answered, "is that there is no secret. I'm as powerless to live up to God's standards as you are, which is why we need Jesus."

I pulled out a Bible and showed him "his" quote as the apostle Paul expressed it in Romans 7:15. Paul's words of frustration often resonate with both pre-Christians *and* Christians who find themselves trying to be good enough to deserve God but falling short. Maybe it resonates with you. If so, Paul's declaration that Christ is the author of our salvation and its resulting changes (7:25–8:2) should thrill you. Jesus has already done the work to free us from the very things that have us so puzzled with ourselves!

The barrier between us and God, the barrier of sin, has been removed without any work on our part. Salvation—and the changes made by the Holy Spirit in the process of our growth—is what God desires for all. He knocks on the door of our souls. Answer His knock today. It's no secret that He's the answer! ❧

RANDY KILGORE

> TODAY'S READING
> **Romans 7:14–25**
>
> **I do not understand what I do. For what I want to do I do not do, but what I hate I do.** Romans 7:15

Without Jesus, salvation and spiritual growth are both gifts beyond our reach.

The "Hope for a Baby" Tree

After wrapping the tree with clear twinkle lights, I tied pink and blue bows on its branches and christened it our "Hope for a Baby" Christmas tree. My husband and I had been waiting for a baby through adoption for more than four years. Surely by Christmas!

Every morning I stopped at the tree and prayed, reminding myself of God's faithfulness. On December 21 we received the news: no baby by Christmas. Devastated, I paused by the tree that had become a symbol of God's provision. *Was God still faithful? Was I doing something wrong?*

TODAY'S READING
Lam. 3:1–3, 13–24

His compassions never fail. They are new every morning; great is your faithfulness.

Lamentations 3:22–23

At times, God's apparent withholding results from His loving discipline. And other times God lovingly delays to renew our trust. In Lamentations, the prophet Jeremiah describes God's correction of Israel. The pain is palpable: "He pierced my heart with arrows from his quiver" (3:13). Through it all, Jeremiah also expresses ultimate trust in God's faithfulness: "His compassions never fail. They are new every morning; great is your faithfulness" (vv. 22–23).

I left the tree standing well beyond Christmas and continued my morning prayer. At last, on Easter weekend, we received our baby girl. God is always faithful, though not necessarily on our timeline nor always according to our desires.

My children are now in their thirties, but each year I set up a miniature version of the tree, reminding myself and others to hope in God's faithfulness. ❧

ELISA MORGAN

Dear God, help me trust You today even when I can't see
what You are doing. You are faithful.

The best reason for hope is God's faithfulness.

Heaven's Love Song

n 1936, songwriter **Billy Hill** released a popular hit song titled "The Glory of Love." Before long a nation was singing about the joy of doing even little things out of love for one another. Fifty years later, lyricist Peter Cetera wrote a more romantic song with a similar title. He imagined two people living forever, knowing together they did it all—for the glory of love.

Revelation, the last book in the Bible, describes a new love song that will someday lift the voices of everyone in heaven and earth (REVELATION 5:9, 13). The music begins, however, in a minor key of mourning. John, our narrator, cries, seeing no answer to all that has gone wrong with the world (VV. 3-4). But his mood brightens and the music builds to a crescendo (VV. 12-13) as John learns the real glory and story of love. Soon he hears all creation praising the powerful Lion-King of Judah (V. 5), who has won the hearts of His subjects by lovingly sacrificing Himself, like a Lamb, for our rescue (V. 13).

> TODAY'S READING
> **Revelation 5:1–13**
>
> **We love him because he first loved us.** 1 John 4:19

In the most moving lyrics ever sung, we see why even simple acts of kindness rise on the wings of a song. The glory we sing about reflects the heart of our God. We sing about Him because He gave us our song.

MART DEHAAN

Father, please help us to see that even the smallest acts of love
and kindness can remind us of Your love for us.

In what ways can you thank God today through simple acts of kindness?

Mosaic of Beauty

Sitting in the courtyard of the Church of the Visitation in Ein Karem, Israel, I was overwhelmed with the beautiful display of sixty-seven mosaics containing the words of Luke 1:46–55 in as many languages. Traditionally known as the *Magnificat* from the Latin "to magnify," these verses are Mary's joyous response to the announcement that she will be the mother of the Messiah.

Each plaque contains Mary's words, including: "My soul glorifies the Lord and my spirit rejoices in God my Savior.... For the Mighty One has done great things for me" (vv. 46–49). The biblical hymn etched in the tiles is a song of praise as Mary recounts the faithfulness of God to her and the nation of Israel.

> **TODAY'S READING**
> Luke 1:46–55
>
> **My soul glorifies the Lord and my spirit rejoices in God my Savior.**
>
> Luke 1:46–47

A grateful recipient of God's grace, Mary rejoices in her salvation (v. 47). She acknowledges that God's mercy has extended to the Israelites for generations (v. 50). Looking back over God's care for the Israelites, Mary praises God for His powerful acts on behalf of His people (v. 51). She also thanks God, recognizing that her daily provision comes from His hand (v. 53).

Mary shows us that recounting the great things God has done for us is a way to express praise and can lead us to rejoice. This Christmas season, consider God's goodness as you reflect on the year. In doing so, you may create a mosaic of great beauty with your words of praise. ❧   *LISA SAMRA*

Father, we praise You for the great things You've done in our lives this year. We rejoice in Your mercy and care for us.

Make a list of the ways God has blessed you this year and reflect on it in silence. Then share stories of His goodness with someone.

Mirrors and Hearers

When I emerged from my hotel in Kampala, Uganda, my hostess, who had come to pick me up for our seminar, looked at me with an amused grin. "What's so funny?" I inquired. She laughed and asked, "Did you comb your hair?" It was my turn to laugh, for I had indeed forgotten to comb my hair. I'd looked at my reflection in the hotel mirror. How come I took no notice of what I saw?

In a practical analogy, James gives us a useful dimension to make our study of Scripture more beneficial. We look in the mirror to examine ourselves to see if anything needs correction—hair combed, face washed, shirt properly buttoned. Like a mirror, the Bible helps us to examine our character, attitude, thoughts, and behavior (JAMES 1:23–24). This enables us to align our lives according to the principles of what God has revealed. We will "keep a tight rein" on our tongues (V. 26) and "look after orphans and widows" (V. 27). We will pay heed to God's Holy Spirit within us and keep ourselves "from being polluted by the world" (V. 27).

> **TODAY'S READING**
> **James 1:16–27**
>
> **Whoever looks intently into the perfect law that gives freedom, and continues in it . . . will be blessed in what they do.**
>
> James 1:25

When we look attentively into "the perfect law that gives freedom" and apply it to our lives, we will be blessed in what we do (V. 25). As we look into the mirror of Scripture, we can "humbly accept the word planted in [us]" (V. 21). ❧

LAWRENCE DARMANI

Heavenly Father, "open my eyes that I may see wonderful things in your law" (PSALM 119:18). Help me to order my life according to what You show me in Scripture.

As a mirror reflects our image, the Bible reveals our inner being.

From Shame to Honor

t's that time of the year again, when families gather to celebrate the festive season together. Some of us, however, dread meeting certain "concerned" relatives whose questions can make those who are still single or childless feel that there's something wrong with them.

Imagine the plight of Elizabeth, who was childless despite being married for many years. In her culture, that was seen as a sign of God's disfavor (SEE 1 SAMUEL 1:5–6) and could actually be considered shameful. So while Elizabeth had been living righteously (LUKE 1:6), her neighbors and relatives may have suspected otherwise.

TODAY'S READING
Luke 1:18–25

[The Lord] has shown his favor and taken away my disgrace among the people. Luke 1:25

Nonetheless, Elizabeth and her husband continued to serve the Lord faithfully. Then, when both were well advanced in years, a miracle occurred. God heard her prayer (V. 13). He loves to show us His favor (V. 25). And though He may seem to delay, His timing is always right and His wisdom always perfect. For Elizabeth and her husband, God had a special gift: a child who would become the Messiah's forerunner (ISAIAH 40:3–5).

Do you feel inadequate because you seem to lack something—a university degree, a spouse, a child, a job, a house? Keep living for Him faithfully and waiting patiently for Him and *His* plan, just as Elizabeth did. No matter our circumstances, God is working in and through us. He knows your heart. He hears your prayers. 🐟   *POH FANG CHIA*

God, You are forever faithful and good. Help us to keep trusting in You,
even when we experience heartache.

Keep living for Him faithfully and waiting patiently for His plan.

The Great Awakening

have a treasured memory of gatherings with family friends when our boys were small. The adults would talk into the night; our children, weary with play would curl up on a couch or chair and fall asleep.

When it was time to leave, I would gather our boys into my arms, carry them to the car, lay them in the back seat, and take them home. When we arrived, I would pick them up again, tuck them into their beds, kiss them goodnight, and turn out the light. In the morning they would awaken—at home.

TODAY'S READING
Deuteronomy 34:1–8

God will bring with Jesus those who have fallen asleep in him.
1 Thessalonians 4:14

This has become a rich metaphor for me of the night on which we "sleep in Jesus" (1 THESSALONIANS 4:14 KJV). We slumber ... and awaken in our eternal home, the home that will heal the weariness that has marked our days.

I came across an Old Testament text the other day that surprised me—a closing comment in Deuteronomy: "Moses ... died there in Moab, as the LORD had said" (34:5). The Hebrew means literally, "Moses died ... *with the mouth of the LORD*," a phrase ancient rabbis translated, "With the kiss of the LORD."

Is it too much to envision God bending over us on our final night on earth, tucking us in and kissing us goodnight? Then, as John Donne so eloquently put it, "One short sleep past, we wake eternally." 🌱

DAVID H. ROPER

Heavenly Father, because Your arms carry us,
we can sleep in peace.

For death is no more than a turning of us over from time to eternity.

WILLIAM PENN

A Christmas Letter

Every Christmas, a friend of mine writes a long letter to his wife, reviewing the events of the year and dreaming about the future. He always tells her how much he loves her, and why. He also writes a letter to each of his daughters. His words of love make an unforgettable Christmas present.

We could say that the original Christmas love letter was Jesus, the Word made flesh. John highlights this truth in his gospel: "In the beginning was the Word, and the Word was with God, and the Word was God" (JOHN 1:1). In ancient philosophy, the Greek for Word, *logos*, suggested a divine mind or order that unites reality, but John expands the definition to reveal the Word as a *person*: Jesus, the Son of God who was "with God in the beginning" (V. 2). This Word, the Father's "one and only Son," "became flesh and made his dwelling among us" (V. 14). Through Jesus the Word, God reveals Himself perfectly.

> **TODAY'S READING**
> **John 1:1–14**
>
> **The Word became flesh and made his dwelling among us. We have seen his glory, the glory of the one and only Son, who came from the Father.**
>
> John 1:14

Theologians have grappled with this beautiful mystery for centuries. However much we may not understand, we can be certain that Jesus as the Word gives light to our dark world (V. 9). If we believe in Him, we can experience the gift of being God's beloved children (V. 12).

Jesus, God's love letter to us, has come and made His home among us. Now that's an amazing Christmas gift! 🕊

AMY BOUCHER PYE

Lord Jesus Christ, You are the Word of God, and You bring light into my life. May I shine forth Your goodness and grace and bring You honor.

How can you share the amazing gift of Jesus with others today?

Following the Leader

I n the sky over our house, three fighter jets scream through the sky—flying in formation so close together they appear to be one. "Wow," I say to my husband, Dan. "Impressive," he agrees. We live near an Air Force base and it's not unusual to see such sights.

TODAY'S READING
Luke 9:21–24

Every time these jets fly over, however, I have the same question: *how can they fly so close together and not lose control?* One obvious reason, I learned, is humility. Trusting that the lead pilot is traveling at precisely the correct speed and trajectory, the wing pilots surrender any desire to switch directions or question their leader's path. Instead, they get in

Whoever wants to be my disciple must deny themselves and take up their cross daily and follow me. Luke 9:23

formation and closely follow. The result? A more powerful team.

It's no different for followers of Jesus. He says, "Whoever wants to be my disciple must deny themselves and take up their cross daily and follow me" (LUKE 9:23).

His path was one of self-denial and suffering, which can be hard to follow. But to be His effective disciples, we too are invited to put aside selfish desires and pick up spiritual burdens daily—serving others first instead of ourselves, for example—as we closely follow Him.

It's quite a sight, this humbling, close walk with God. Following His lead, and staying so close, we can appear with Christ as one. Then others won't see us, they'll see Him. There's a simple word for what that looks like: "Wow!" 🌸

PATRICIA RAYBON

Please, God, draw us close to You. Fill us with Your Spirit of love and joy and peace. Enable us to be a shining light in our world.

Our lives are a window through which others can see Jesus.

Don't Be Afraid!

Nearly every time an angel appears in the Bible, the first words he says are "Don't be afraid!" Little wonder. When the supernatural makes contact with planet Earth, it usually leaves the human observers flat on their faces in fear. But Luke tells of God making an appearance in a form that doesn't frighten. In Jesus, born with the animals and laid in a feeding trough, God takes an approach that we need not fear. What could be less scary than a newborn baby?

> TODAY'S READING
> **Luke 2:42–52**
>
> **The kingdom of God has come near.** Mark 1:15

On Earth Jesus is both God and man. As God, He can work miracles, forgive sins, conquer death, and predict the future. But for Jews accustomed to images of God as a bright cloud or pillar of fire, Jesus also causes much confusion. How could a baby in Bethlehem, a carpenter's son, a man from Nazareth, be the Messiah from God?

Why does God take on human form? The scene of twelve-year-old Jesus debating rabbis in the temple gives one clue. "Everyone who heard him was amazed at his understanding and his answers," Luke tells us (2:47). For the first time, ordinary people could hold a conversation with God in visible form.

Jesus can talk to anyone—His parents, a rabbi, a poor widow—without first having to announce, "Don't be afraid!" In Jesus, God draws near. 🍂

PHILIP YANCEY

Heavenly Father, we pause at Christmas to remember how Your Son came to us in the form of a helpless baby . . . and we worship in amazement and wonder that God came near to us.

Jesus was God and man in one person, that God and man might be happy together again. GEORGE WHITEFIELD

Hope *Is* Our Strategy

My favorite football team has lost eight consecutive games as I write this. With each loss, it's harder to hope this season can be redeemed for them. The coach has made changes weekly, but they haven't resulted in wins. Talking with my coworkers, I've joked that merely wanting a different outcome can't guarantee it. "Hope is not a strategy," I've quipped.

That's true in football. But in our spiritual lives, it's just the opposite. Not only is cultivating hope in God a strategy, but clinging to Him in faith and trust is the *only* strategy. This world often disappoints us, but hope can anchor us in God's truth and power during the turbulent times.

> **TODAY'S READING**
> Micah 7:1–7
>
> **But as for me, I watch in hope for the LORD, I wait for God my Savior; my God will hear me.**
>
> Micah 7:7

Micah understood this reality. He was heartbroken by how Israel had turned away from God. "What misery is mine! . . . The faithful have been swept from the land; not one upright person remains" (7:1–2). But then he refocused on his true hope: "But as for me, I watch in hope for the LORD, I wait for God my Savior; my God will hear me" (v. 7).

What does it take to maintain hope in harsh times? Micah shows us: Watching. Waiting. Praying. Remembering. God hears our cries even when our circumstances are overwhelming. In these moments, clinging to and acting in response to our hope in God *is* our strategy, the only strategy that will help us weather life's storms. 🌱
ADAM HOLZ

Father, You've promised to be an anchor for our hearts
when circumstances look discouraging. Help us call out to You in faith
and hope, believing that You hear our hearts' cries.

What does it take to maintain hope in harsh times?
Watching. Waiting. Praying. Remembering.

In Abundance or Affliction

Ann Voskamp's book *One Thousand Gifts* encourages readers to search their lives each day for what the Lord has done for them. In it, she daily notes God's abundant generosity to her in gifts both large and small, ranging from the simple beauty of iridescent bubbles in the dish sink to the incomparable salvation of sinners like herself (and the rest of us!). Ann contends that gratitude is the key to seeing God in even the most troubling of life's moments.

TODAY'S READING
Job 1:13–22

The LORD gave and the LORD has taken away; may the name of the LORD be praised. Job 1:21

Job is famous for a life of such "troubling" moments. Indeed, his losses were deep and many. Just moments after losing all his livestock, he learns of the simultaneous death of all his ten children. Job's profound grief was evidenced in his response: he "tore his robe and shaved his head" (1:20). His words in that painful hour make me think Job knew the practice of gratitude, for he acknowledges that God had given him everything he'd lost (v. 21). How else could he worship in the midst of such incapacitating grief?

The practice of daily gratitude can't erase the magnitude of pain we feel in seasons of loss. Job questioned and grappled through his grief as the rest of the book describes. But recognizing God's goodness to us—in even the smallest of ways—*can* prepare us to kneel in worship before our all-powerful God in the darkest hours of our earthly lives. 🌼   *KIRSTEN HOLMBERG*

O God, You are the Giver of all good things.
Help me to recognize Your generosity in even the smallest ways
and to trust You in seasons of loss and hardship.

*Why not start a gratitude list? Watch how the regular practice of
thankfulness changes your daily life.*

Ponder It

During **Oswald Chambers'** years at the Bible Training College in London (1911–15), he often startled the students with things he said during his lectures. One young woman explained that because discussion was reserved for the following mealtime together, Chambers would frequently be bombarded with questions and objections. She recalled that Oswald would often simply smile and say, "Just leave it for now; it will come to you later." He encouraged them to ponder the issues and allow God to reveal His truth to them.

TODAY'S READING
Luke 2:8–20

Mary treasured up all these things and pondered them in her heart.
Luke 2:19

To ponder something is to concentrate and think deeply about it. After the events leading to the birth of Jesus in Bethlehem, followed by the appearance of angels and the shepherds who came to see the Messiah, "Mary treasured up all these things and pondered them in her heart" (LUKE 2:19). New Testament scholar W. E. Vine said that *ponder* means "... to throw together, confer, to put one thing with another in considering circumstances" (*Expository Dictionary of New Testament Words*).

When we struggle to understand the meaning of what's happening in our lives, we have Mary's wonderful example of what it means to seek God and His wisdom.

When we, like her, accept God's leading in our lives, we have many new things about His loving guidance to treasure and ponder in our hearts. ❧   *DAVID C. MCCASLAND*

Father, guide us by Your Holy Spirit as we consider Your great love
and embrace Your plan for our lives.

Allow yourself a few minutes of quiet during this busy season to sit and listen for what God might be saying to you.

Winter Snow

n winter, I often wake to the beautiful surprise of a world blanketed in the peace and quiet of an early morning snow. Not loudly like a spring thunderstorm that announces its presence in the night, snow comes softly.

In "Winter Snow Song," Audrey Assad sings that Jesus could have come to earth in power like a hurricane, but instead He came quietly and slowly like the winter snow falling softly in the night outside my window.

TODAY'S READING
Isaiah 42:1–4

> He will not shout or cry out, or raise his voice in the streets. A bruised reed he will not break. Isaiah 42:2–3

Jesus's arrival took many by quiet surprise. Instead of being born in a palace, He was born in an unlikely place, a humble dwelling outside Bethlehem. And He slept in the only bed available, a manger (LUKE 2:7). Instead of being attended by royalty and government officials, Jesus was welcomed by lowly shepherds (VV. 15–16). Instead of having wealth, Jesus's parents could only afford the inexpensive sacrifice of two birds when they presented Him at the temple (V. 24).

The unassuming way Jesus entered the world was foreshadowed by the prophet Isaiah, who prophesied the coming Savior would "not shout or cry out" (ISAIAH 42:2) nor would He come in power that might break a damaged reed or extinguish a struggling flame (V. 3). Instead He came gently in order to draw us to Himself with His offer of peace with God—a peace still available to anyone who believes the unexpected story of a Savior born in a manger. 🌱   LISA SAMRA

Lord Jesus, thank You for willingly giving up Your majesty and coming to earth in order to offer peace.

How silently, how silently the wondrous gift is given!
—O LITTLE TOWN OF BETHLEHEM

Just Another Day?

n *Christmas Every Day*, William Dean Howells tells of a little girl who gets her wish. For one long, horrible year it is indeed Christmas every day. By day three, the yuletide joy has already begun to wear thin. Before long everyone hates candy. Turkeys become scarce and sell for outrageous prices. Presents are no longer received with gratitude as they pile up everywhere. People angrily snap at each other.

Thankfully, Howell's story is just a satirical tale. But what an incredible blessing that the subject of the Christmas celebration never wearies us despite the fact that we see Him throughout the Bible.

After Jesus had ascended to His Father, the apostle Peter proclaimed to a crowd at the temple in Jerusalem that Jesus was the one Moses foretold when he said, "God will raise up for you a prophet like me" (ACTS 3:22; DEUTERONOMY 18:18). God's promise to Abraham, "Through your offspring all peoples on earth will be blessed," was really a reference to Jesus (ACTS 3:25; GENESIS 22:18). Peter noted, "All the prophets who have spoken have foretold these days"—the arrival of the Messiah (ACTS 3:24).

We can keep the spirit of Christmas alive long after the celebrations have ended. By seeing Christ in the whole story of the Bible we can appreciate how Christmas is so much more than just another day. 🌿   *TIM GUSTAFSON*

Father, thank You for giving us Your Son, and for giving us His Story on the pages of the Bible.

This year, as you pack up the Christmas decorations, don't put away the spirit of Christmas.

The Highest Place

My husband invited a friend to church. After the service his friend said, "I liked the songs and the atmosphere, but I don't get it. Why do you give Jesus such a high place of honor?" My husband then explained to him that Christianity is a relationship with Christ. Without Him, Christianity would be meaningless. It's because of what Jesus has done in our lives that we meet together and praise Him.

TODAY'S READING
Colossians 1:15–23

He is before all things, and in him all things hold together. Colossians 1:17

Who is Jesus and what has He done? The apostle Paul answered this question in Colossians 1. No one has seen God, but Jesus came to reflect and reveal Him (V. 15). Jesus, as the Son of God, came to die for us and free us from sin. Sin has separated us from God's holiness, so peace could only be made through someone perfect. That was Jesus (VV. 14, 20). In other words, Jesus has given us what no one else could—access to God and eternal life (JOHN 17:3).

Why does He deserve such a place of honor? He conquered death. He won our hearts by His love and sacrifice. He gives us new strength every day. He is everything to us!

We give Him the glory because He deserves it. We lift Him up because that is His rightful place. Let's give Him the highest place in our hearts. ❧ *KEILA OCHOA*

Jesus, You are my Savior and my Lord, and I want to give You the highest place of honor in my life.

Jesus is the center of our worship.

Good Riddance Day

Since 2006 a group of people have celebrated an unusual event around the New Year. It's called Good Riddance Day. Based on a Latin American tradition, individuals write down unpleasant, embarrassing memories and bad issues from the past year and throw them into an industrial-strength shredder. Or some take a sledgehammer to their good riddance item.

> **TODAY'S READING**
> **Psalm 103:1–12**
>
> **As far as the east is from the west, so far has he removed our transgressions from us.** Psalm 103:12

The writer of Psalm 103 goes beyond suggesting that people say good riddance to unpleasant memories. He reminded us that God bids good riddance to our sins. In his attempt to express God's vast love for His people, the psalmist used word pictures. He compared the vastness of God's love to the distance between the heavens and the earth (v. 11). Then the psalmist talked about His forgiveness in spatial terms. As far as the place where the sun rises is from the place where the sun sets, so the Lord has removed His people's sins from them (v. 12). The psalmist wanted God's people to know that His love and forgiveness were infinite and complete. God freed His people from the power of their transgressions by fully pardoning them.

Good news! We don't have to wait until the New Year to experience Good Riddance Day. Through our faith in Jesus, when we confess and turn from our sins, He bids good riddance to them and casts them into the depths of the sea. Today can be a Good Riddance Day! 🌿

MARVIN WILLIAMS

Thank You, Father, for freedom from sin.

What sins do you need to say goodbye to? How does it make you feel knowing that God infinitely and completely forgets your sins?

When God Says No

When I was conscripted into the military at age eighteen, as all young Singaporean men are, I prayed desperately for an easy posting. A clerk or driver, perhaps. Not being particularly strong, I hoped to be spared the rigors of combat training. But one evening as I read my Bible, one verse leaped off the page: "My grace is sufficient for you ..." (2 CORINTHIANS 12:9).

My heart dropped—but it shouldn't have. God had answered my prayers. Even if I received a difficult assignment, He would provide for me.

So I ended up as an armored infantryman, doing things I didn't always enjoy. Looking back now, I'm grateful God didn't give me what I wanted. The training and experience toughened me physically and mentally and gave me confidence to enter adulthood.

> TODAY'S READING
> **Isaiah 25:1–5**
>
> **In perfect faithfulness you have done wonderful things, things planned long ago.** Isaiah 25:1

In Isaiah 25:1–5, after prophesying Israel's punishment and subsequent deliverance from her enemies, the prophet praises God for His plans. All these "wonderful things," Isaiah notes, had been "planned long ago" (v. 1), yet they included some arduous times.

It can be hard to hear God saying no, and even harder to understand when we're praying for something good—like someone's deliverance from a crisis. That's when we need to hold on to the truth of God's good plans. We may not understand why, but we can keep trusting in His love, goodness, and faithfulness. ❧

LESLIE KOH

Lord, give me the faith to keep trusting You even when You say no.
When God says no, He has a plan. Keep trusting Him!

All Things New

Junkyards intrigue me. I enjoy working on cars, so I frequently make trips to the one near our home. It's a lonely place, where the wind whispers through discarded hulks that were once someone's prized possession. Some were wrecked, some wore out, and others simply outlived their usefulness. As I walk between the rows, a car will sometimes catch my eye, and I'll find myself wondering about the adventures it had during its "lifetime." Like a portal to the past, each has a story to tell—of human hankering after the latest model and the inescapable passage of time.

But I take particular pleasure in finding new life for an old part. Whenever I can take something discarded and give it new life in a restored vehicle, it feels like a small victory against time and decline.

TODAY'S READING
Revelation 21:1–7

If anyone is in Christ, the new creation has come: The old has gone, the new is here!
2 Corinthians 5:17

It sometimes makes me think of Jesus's words at the end of the Bible: "I am making everything new!" (REVELATION 21:5). These words refer to God's renewal of creation, which includes believers. Already, all who've received Jesus are a "new creation" in Him (2 CORINTHIANS 5:17).

And one day we will enter into His promise of unending days with Him (JOHN 14:3). Age and disease will no longer take their toll, and we will continue the adventure of an eternal lifetime. What stories each of us will have to tell—stories of our Savior's redeeming love and undying faithfulness. 🌿   *JAMES BANKS*

Loving Lord, I praise You that I am a new creation in You, and that in Your kindness and mercy You have given me the promise of eternal life.

The end of a year and beginning of another is an opportunity for a fresh start. What might God be making new in your life?

The Messenger

" **I have a message for you!**" A woman working at the conference I was attending handed me a piece of paper, and I wondered if I should be nervous or excited. But when I read, "You have a nephew!" I knew I could rejoice.

Messages can bring good news, bad news, or words that challenge. In the Old Testament, God used His prophets to communicate messages of hope or judgment. But when we look closely, we see that even His words of judgment were intended to lead to repentance, healing, and restoration.

> TODAY'S READING
> **Malachi 3:1–5**
>
> **I will send my messenger, who will prepare the way before me.**
>
> Malachi 3:1

Both types of messages appear in Malachi 3 when the Lord promised to send a messenger who would prepare the way for Him. John the Baptist announced the coming of the true Messenger, Jesus (SEE MATTHEW 3:11)—"the messenger of the covenant" (MALACHI 3:1) who will fulfill God's promises. But He will act "like a refiner's fire or a launderer's soap" (V. 2), for He will purify those who believe in His word. The Lord sent His word to cleanse His people because of His loving concern for their well-being.

God's message is one of love, hope, and freedom. He sent His Son to be a messenger who speaks our language—sometimes with messages of correction, but always those of hope. We can trust His message. ❧   *AMY BOUCHER PYE*

Lord Jesus Christ, help me not only to understand Your message
but to live it.

Ask the Lord to help you share His good news with others in the new year.

Making It Personal

SOMEONE HAS SAID, "Knowing Christ died— that's history. Believing He died for me—that's salvation." A personal relationship with Christ begins at the moment of our salvation. Jesus referred to this event as a second birth (JOHN 3:3). Only when we are born spiritually into God's family do we become His children, His friends, His servants, and members of His spiritual kingdom.

> **A Final Thought**

While we may not know exactly when this new life begins, we can understand the steps we need to take to begin this relationship.

1 Admit our lost condition.

All of us are born to the parents of a fallen humanity. We come into this world separated from the life of God and absorbed with an interest in finding satisfaction and significance on our own terms. We don't show a natural desire for God who made us for Himself (ROMANS 3:11–12).

> We come into this world...absorbed with an interest in finding significance on our own terms.

While we may look good to ourselves as long as we measure ourselves by ourselves, Jesus Christ showed us our sin. He is the One who showed us what it means to have a personal relationship with God. He is also the One who said that He didn't come into this world to help good people, but "to seek and to save the lost" (LUKE 19:10).

The Bible says we all come into this physical world physically alive but spiritually dead—missing out on the quality of life for which God made us. The apostle Paul wrote, "All have sinned and fall short of the glory of God" (ROMANS 3:23), "There is no one righteous, not even one" (ROMANS 3:10), and "The wages of sin is death" (ROMANS 6:23).

2 Acknowledge what God has done for us.

The word gospel means "good news." The gospel of Christ is that God Himself loved us enough to send His own Son into this world to rescue us from ourselves and our sin (JOHN 1:1–4; 3:16). The good news is that Jesus lived the quality of life that God intended for us to live. Without flaw, He loved His heavenly Father with all of His heart, soul, and mind. Without fail, He showed us what it means to love our neighbor as ourselves.

> Jesus's death was of infinite value. When He rose from the dead, He proved that He had died in our place to pay the price of all sin— past, present, and future.

Then, to solve the problem of our lost relationship with His Father, Jesus died in our place, offering Himself as a perfect sacrifice to pay the price of sin. Because He was not only man but God our Creator as well (JOHN 1:1–14), His death was of infinite value. When He rose from the dead, He proved that He had died in our place to pay the price of all sin—past, present, and future. With one sacrifice, He paid for the least—and the worst—of our sin.

3 Personally believe and receive God's gift.

While we all have earned the wages of spiritual death and separation from God (ROMANS 6:23), no one can earn a relationship with God. It is a gift of His love and mercy—not a reward for our effort. No one is saved by trying to be good. We are saved by trusting in Christ. This is why the apostle Paul could write, "For it is by grace you have been saved, through faith—and this is not from yourselves,

> No one is saved by trying to be good. We are saved by trusting in Christ.

it is the gift of God—not by works, so that no one can boast" (EPHESIANS 2:8–9; SEE ALSO ROMANS 4:5; TITUS 3:5).

This may sound too simple. But it takes a miracle of God's grace to break our pride and self-sufficiency. It takes God's Spirit to draw us into this kind of personal relationship. If this is your desire, this is how you can begin.

The actual words we say to God to receive this gift may vary (LUKE 18:13; 23:42-43). What is important is that we believe God enough to be able to say, "Father, I know I have sinned against You. I believe that Jesus is Your Son, that He died for my sins, and that He rose from the dead to prove it. Now I accept Your offer of eternal life. I accept Jesus as Your gift for my salvation."

If this is the honest expression of your heart, welcome to God's family! By simple, childlike faith you have entered into a personal relationship with the One who made you and saved you for Himself. ❧

OUR DAILY BREAD MINISTRIES OFFICES

For information on our resources, please write to the office nearest you from the list below, or go to **ourdailybread.org/locations** for the complete list of offices.

AFRICA REGION

SOUTH AFRICA
Our Daily Bread Ministries, PO Box 2637, Umhlanga Rocks, Durban 4320
PH: +27 31 563 6322 / 825 2001 • FX: +27 31 563 1963
Email: southafrica@odb.org

KENYA
Our Daily Bread Ministries, PO Box 2761, 00200 City Square, Nairobi
PH: +254 20 5201415 • M: +254 717 805557/727 207899
Email: kenya@odb.org

NIGERIA (REGIONAL OFFICE)
Our Daily Bread Ministries, PO Box 80125, Lafiaji Post Office 101006, Lagos State
PH: +234 1 462 0199 • M: +234 80 5462 7884
Email: nigeria@odb.org

IBERO-AMERICA & CARIBBEAN REGION

BRAZIL (REGIONAL OFFICE)
Our Daily Bread Ministries, Caixa Postal 4190, 82501-970, Curitiba/PR
PH: +55 41 3257 4028
Email: brazil@odb.org

GUYANA
Our Daily Bread Ministries, PO Box 101070, Georgetown
PH: +592 231 6704
Email: guyana@odb.org

JAMAICA W.I.
Our Daily Bread Ministries, 23 Parkington Plaza, PO Box 139, Kingston 10
PH: +1 876 926 5552
Email: jamaica@odb.org

TRINIDAD & TOBAGO W.I.
Our Daily Bread Ministries, PO Box 4938, Tunapuna, Trinidad W.I.
PH: +1 868 645 7402
Email: trinidad@odb.org

USA
Our Daily Bread, PO Box 2222, Grand Rapids, MI 49501 USA
PH: +1 616 974-2210
Email: odb@odb.org

Our Daily Bread

Topic Index

ANNUAL EDITION 2020

Topic Index

ANNUAL EDITION 2020

Topic Index

ANNUAL EDITION 2020